Epilogue 58>> First Shrine Visit of the Year

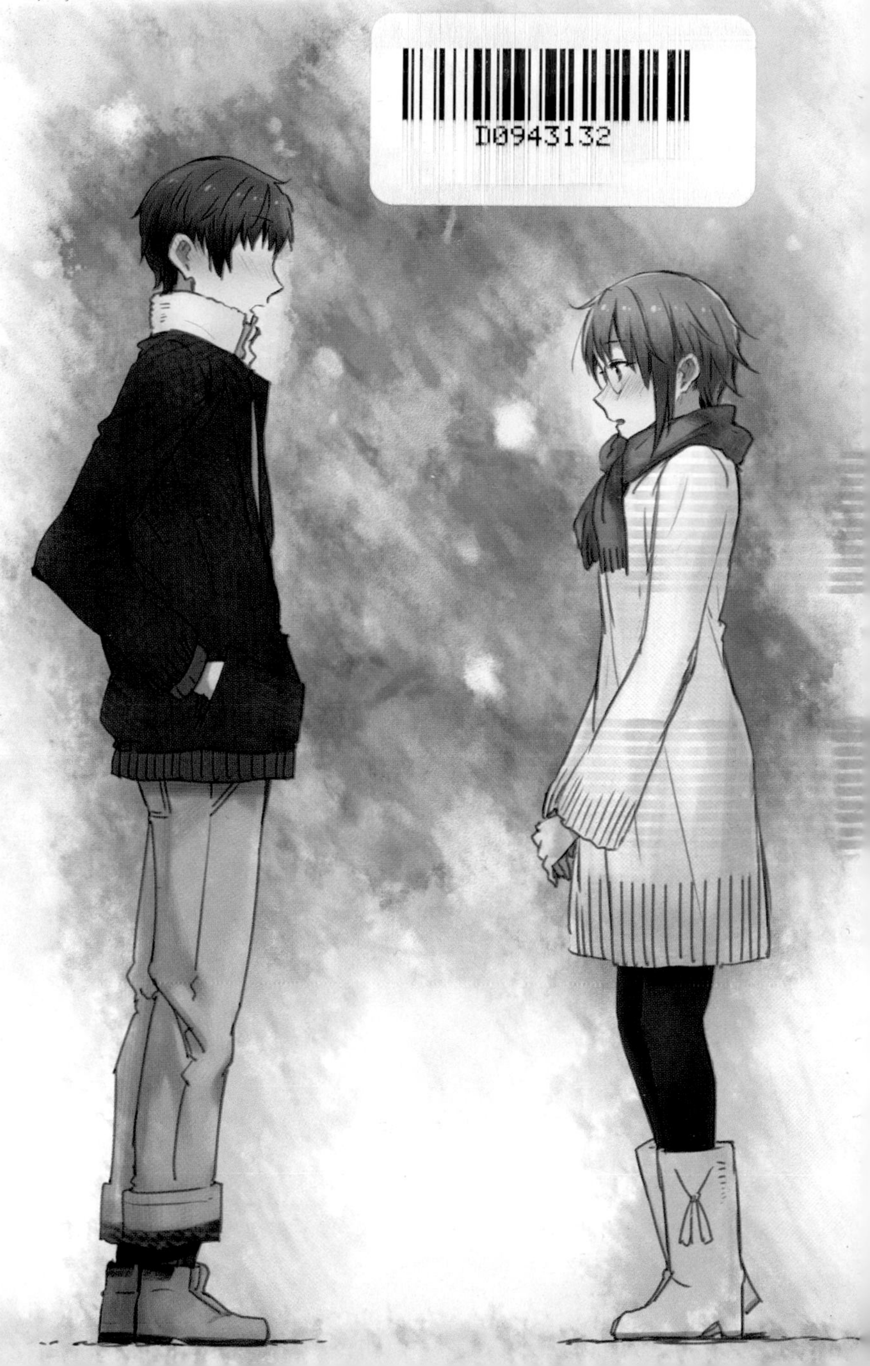

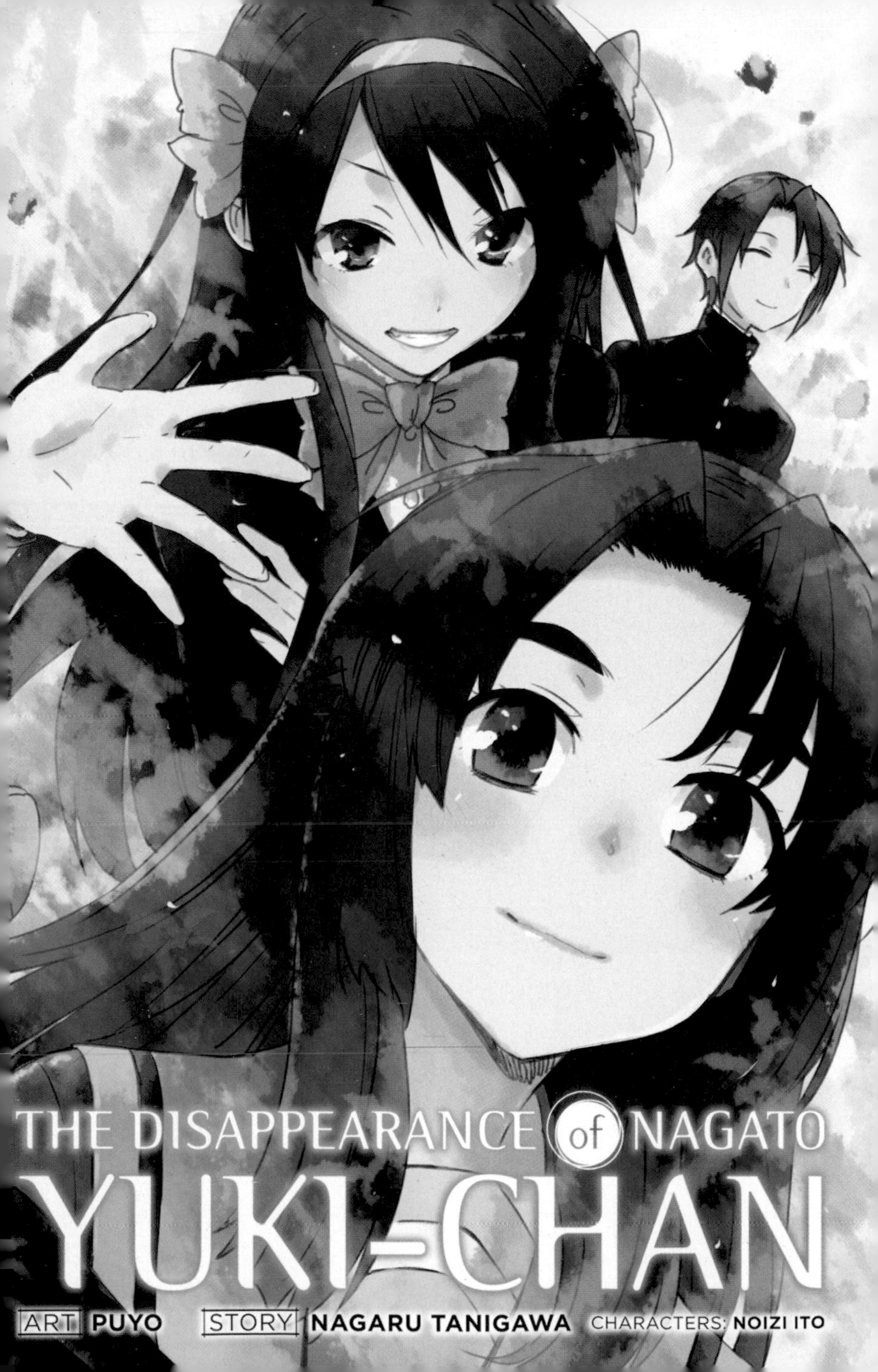
THE DISAPPEARANCE of NAGATO
YUKI-CHAN
ART PUYO
STORY NAGARU TANIGAWA
CHARACTERS: NOIZI ITO

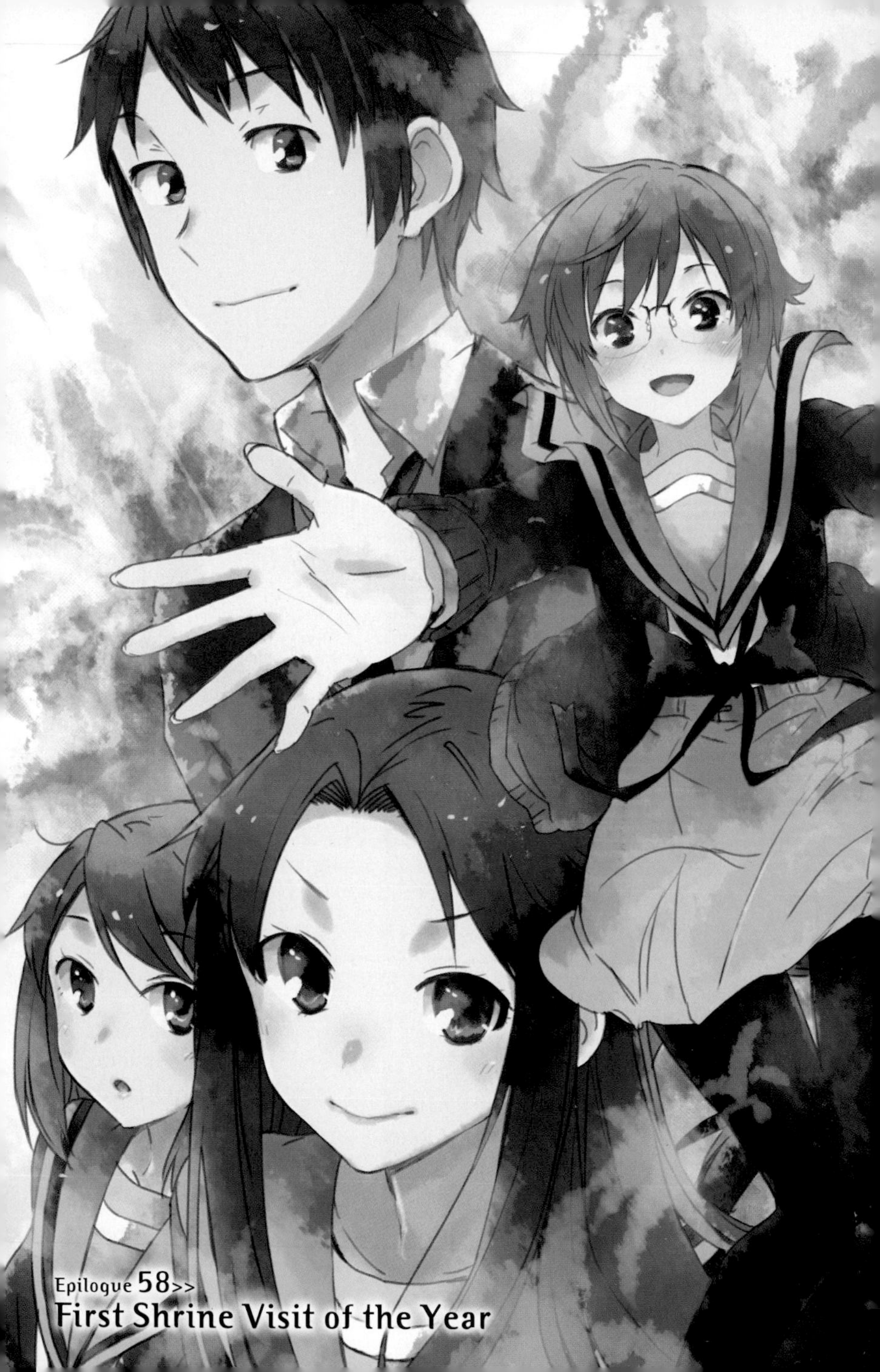

Epilogue 58>>

First Shrine Visit of the Year

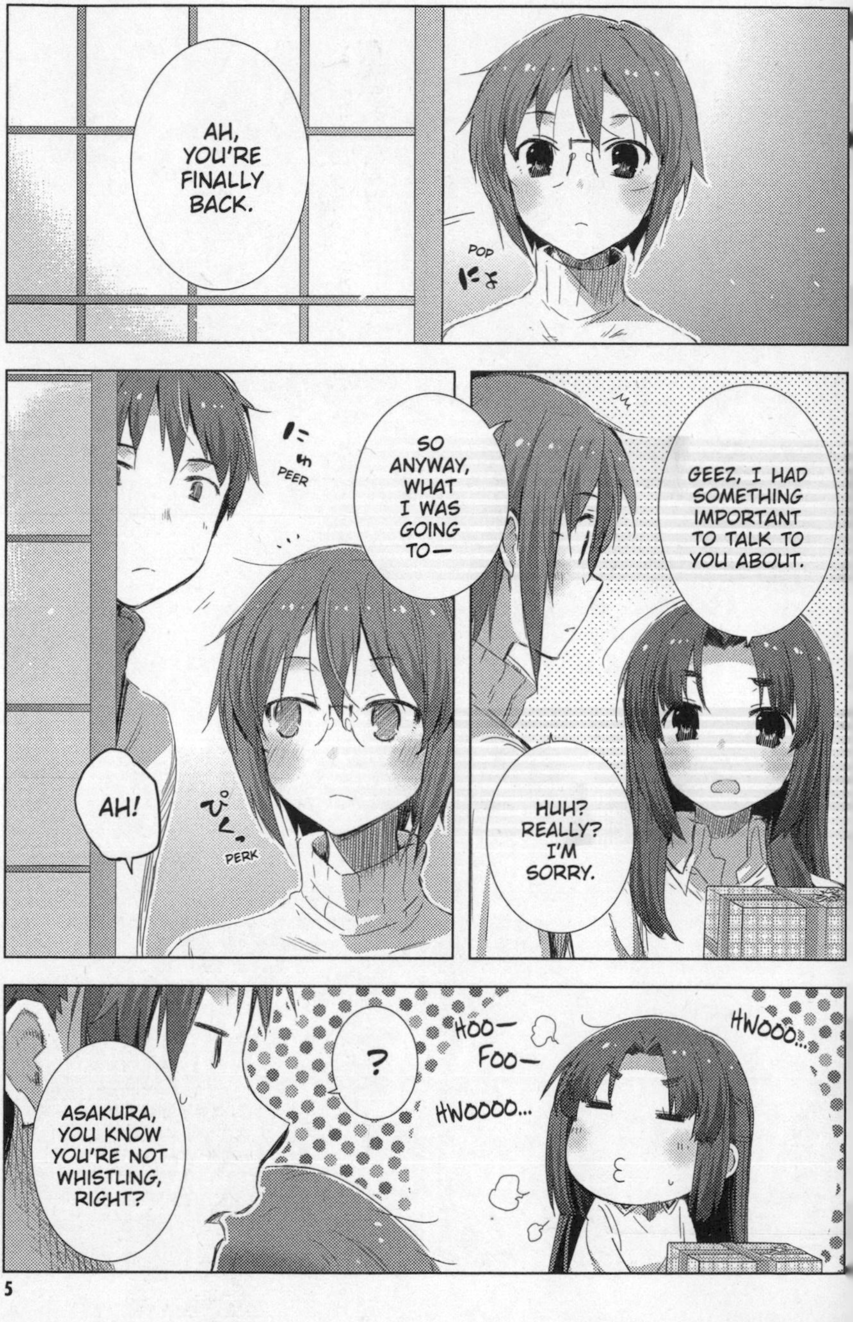
POP
にょ
AH, YOU'RE FINALLY BACK.
GEEZ, I HAD SOMETHING IMPORTANT TO TALK TO YOU ABOUT.
HUH? REALLY? I'M SORRY.
SO ANYWAY, WHAT I WAS GOING TO—
にゅ
PEER
ぴくっ
PERK
AH!
HWOOO...
HOO— FOO—
HWOOOO...
?
ASAKURA, YOU KNOW YOU'RE NOT WHISTLING, RIGHT?

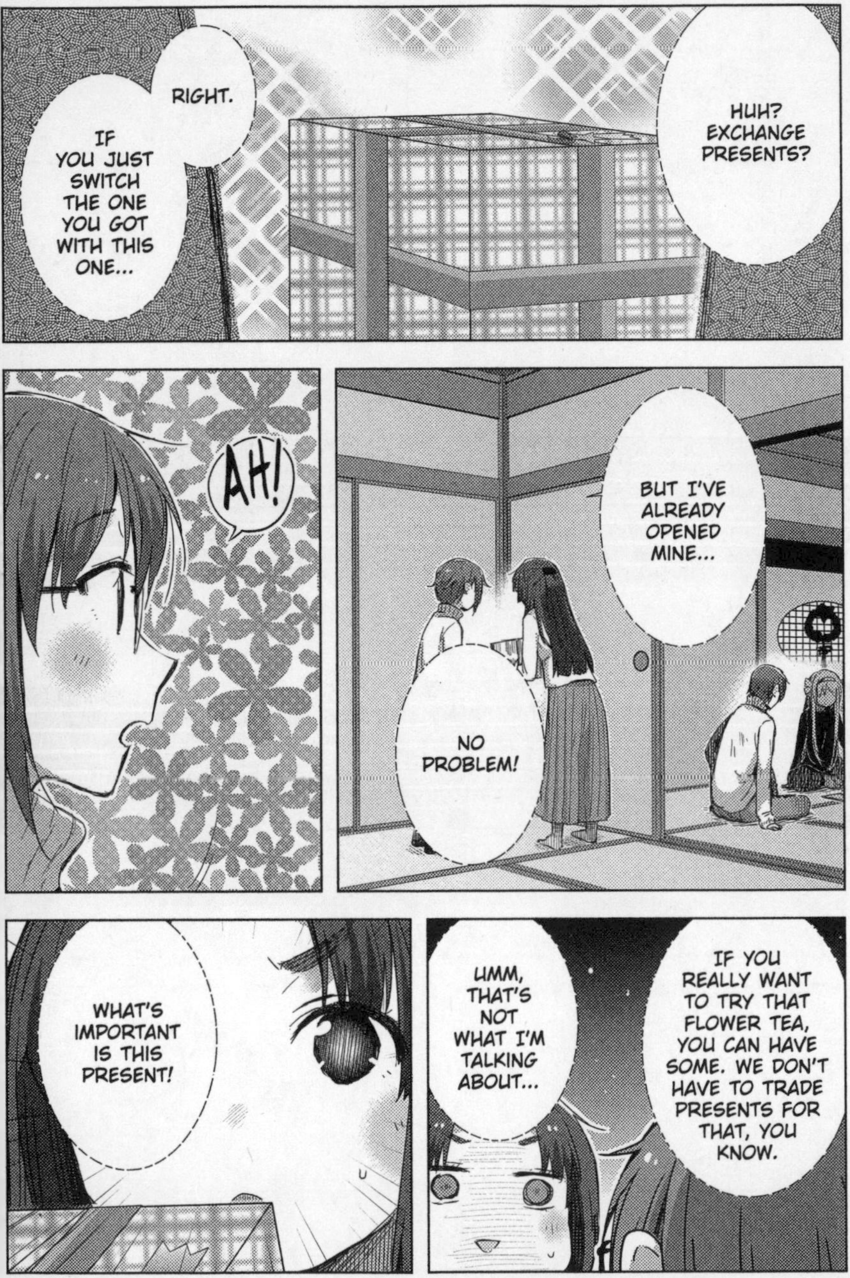
HUH? EXCHANGE PRESENTS?
RIGHT.
IF YOU JUST SWITCH THE ONE YOU GOT WITH THIS ONE...
BUT I'VE ALREADY OPENED MINE...
NO PROBLEM!
AH!
IF YOU REALLY WANT TO TRY THAT FLOWER TEA, YOU CAN HAVE SOME. WE DON'T HAVE TO TRADE PRESENTS FOR THAT, YOU KNOW.
UMM, THAT'S NOT WHAT I'M TALKING ABOUT...
WHAT'S IMPORTANT IS THIS PRESENT!

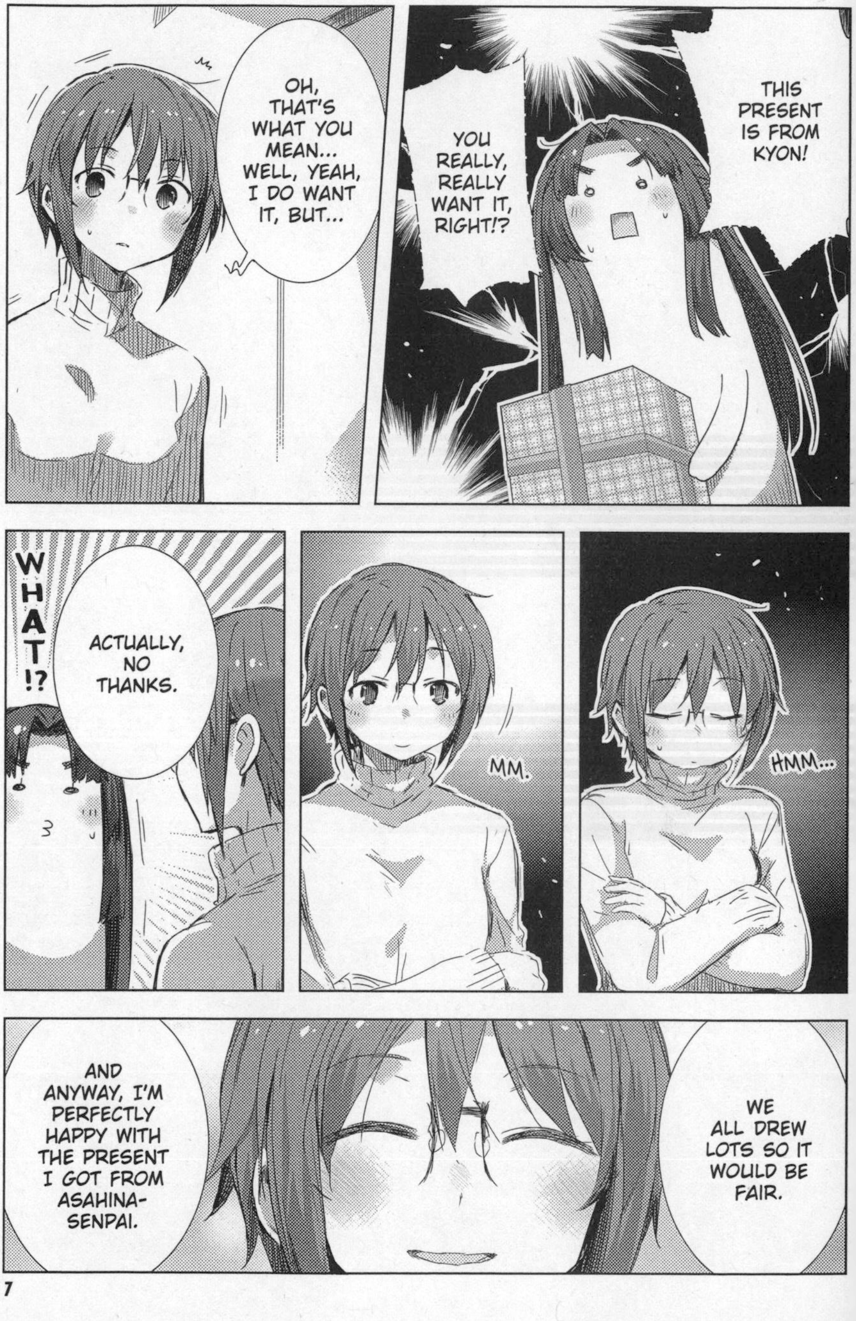
THIS PRESENT IS FROM KYON!
YOU REALLY, REALLY WANT IT, RIGHT!?
OH, THAT'S WHAT YOU MEAN... WELL, YEAH, I DO WANT IT, BUT...
HMM...
MM.
ACTUALLY, NO THANKS.
WHAT!?
WE ALL DREW LOTS SO IT WOULD BE FAIR.
AND ANYWAY, I'M PERFECTLY HAPPY WITH THE PRESENT I GOT FROM ASAHINA-SENPAI.

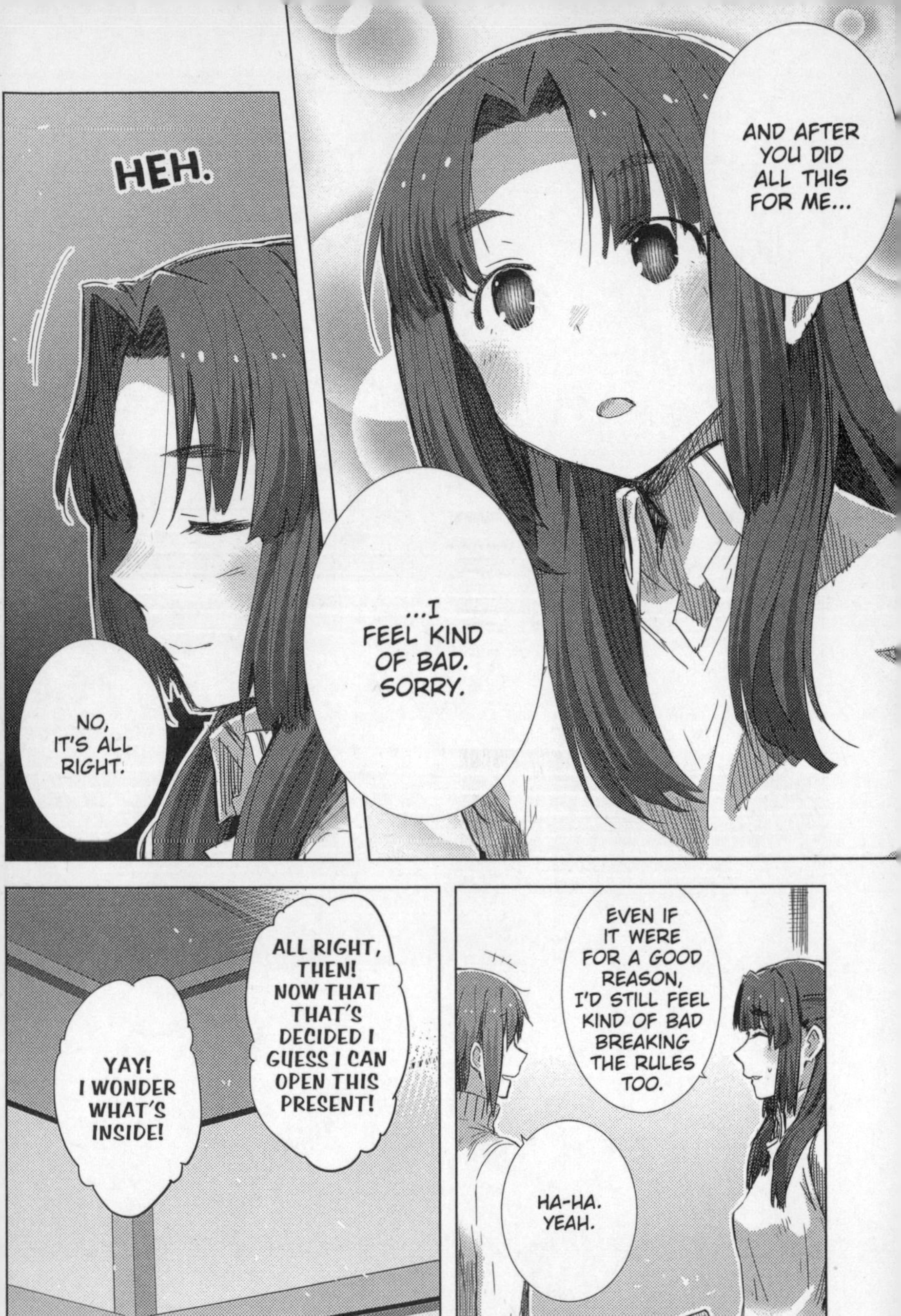
AND AFTER YOU DID ALL THIS FOR ME...
...I FEEL KIND OF BAD. SORRY.
HEH.
NO, IT'S ALL RIGHT.
EVEN IF IT WERE FOR A GOOD REASON, I'D STILL FEEL KIND OF BAD BREAKING THE RULES TOO.
HA-HA. YEAH.
ALL RIGHT, THEN! NOW THAT THAT'S DECIDED I GUESS I CAN OPEN THIS PRESENT!
YAY! I WONDER WHAT'S INSIDE!

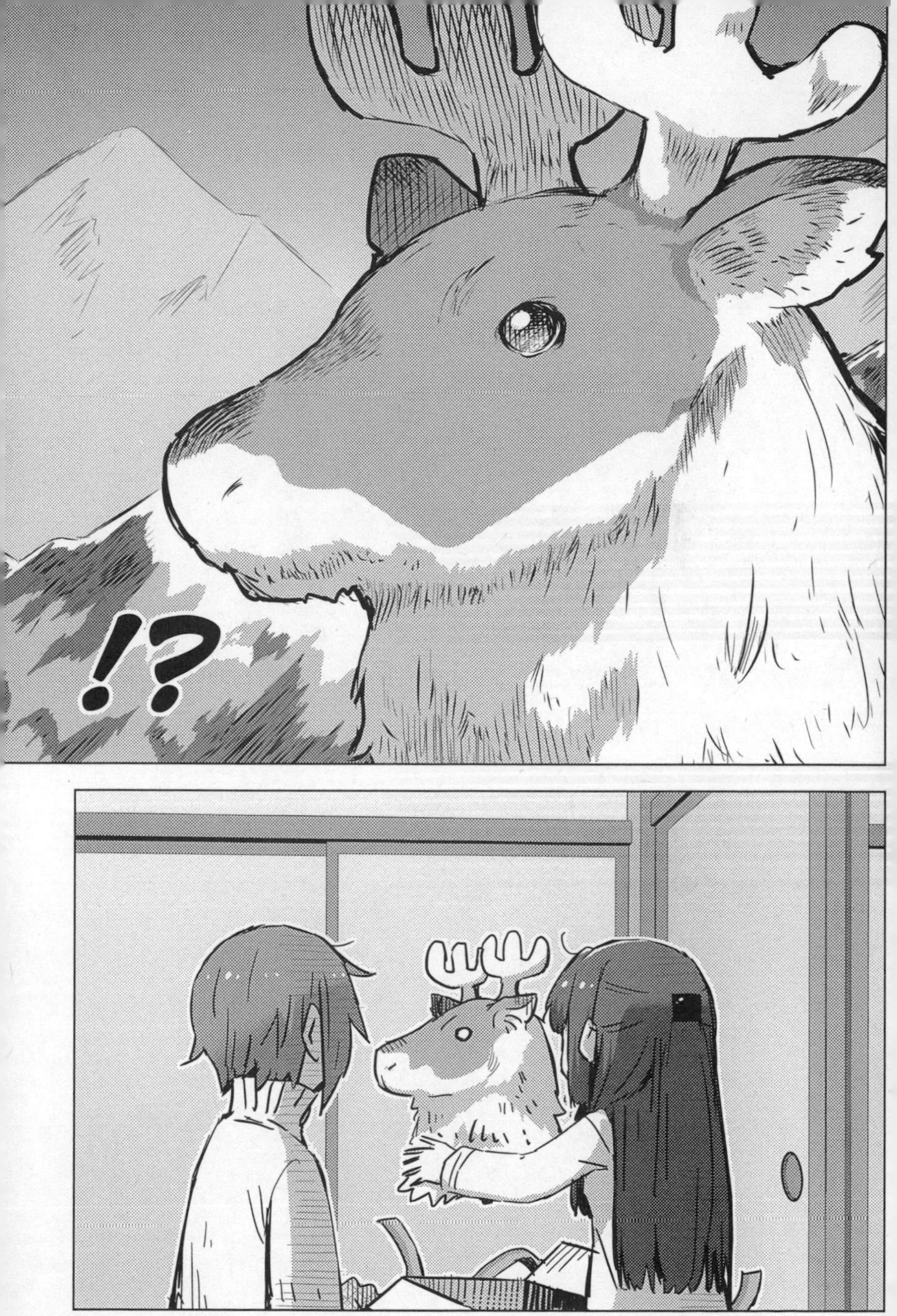
!?

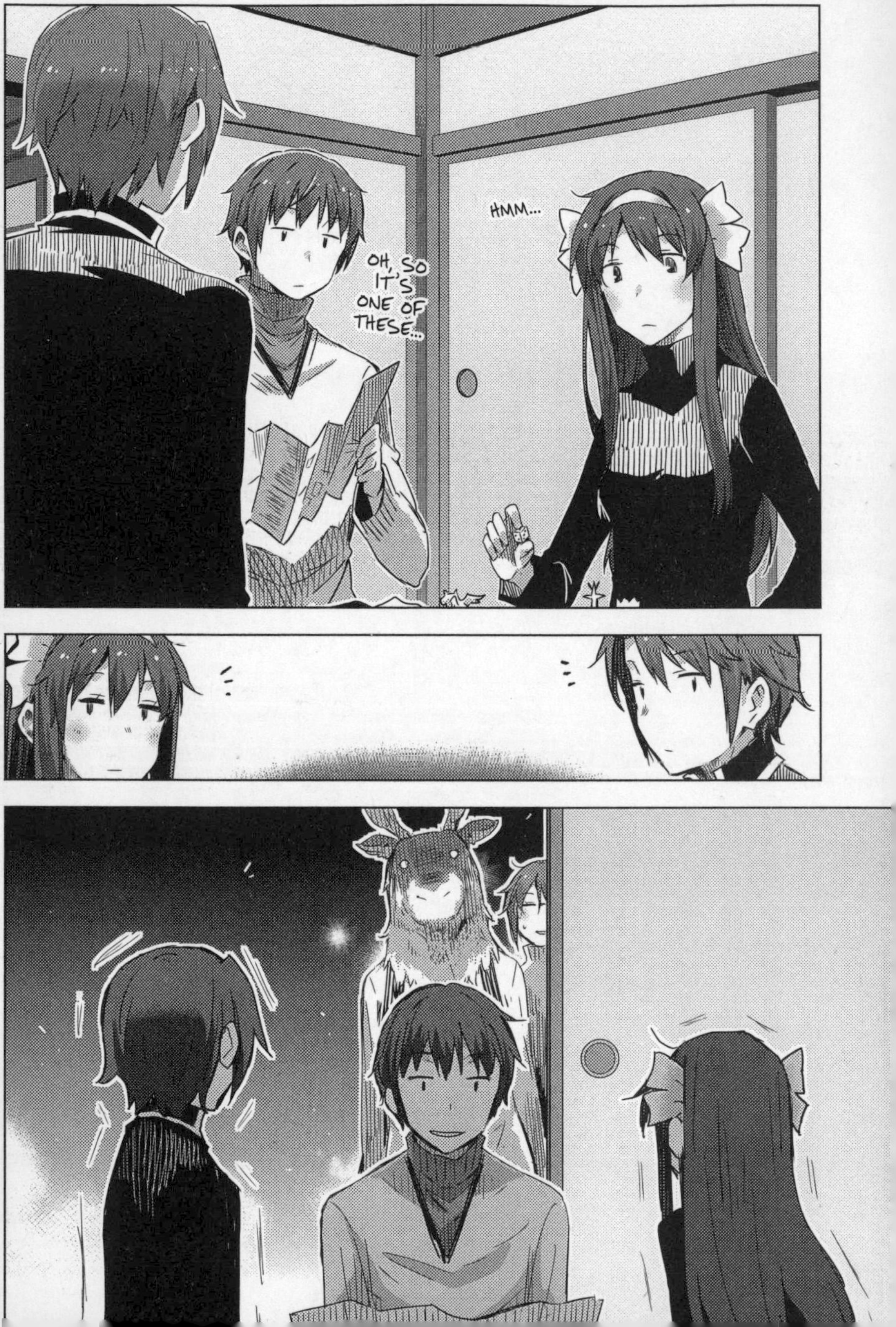
HMM...
OH, SO IT'S ONE OF THESE...

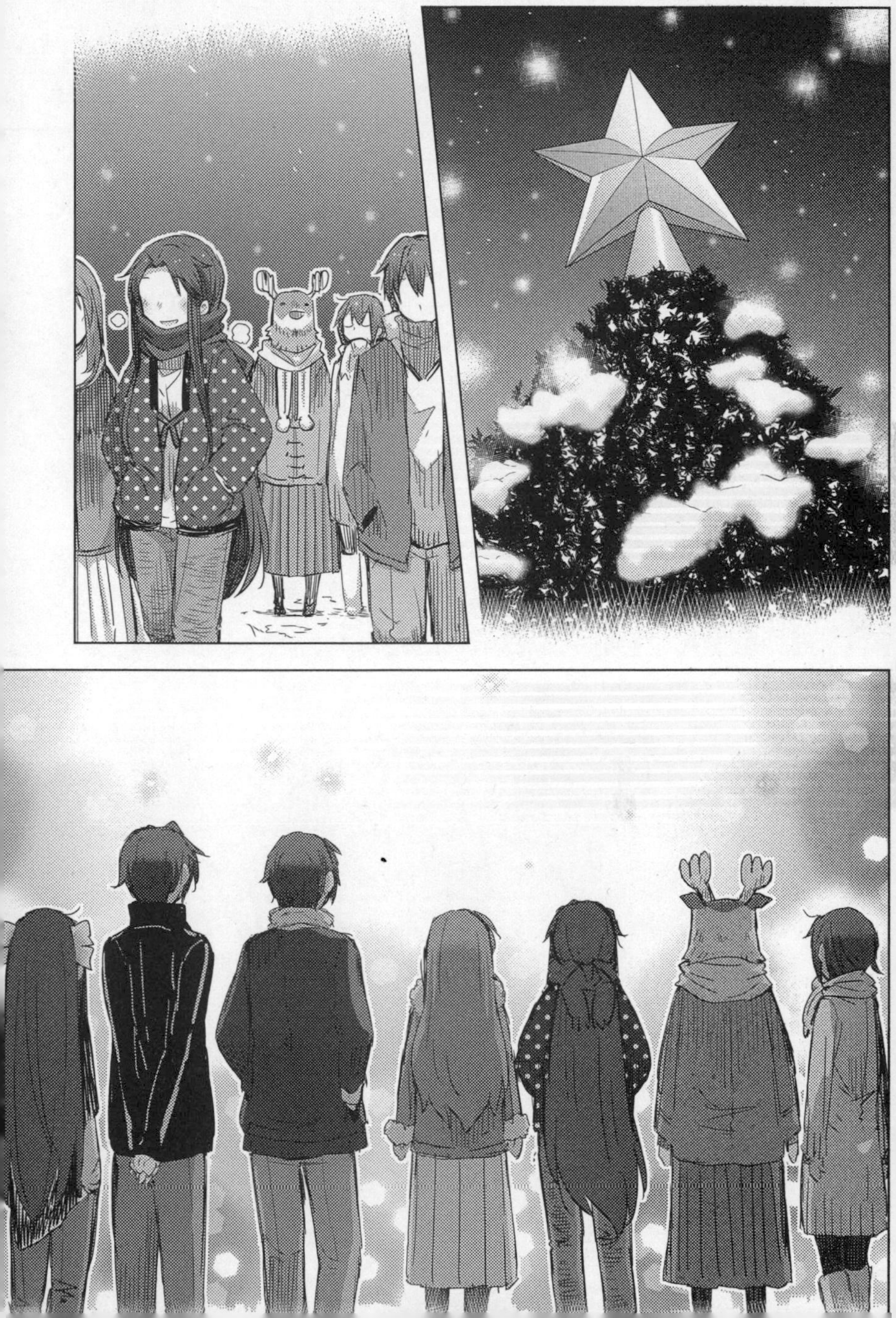

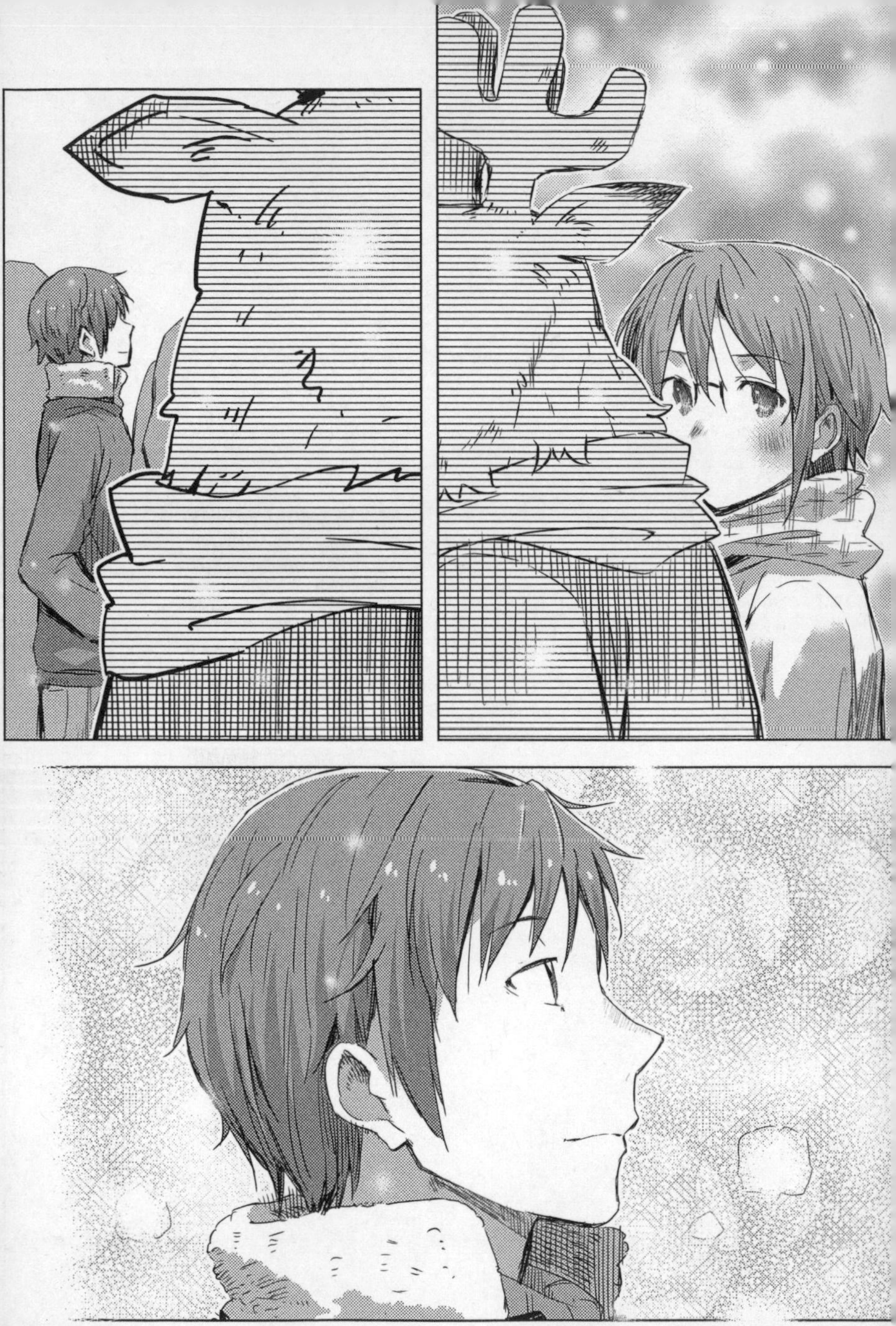

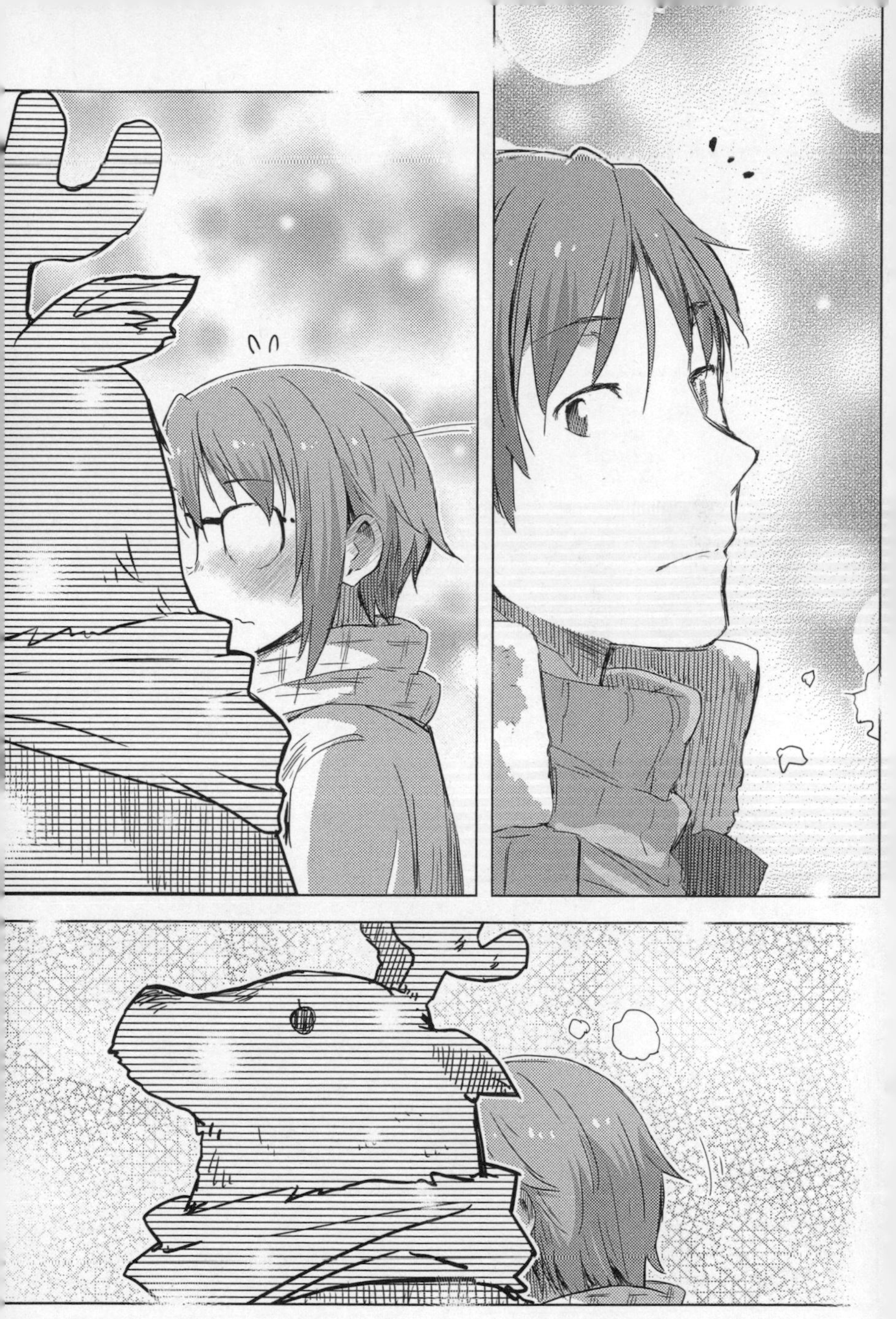

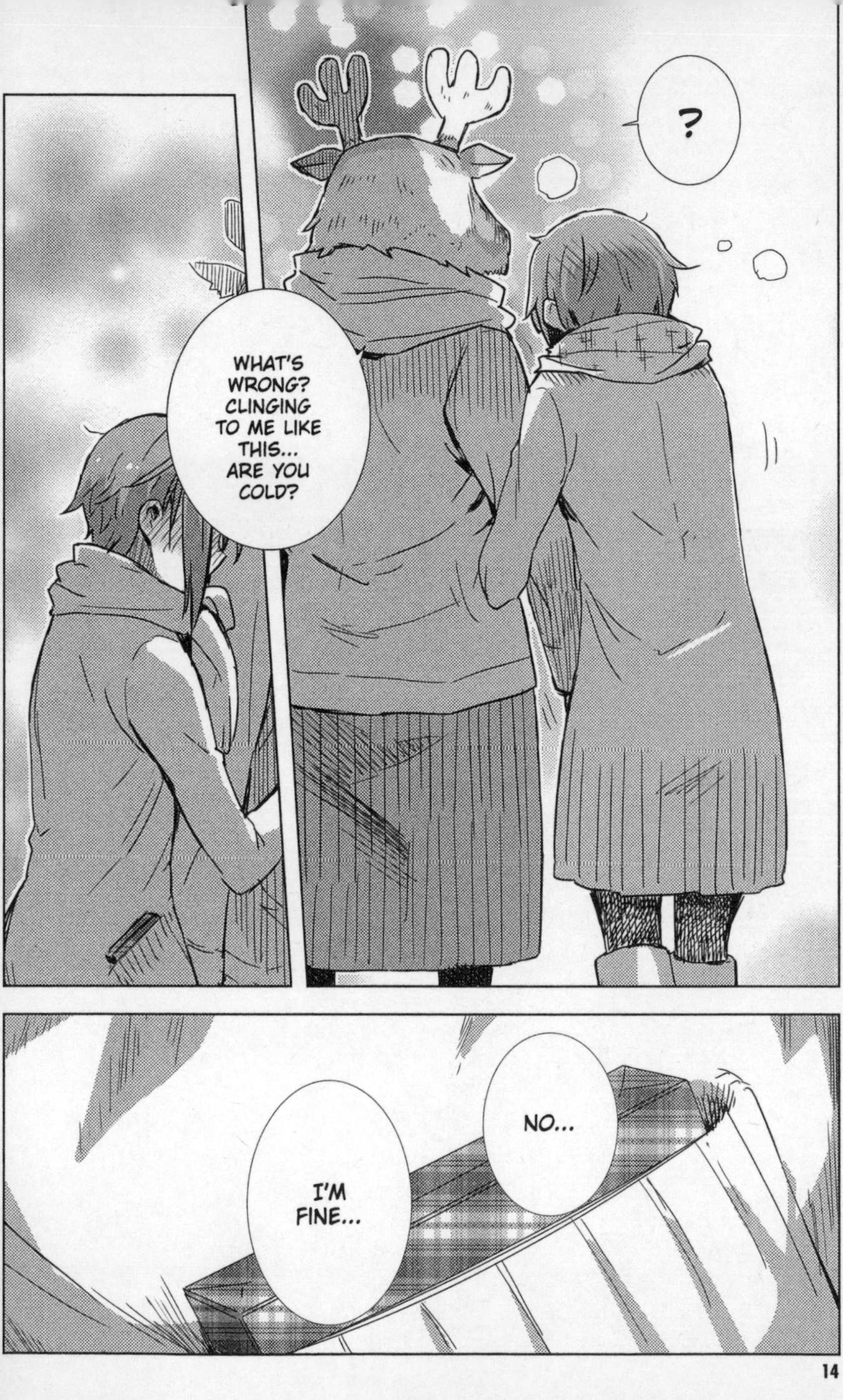
?
WHAT'S WRONG? CLINGING TO ME LIKE THIS... ARE YOU COLD?
NO...
I'M FINE...

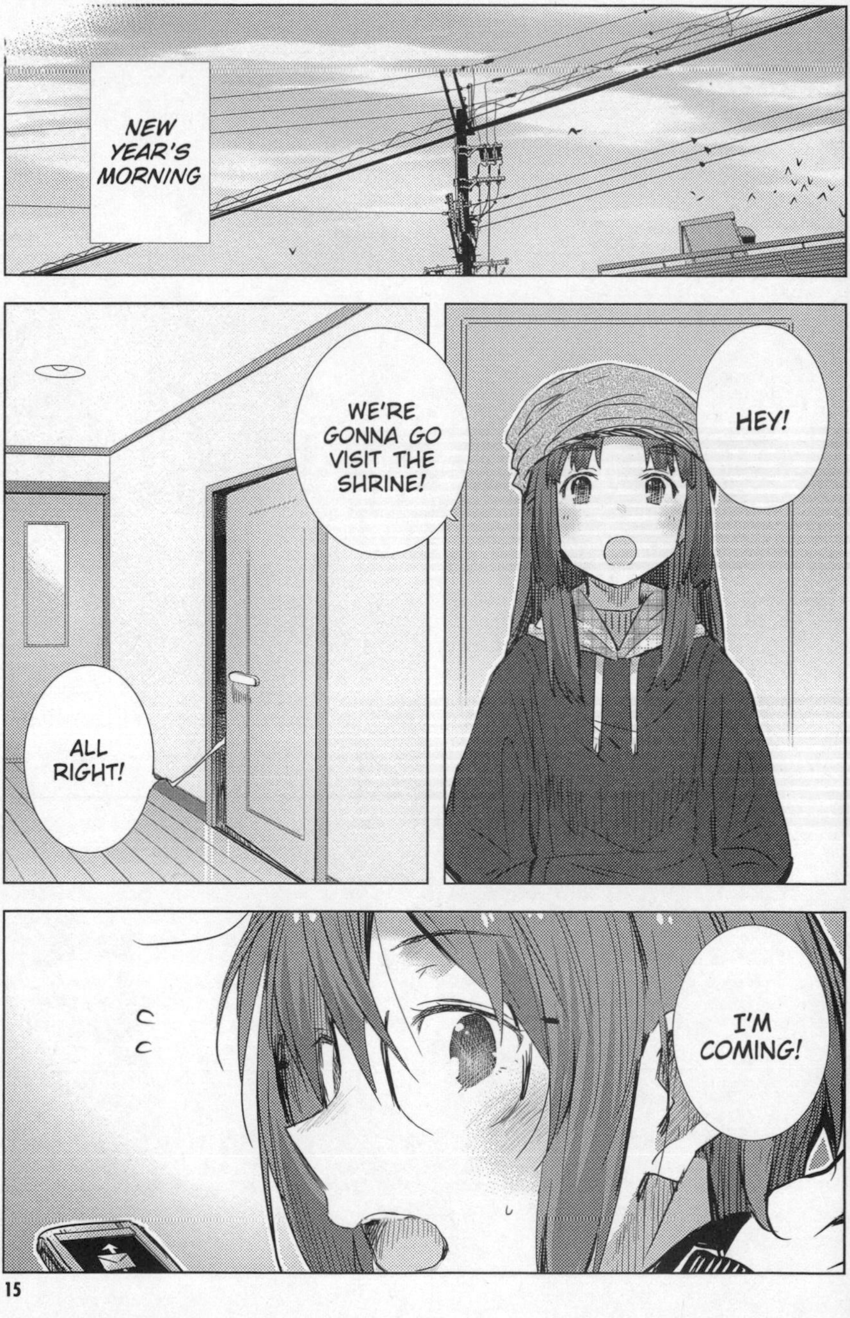
NEW YEAR'S MORNING
HEY!
WE'RE GONNA GO VISIT THE SHRINE!
ALL RIGHT!
I'M COMING!

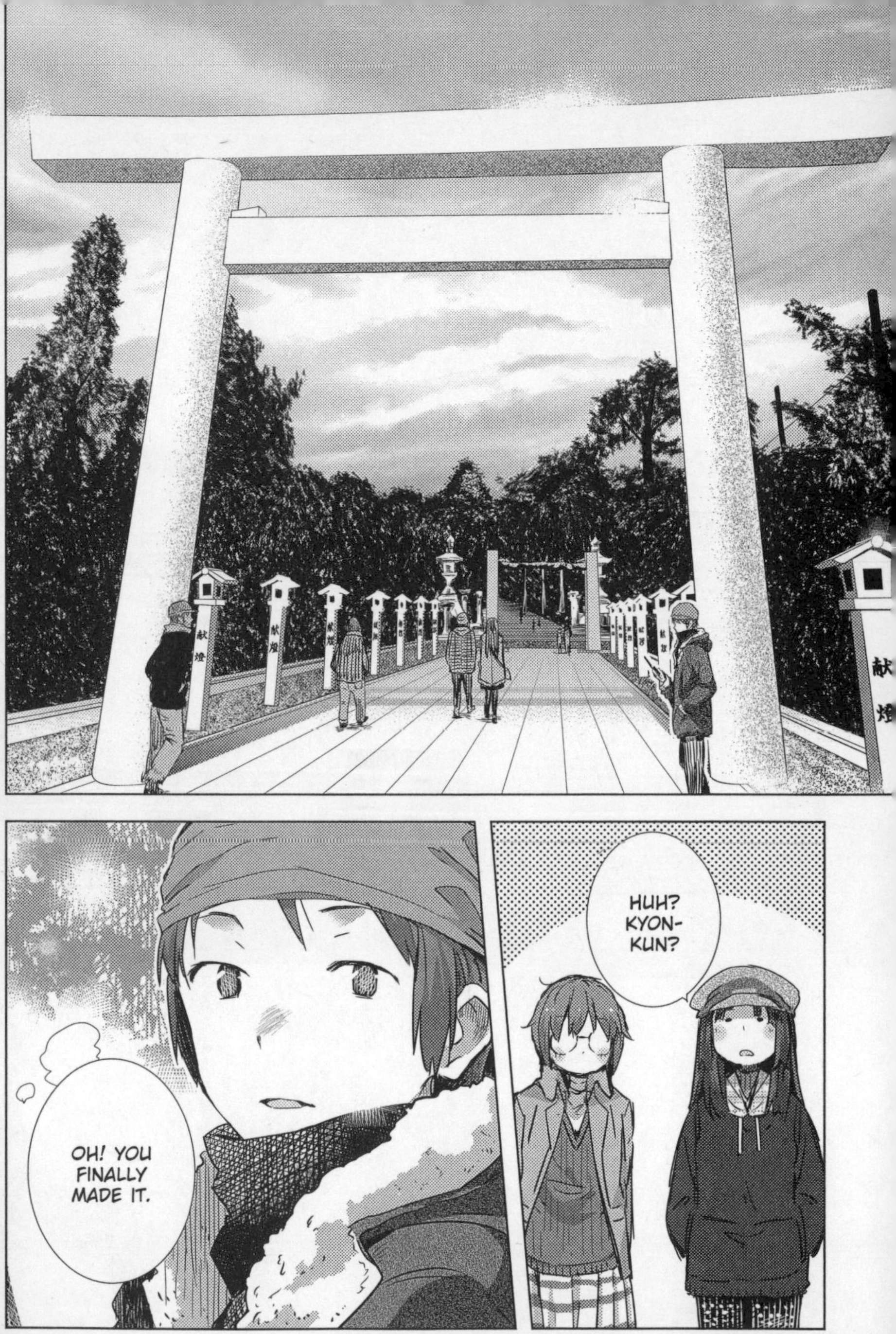
献燈
HUH? KYON-KUN?
OH! YOU FINALLY MADE IT.

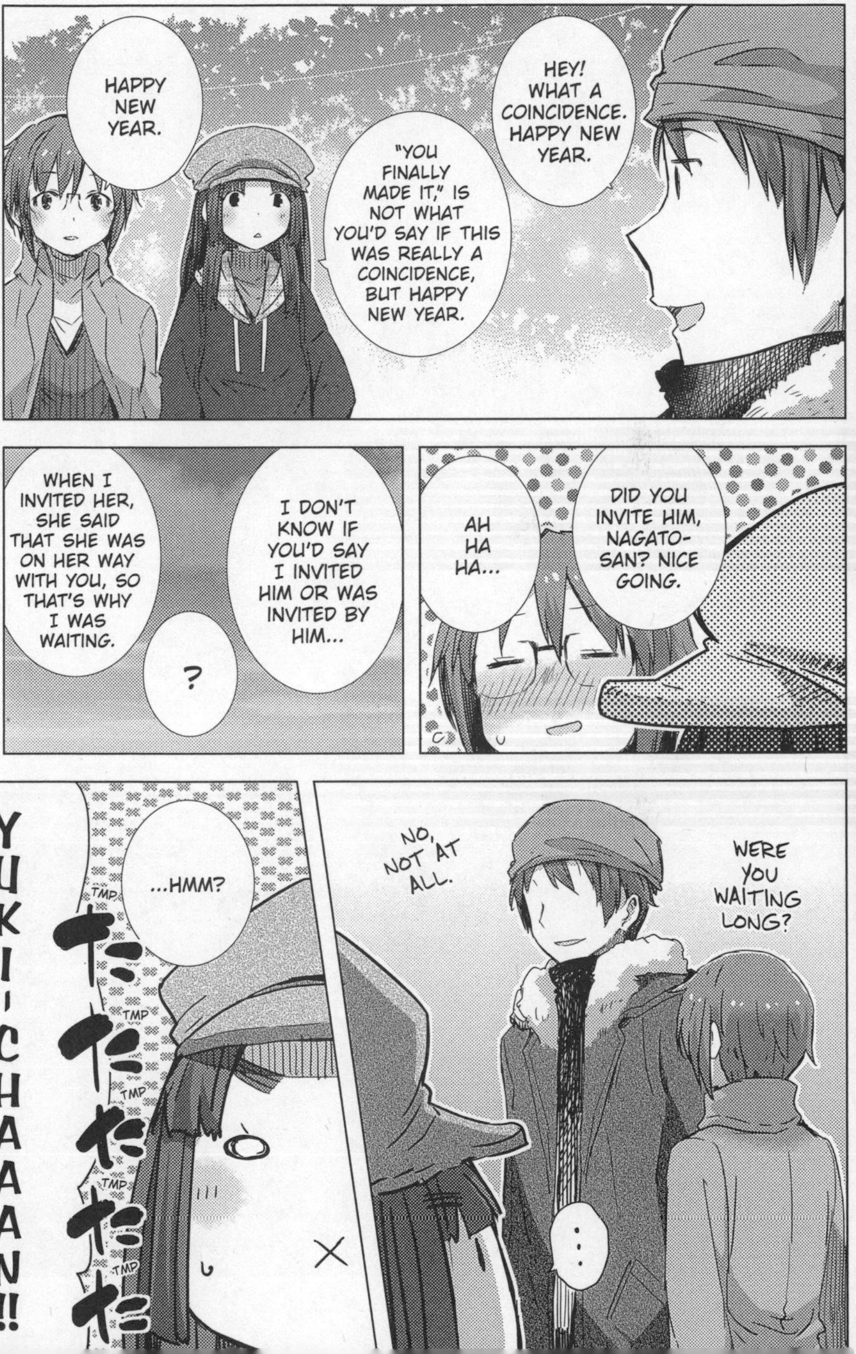
HEY! WHAT A COINCIDENCE. HAPPY NEW YEAR.
"YOU FINALLY MADE IT," IS NOT WHAT YOU'D SAY IF THIS WAS REALLY A COINCIDENCE, BUT HAPPY NEW YEAR.
HAPPY NEW YEAR.
DID YOU INVITE HIM, NAGATO-SAN? NICE GOING.
AH HA HA...
I DON'T KNOW IF YOU'D SAY I INVITED HIM OR WAS INVITED BY HIM...
?
WHEN I INVITED HER, SHE SAID THAT SHE WAS ON HER WAY WITH YOU, SO THAT'S WHY I WAS WAITING.
WERE YOU WAITING LONG?
NO, NOT AT ALL.
...
...HMM?
TMP TMP TMP TMP TMP
YUKI-CHAAAN!!

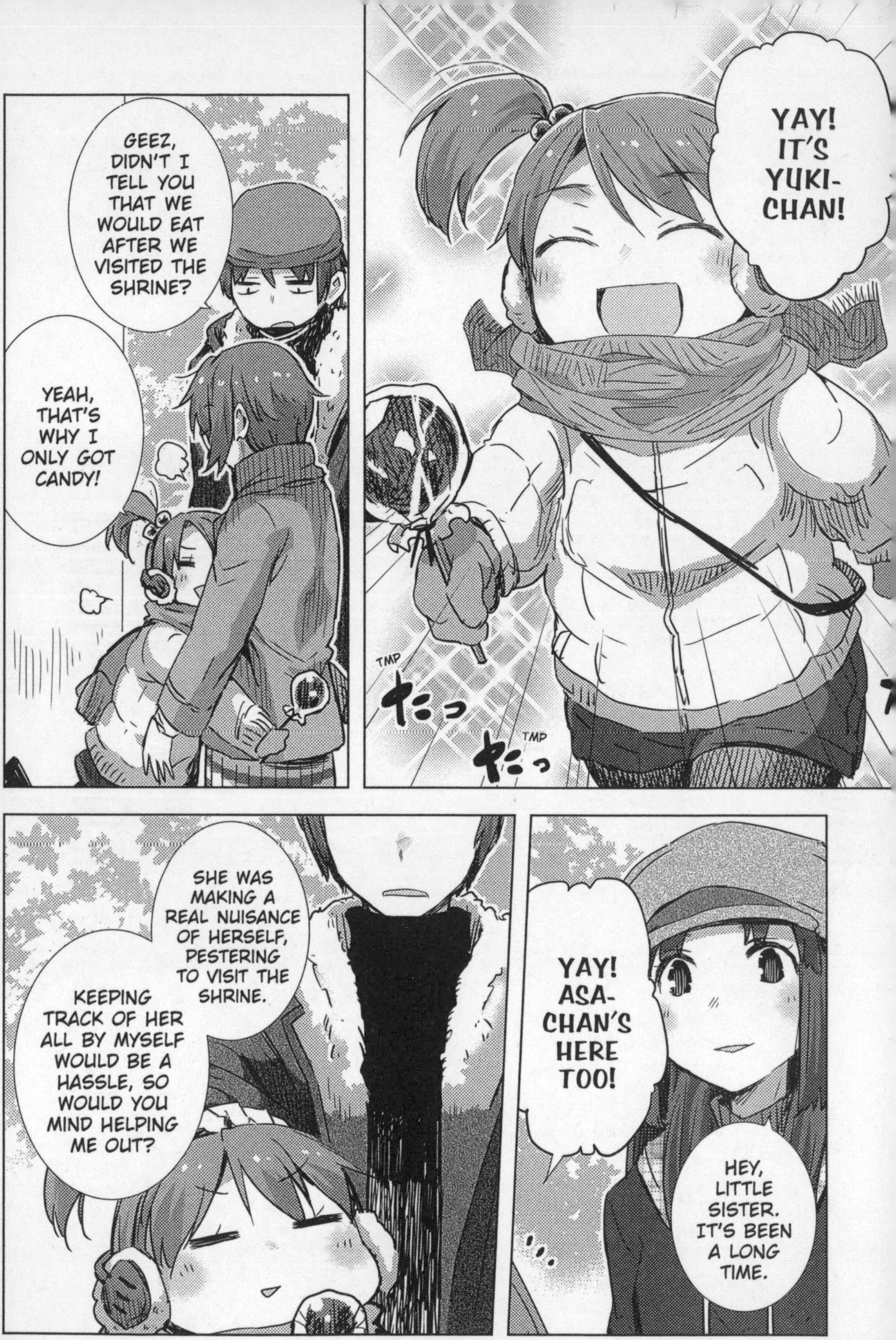
YAY! IT'S YUKI-CHAN!
TMP
TMP
GEEZ, DIDN'T I TELL YOU THAT WE WOULD EAT AFTER WE VISITED THE SHRINE?
YEAH, THAT'S WHY I ONLY GOT CANDY!
YAY! ASA-CHAN'S HERE TOO!
...
HEY, LITTLE SISTER. IT'S BEEN A LONG TIME.
SHE WAS MAKING A REAL NUISANCE OF HERSELF, PESTERING TO VISIT THE SHRINE.
KEEPING TRACK OF HER ALL BY MYSELF WOULD BE A HASSLE, SO WOULD YOU MIND HELPING ME OUT?

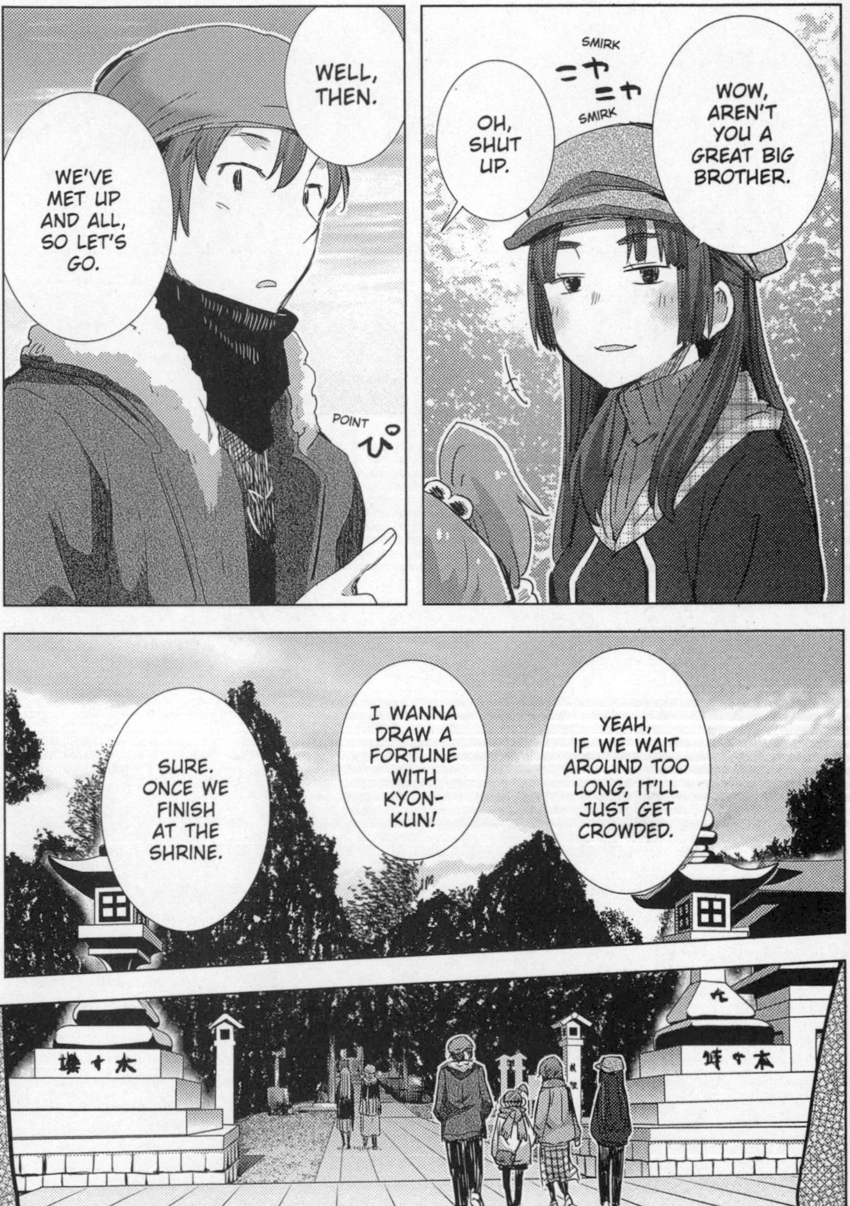
WOW, AREN'T YOU A GREAT BIG BROTHER.
SMIRK
SMIRK
OH, SHUT UP.
WELL, THEN.
WE'VE MET UP AND ALL, SO LET'S GO.
POINT
YEAH, IF WE WAIT AROUND TOO LONG, IT'LL JUST GET CROWDED.
I WANNA DRAW A FORTUNE WITH KYON-KUN!
SURE. ONCE WE FINISH AT THE SHRINE.

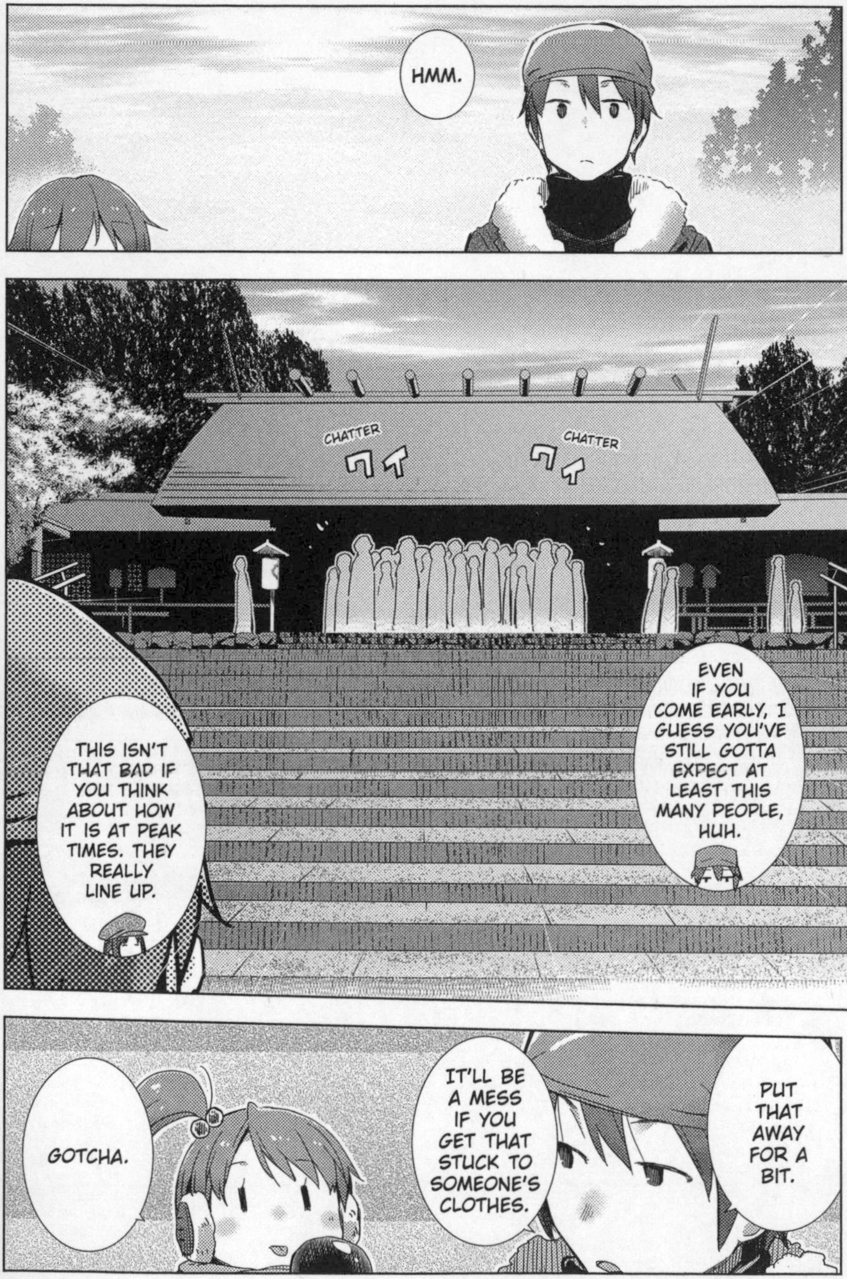
HMM.
CHATTER ワイ
CHATTER ワイ
EVEN IF YOU COME EARLY, I GUESS YOU'VE STILL GOTTA EXPECT AT LEAST THIS MANY PEOPLE, HUH.
THIS ISN'T THAT BAD IF YOU THINK ABOUT HOW IT IS AT PEAK TIMES. THEY REALLY LINE UP.
PUT THAT AWAY FOR A BIT.
IT'LL BE A MESS IF YOU GET THAT STUCK TO SOMEONE'S CLOTHES.
GOTCHA.

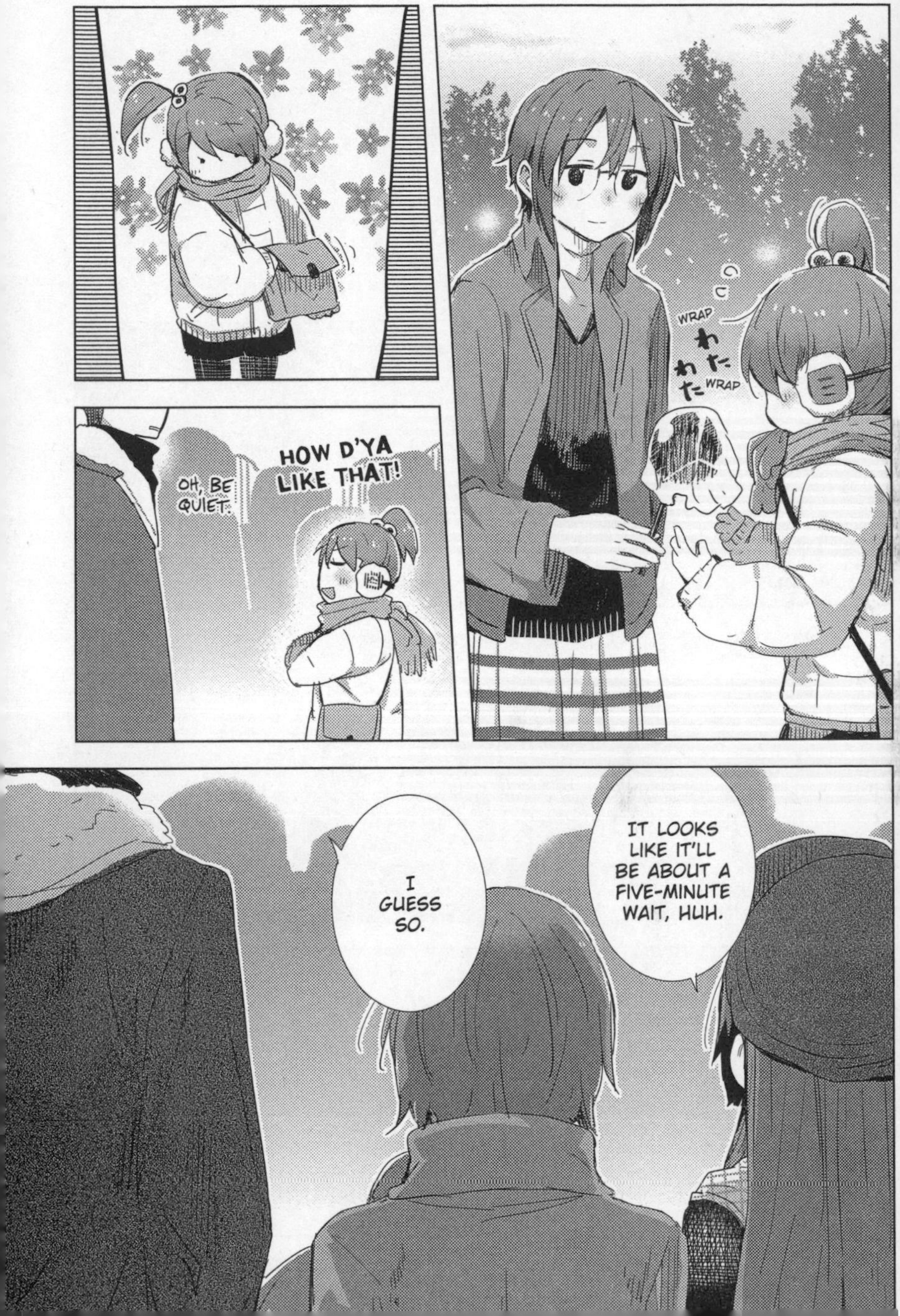
WRAP
わた
わた
WRAP
HOW D'YA LIKE THAT!
OH, BE QUIET.
IT LOOKS LIKE IT'LL BE ABOUT A FIVE-MINUTE WAIT, HUH.
I GUESS SO.

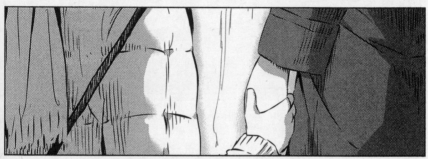

OKAY.

FIVE YEN, PLEASE!

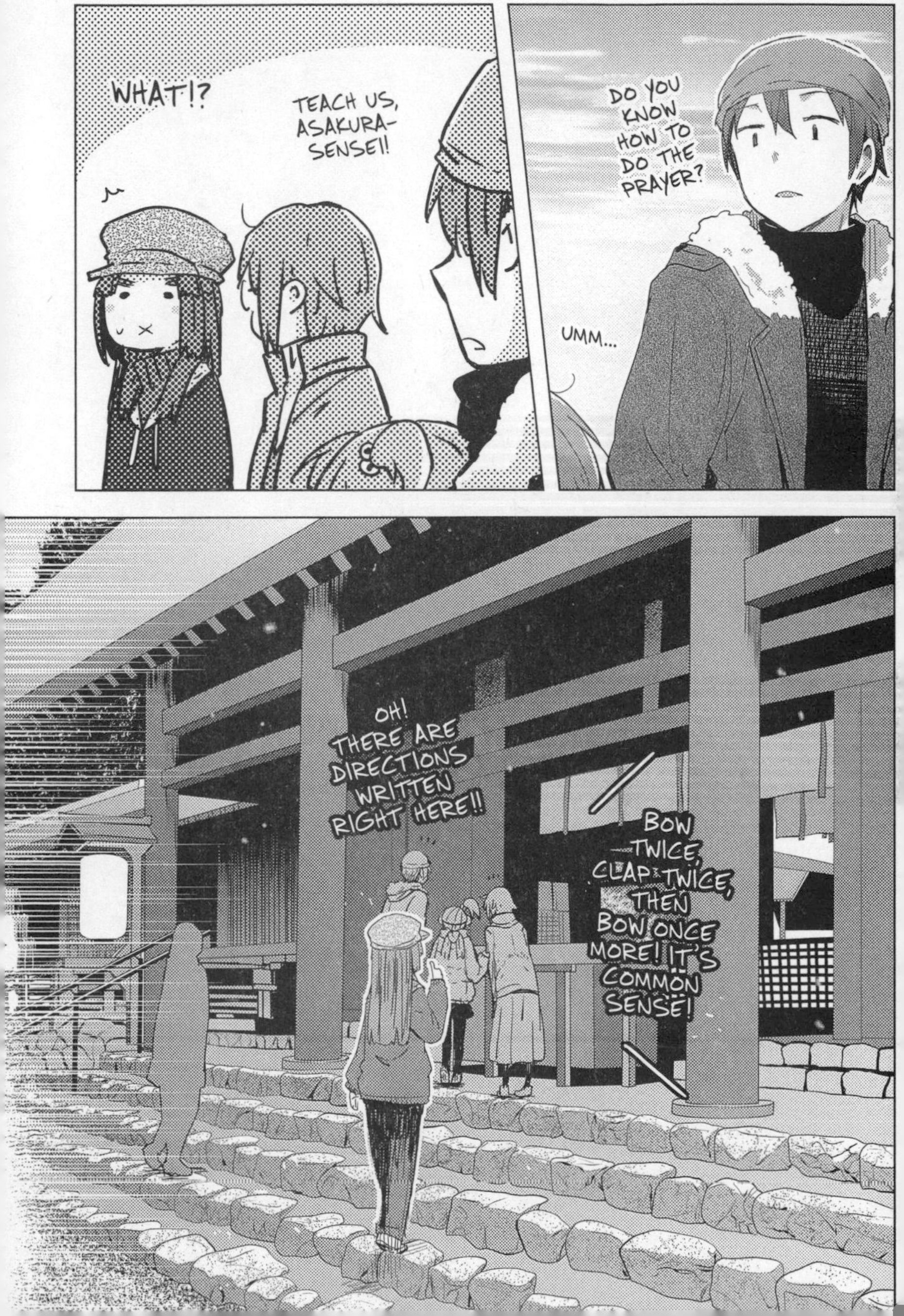
DO YOU KNOW HOW TO DO THE PRAYER?
UMM...
TEACH US, ASAKURA-SENSEI!!
WHAT!?
BOW TWICE, CLAP TWICE, THEN BOW ONCE MORE! IT'S COMMON SENSE!
OH! THERE ARE DIRECTIONS WRITTEN RIGHT HERE!!

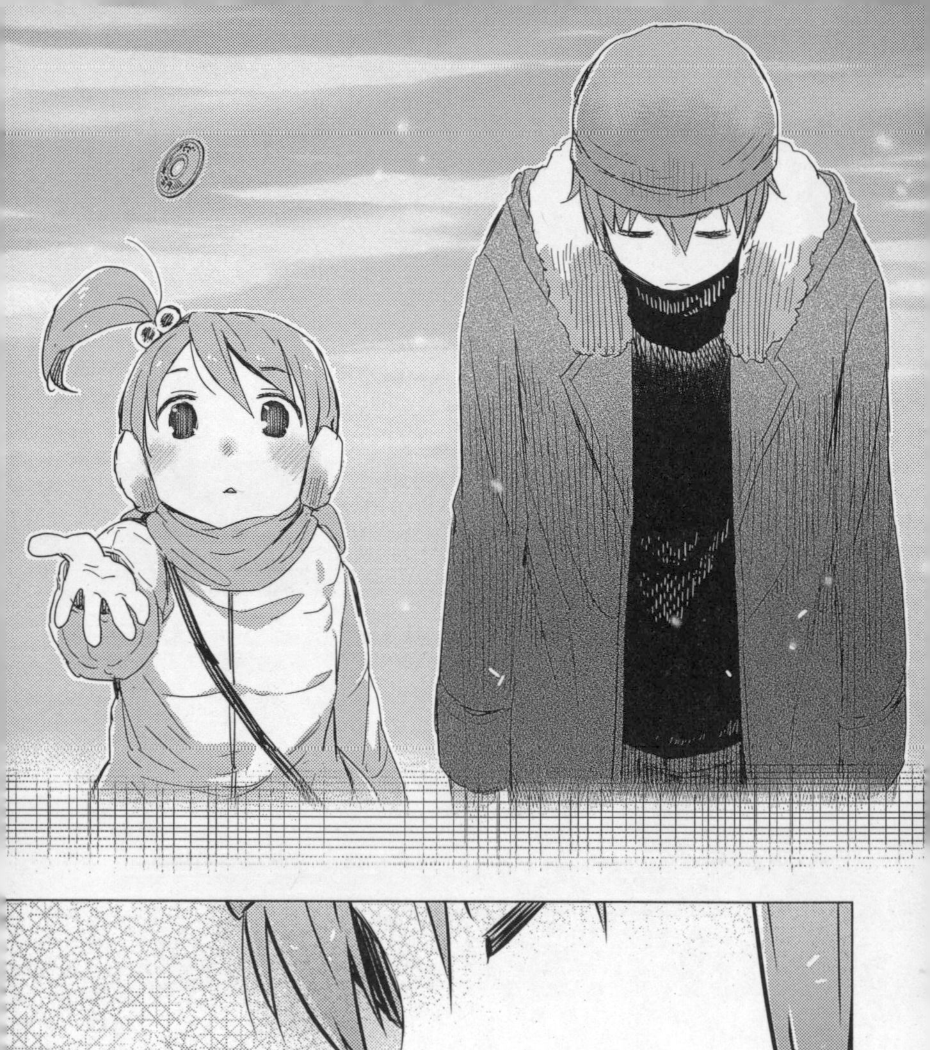

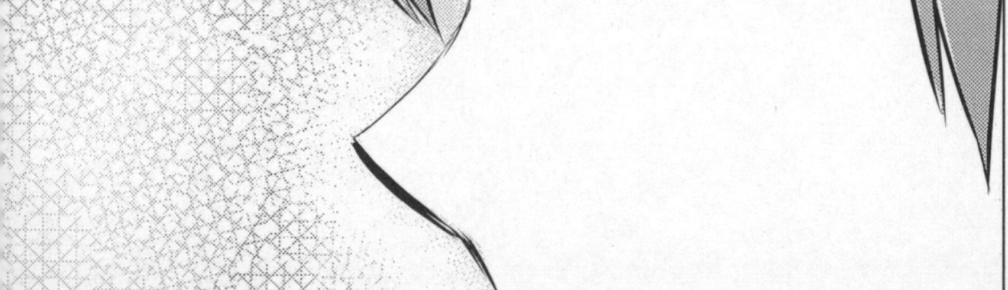

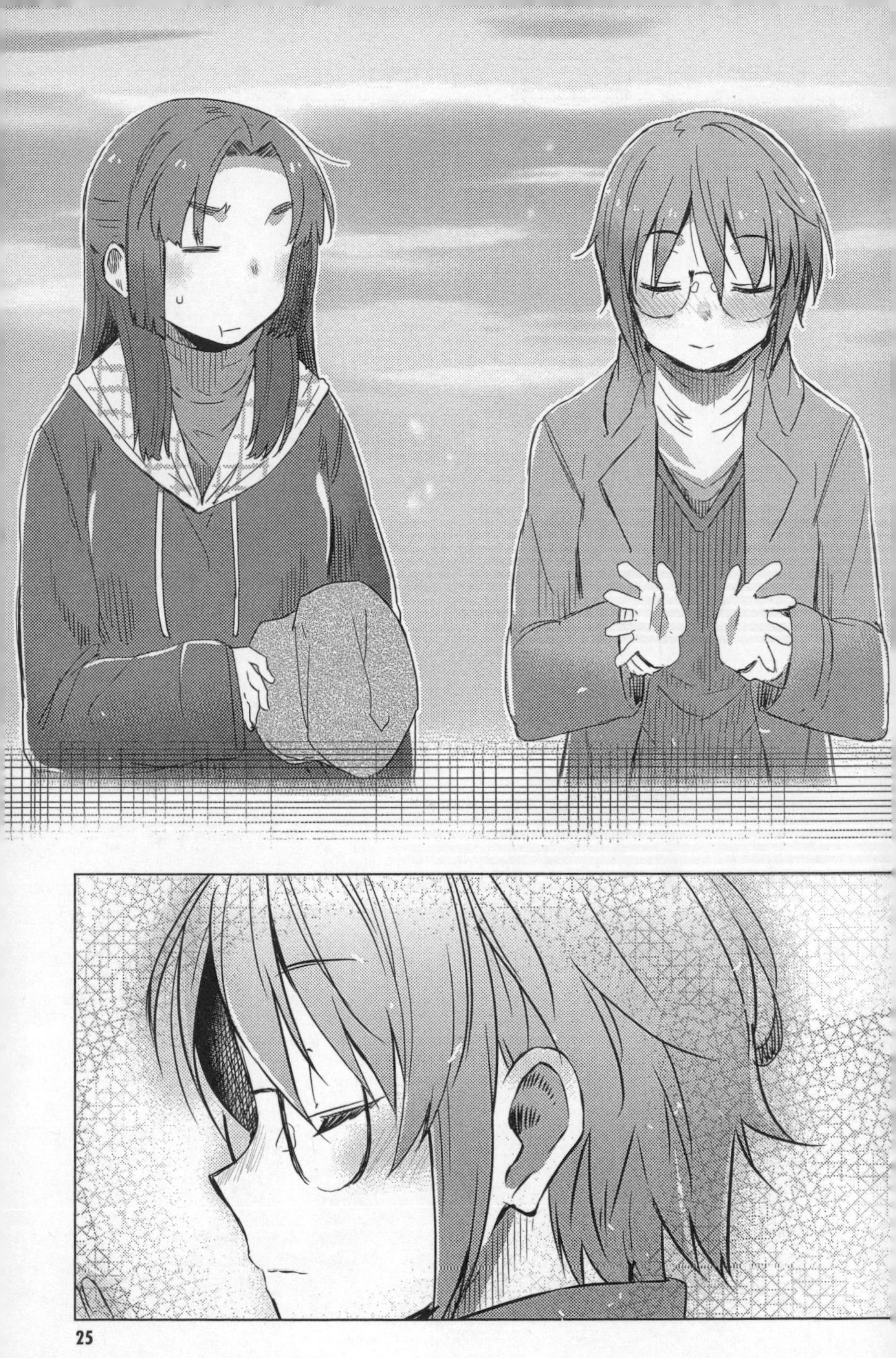

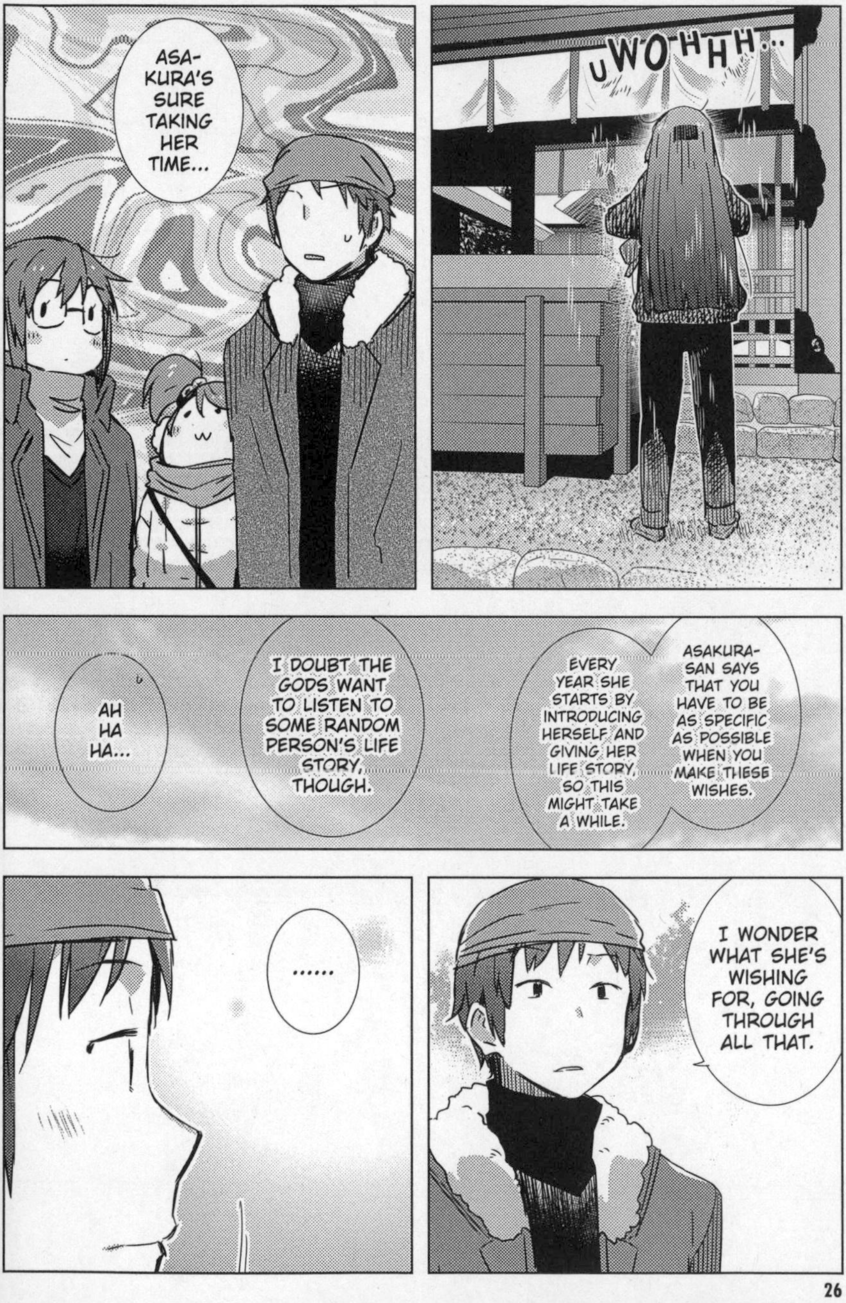
UWOHHH...
ASA-KURA'S SURE TAKING HER TIME...
ASAKURA-SAN SAYS THAT YOU HAVE TO BE AS SPECIFIC AS POSSIBLE WHEN YOU MAKE THESE WISHES.
EVERY YEAR SHE STARTS BY INTRODUCING HERSELF AND GIVING HER LIFE STORY, SO THIS MIGHT TAKE A WHILE.
I DOUBT THE GODS WANT TO LISTEN TO SOME RANDOM PERSON'S LIFE STORY, THOUGH.
AH HA HA...
I WONDER WHAT SHE'S WISHING FOR, GOING THROUGH ALL THAT.
......

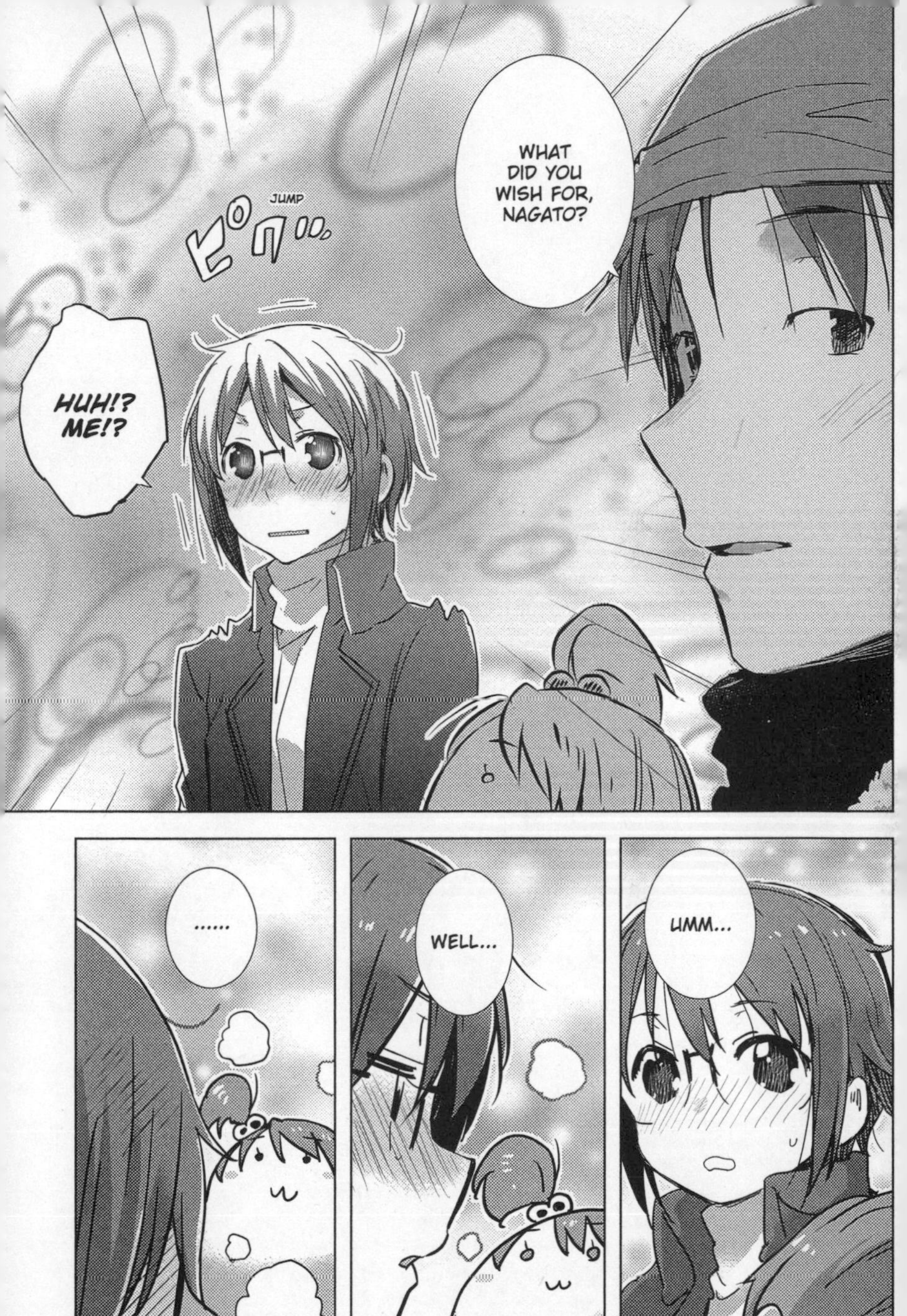
WHAT DID YOU WISH FOR, NAGATO?
JUMP
HUH!? ME!?
UMM...
WELL...
......

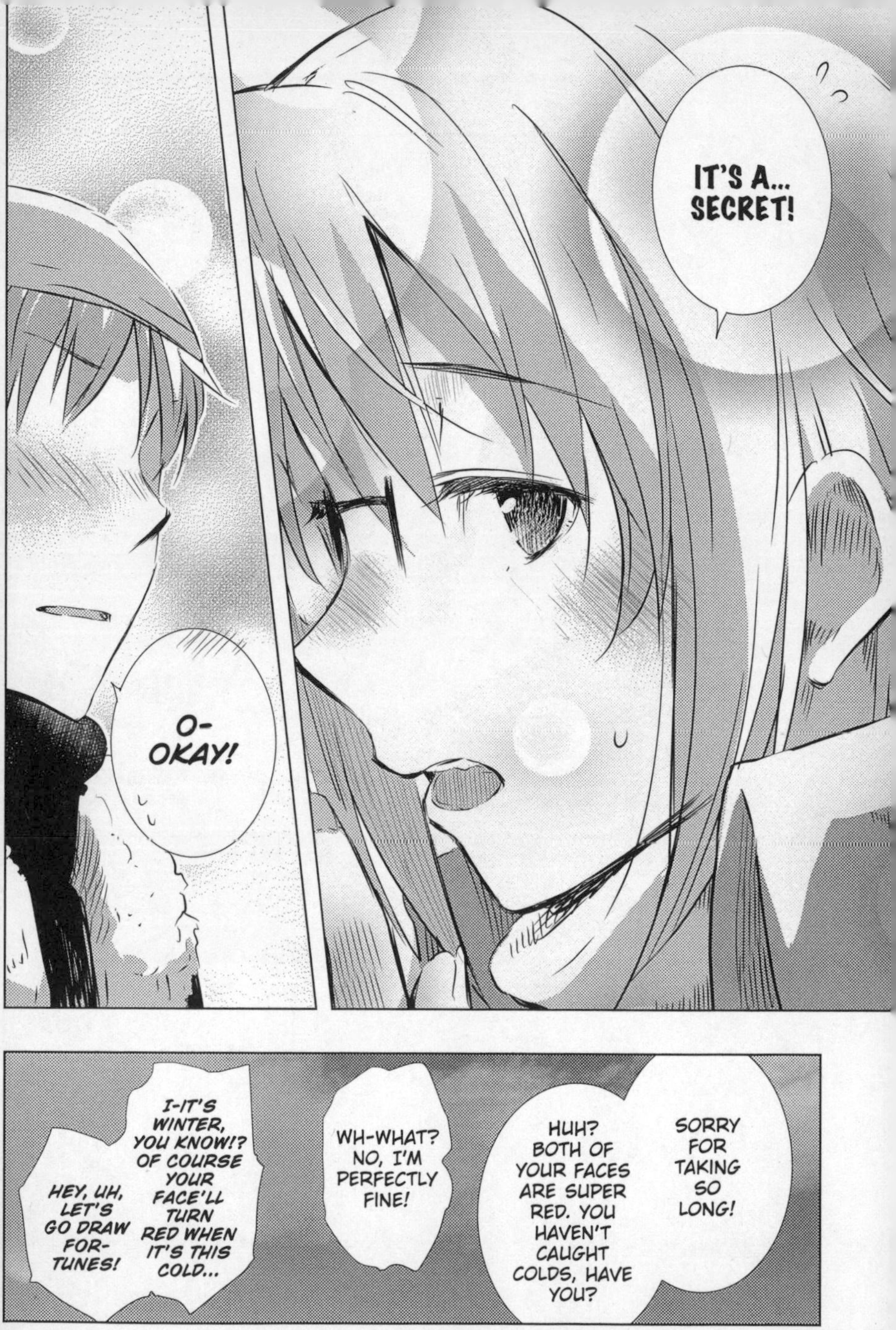
IT'S A... SECRET!
O-OKAY!
SORRY FOR TAKING SO LONG!
HUH? BOTH OF YOUR FACES ARE SUPER RED. YOU HAVEN'T CAUGHT COLDS, HAVE YOU?
WH-WHAT? NO, I'M PERFECTLY FINE!
I-IT'S WINTER, YOU KNOW!? OF COURSE YOUR FACE'LL TURN RED WHEN IT'S THIS COLD...
HEY, UH, LET'S GO DRAW FOR-TUNES!

DUHHHH...

I LOVE DRAWING HER WHEN SHE'S LISTENING TO OTHER PEOPLE'S CONVERSA- TIONS WITHOUT INTERRUPTING BUT JUST SORT OF SPACING OUT.

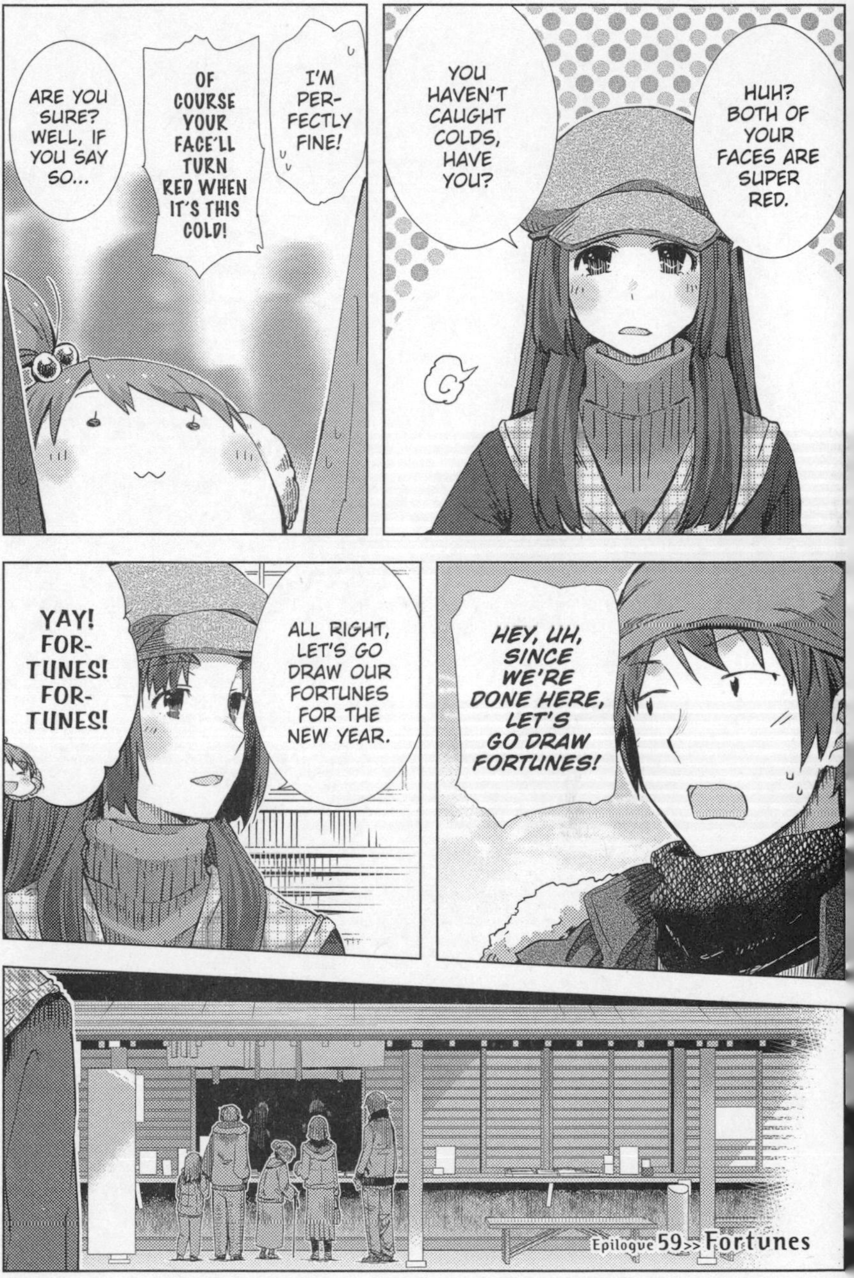
HUH? BOTH OF YOUR FACES ARE SUPER RED.
YOU HAVEN'T CAUGHT COLDS, HAVE YOU?
I'M PER-FECTLY FINE!
OF COURSE YOUR FACE'LL TURN RED WHEN IT'S THIS COLD!
ARE YOU SURE? WELL, IF YOU SAY SO...
HEY, UH, SINCE WE'RE DONE HERE, LET'S GO DRAW FORTUNES!
ALL RIGHT, LET'S GO DRAW OUR FORTUNES FOR THE NEW YEAR.
YAY! FOR-TUNES! FOR-TUNES!
Epilogue 59>> Fortunes

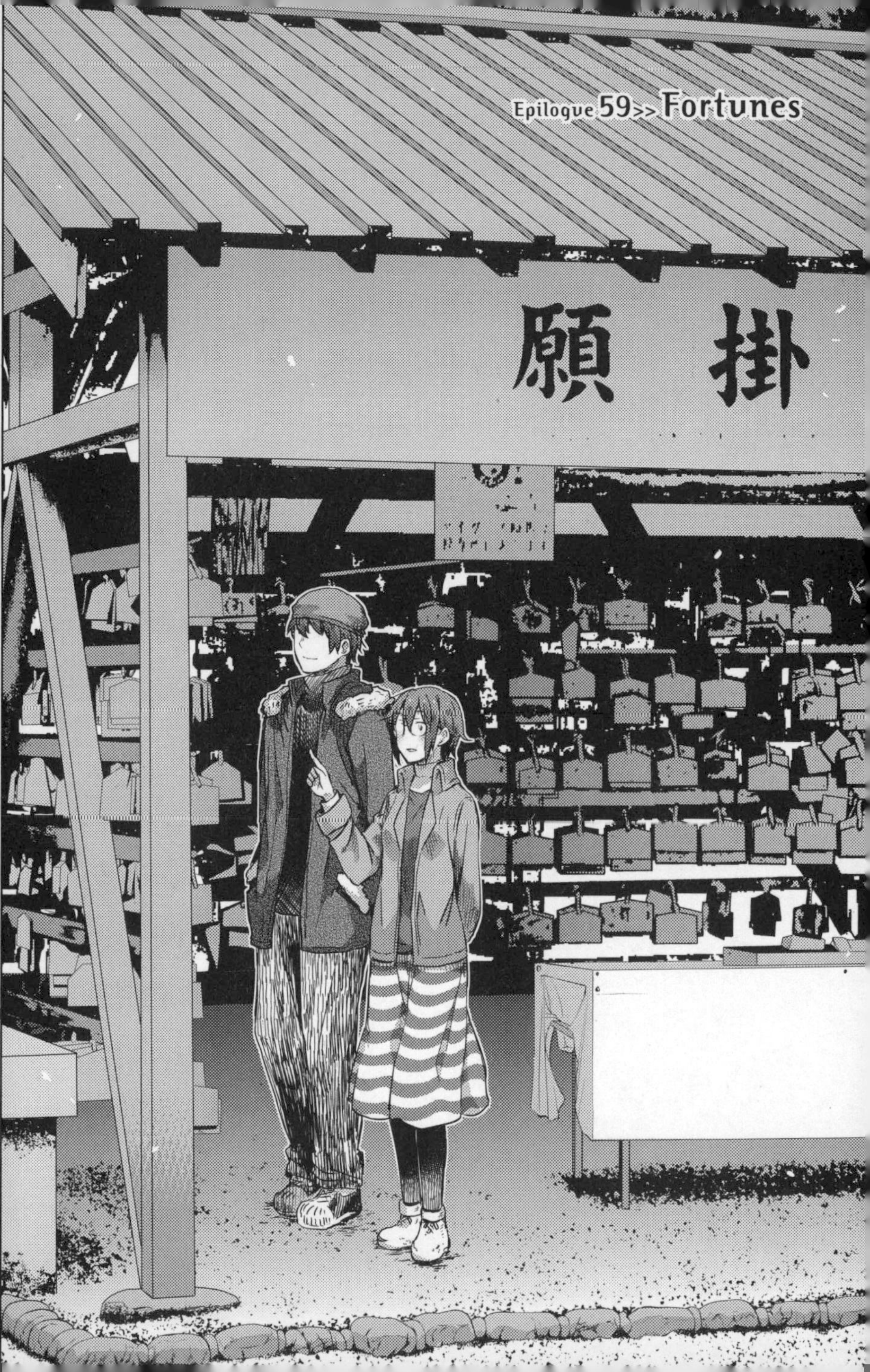
Epilogue 59>> Fortunes
願掛

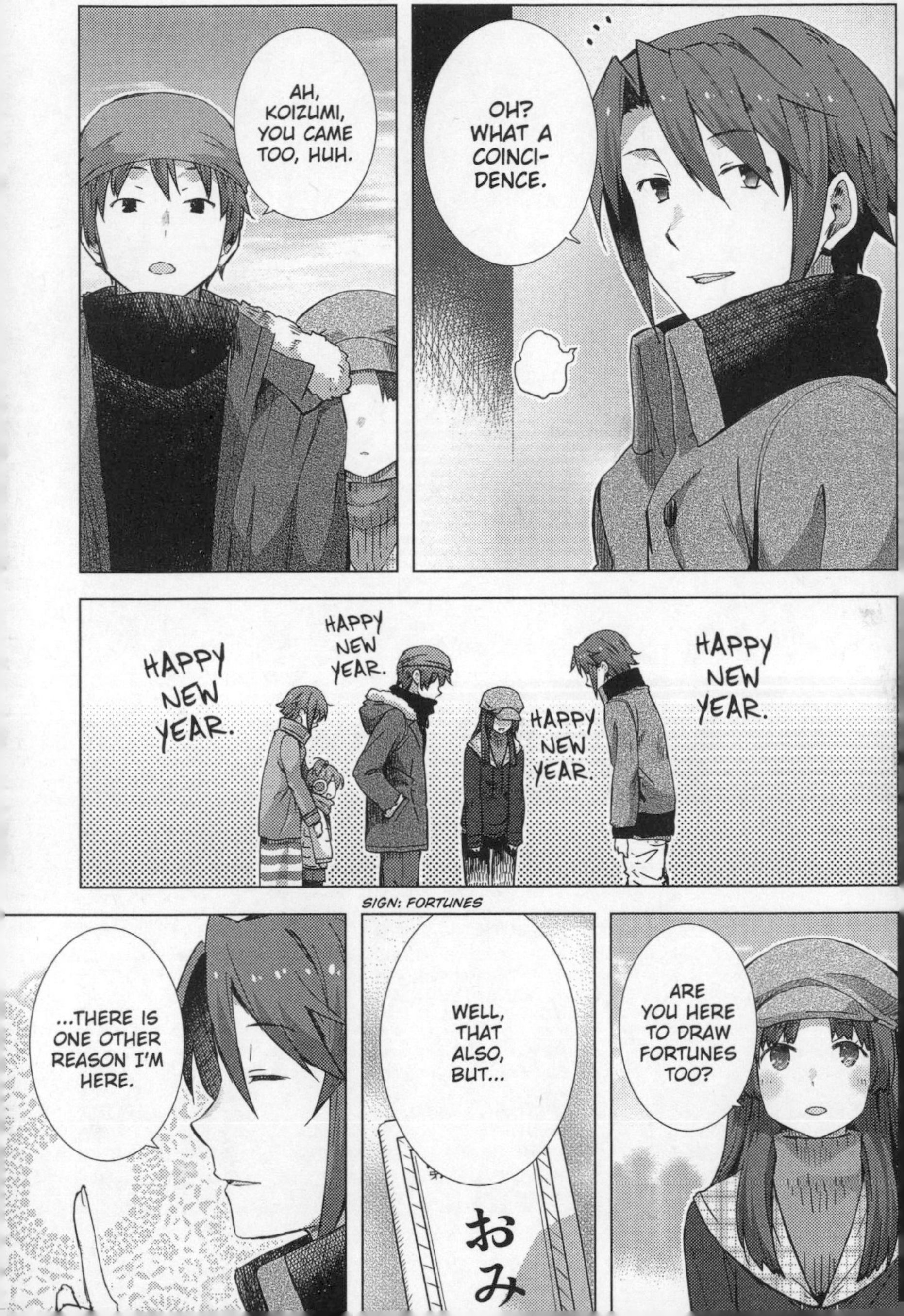
OH? WHAT A COINCIDENCE.
AH, KOIZUMI, YOU CAME TOO, HUH.
HAPPY NEW YEAR.
HAPPY NEW YEAR.
HAPPY NEW YEAR.
HAPPY NEW YEAR.
SIGN: FORTUNES
ARE YOU HERE TO DRAW FORTUNES TOO?
WELL, THAT ALSO, BUT...
おみ
...THERE IS ONE OTHER REASON I'M HERE.

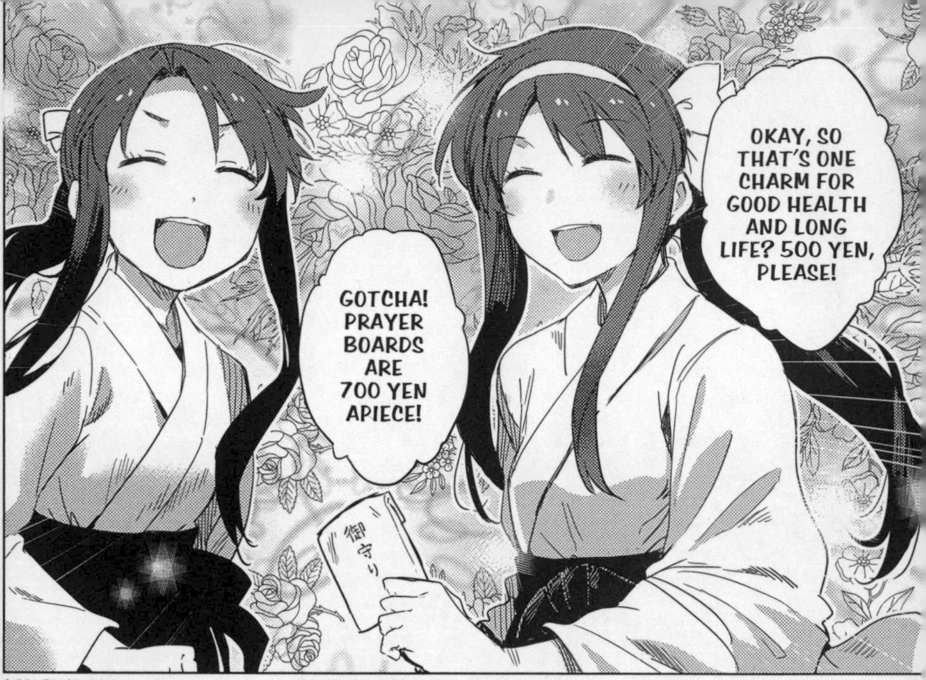
OKAY, SO THAT'S ONE CHARM FOR GOOD HEALTH AND LONG LIFE? 500 YEN, PLEASE!
GOTCHA! PRAYER BOARDS ARE 700 YEN APIECE!
御守り

*TSURUYA-SAN

ENVELOPE: PROTECTION CHARM

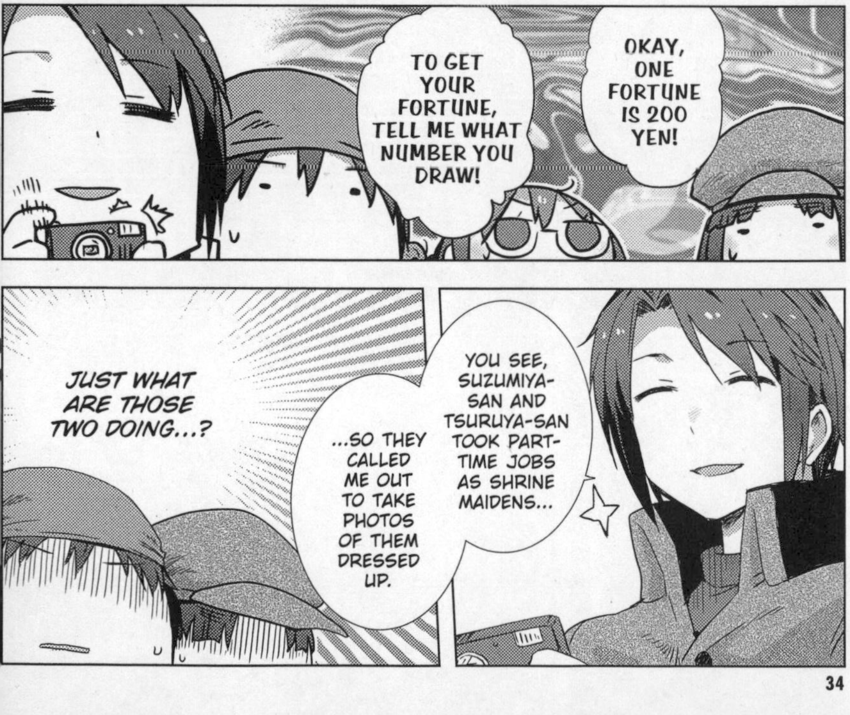
OKAY, ONE FORTUNE IS 200 YEN!
TO GET YOUR FORTUNE, TELL ME WHAT NUMBER YOU DRAW!
YOU SEE, SUZUMIYA-SAN AND TSURUYA-SAN TOOK PART-TIME JOBS AS SHRINE MAIDENS...
...SO THEY CALLED ME OUT TO TAKE PHOTOS OF THEM DRESSED UP.
JUST WHAT ARE THOSE TWO DOING...?

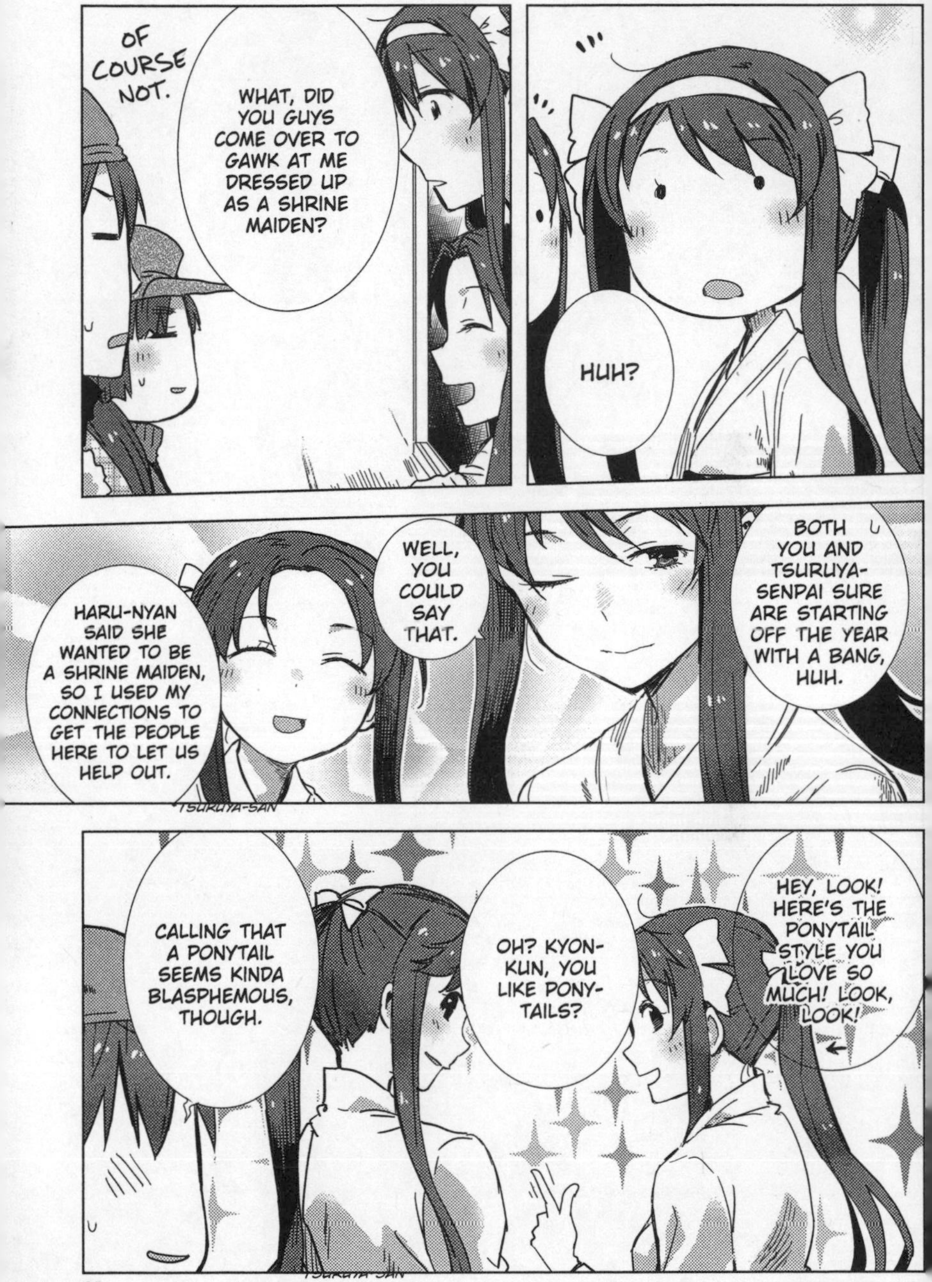
HUH?
WHAT, DID YOU GUYS COME OVER TO GAWK AT ME DRESSED UP AS A SHRINE MAIDEN?
OF COURSE NOT.
BOTH YOU AND TSURUYA-SENPAI SURE ARE STARTING OFF THE YEAR WITH A BANG, HUH.
WELL, YOU COULD SAY THAT.
HARU-NYAN SAID SHE WANTED TO BE A SHRINE MAIDEN, SO I USED MY CONNECTIONS TO GET THE PEOPLE HERE TO LET US HELP OUT.
TSURUYA-SAN
HEY, LOOK! HERE'S THE PONYTAIL STYLE YOU LOVE SO MUCH! LOOK, LOOK!
OH? KYON-KUN, YOU LIKE PONY-TAILS?
CALLING THAT A PONYTAIL SEEMS KINDA BLASPHEMOUS, THOUGH.
TSURUYA-SAN

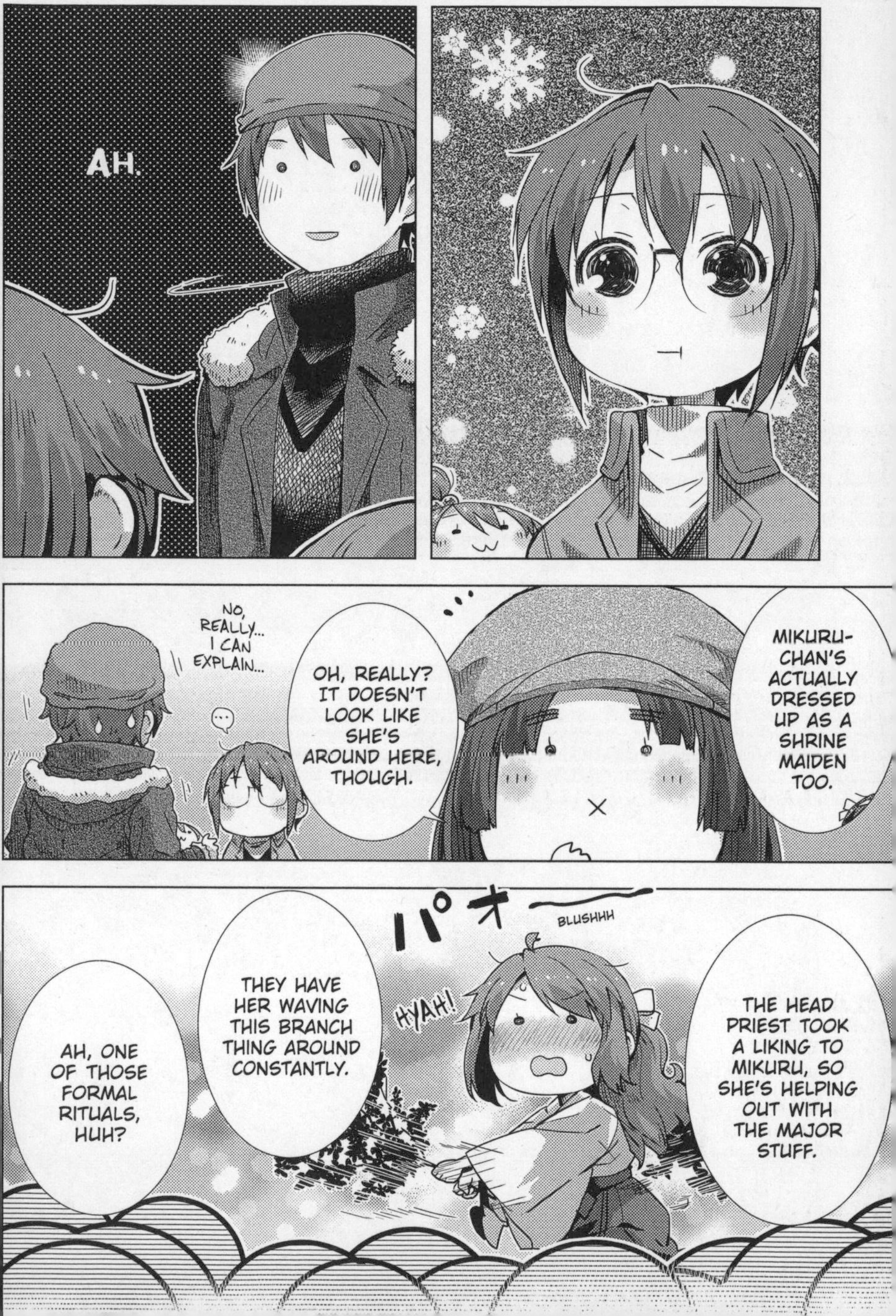
AH.
MIKURU-CHAN'S ACTUALLY DRESSED UP AS A SHRINE MAIDEN TOO.
OH, REALLY? IT DOESN'T LOOK LIKE SHE'S AROUND HERE, THOUGH.
NO, REALLY... I CAN EXPLAIN...
...
パオーー
BLUSHHH
THE HEAD PRIEST TOOK A LIKING TO MIKURU, SO SHE'S HELPING OUT WITH THE MAJOR STUFF.
HYAH!
THEY HAVE HER WAVING THIS BRANCH THING AROUND CONSTANTLY.
AH, ONE OF THOSE FORMAL RITUALS, HUH?

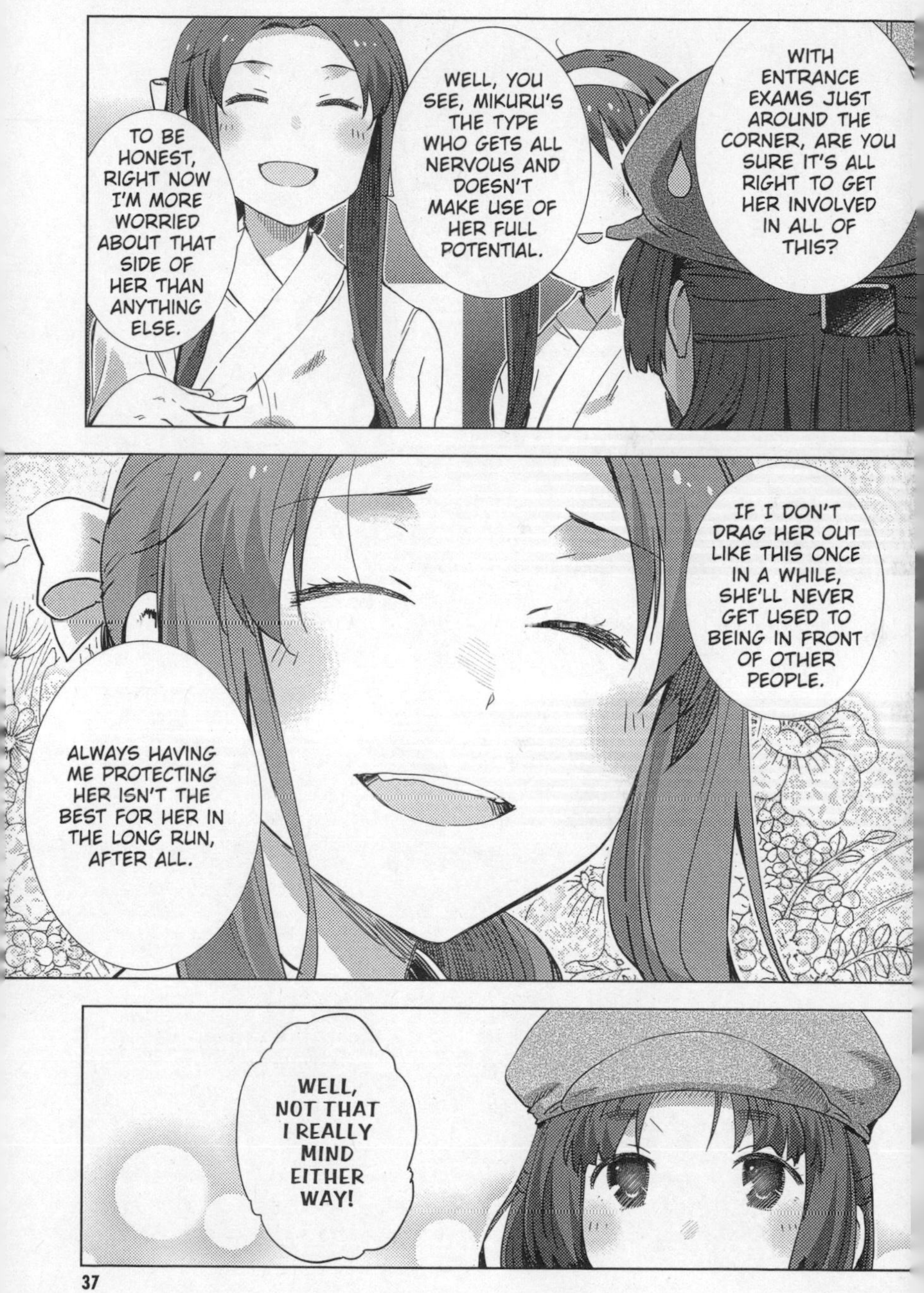
WITH ENTRANCE EXAMS JUST AROUND THE CORNER, ARE YOU SURE IT'S ALL RIGHT TO GET HER INVOLVED IN ALL OF THIS?
WELL, YOU SEE, MIKURU'S THE TYPE WHO GETS ALL NERVOUS AND DOESN'T MAKE USE OF HER FULL POTENTIAL.
TO BE HONEST, RIGHT NOW I'M MORE WORRIED ABOUT THAT SIDE OF HER THAN ANYTHING ELSE.
IF I DON'T DRAG HER OUT LIKE THIS ONCE IN A WHILE, SHE'LL NEVER GET USED TO BEING IN FRONT OF OTHER PEOPLE.
ALWAYS HAVING ME PROTECTING HER ISN'T THE BEST FOR HER IN THE LONG RUN, AFTER ALL.
WELL, NOT THAT I REALLY MIND EITHER WAY!

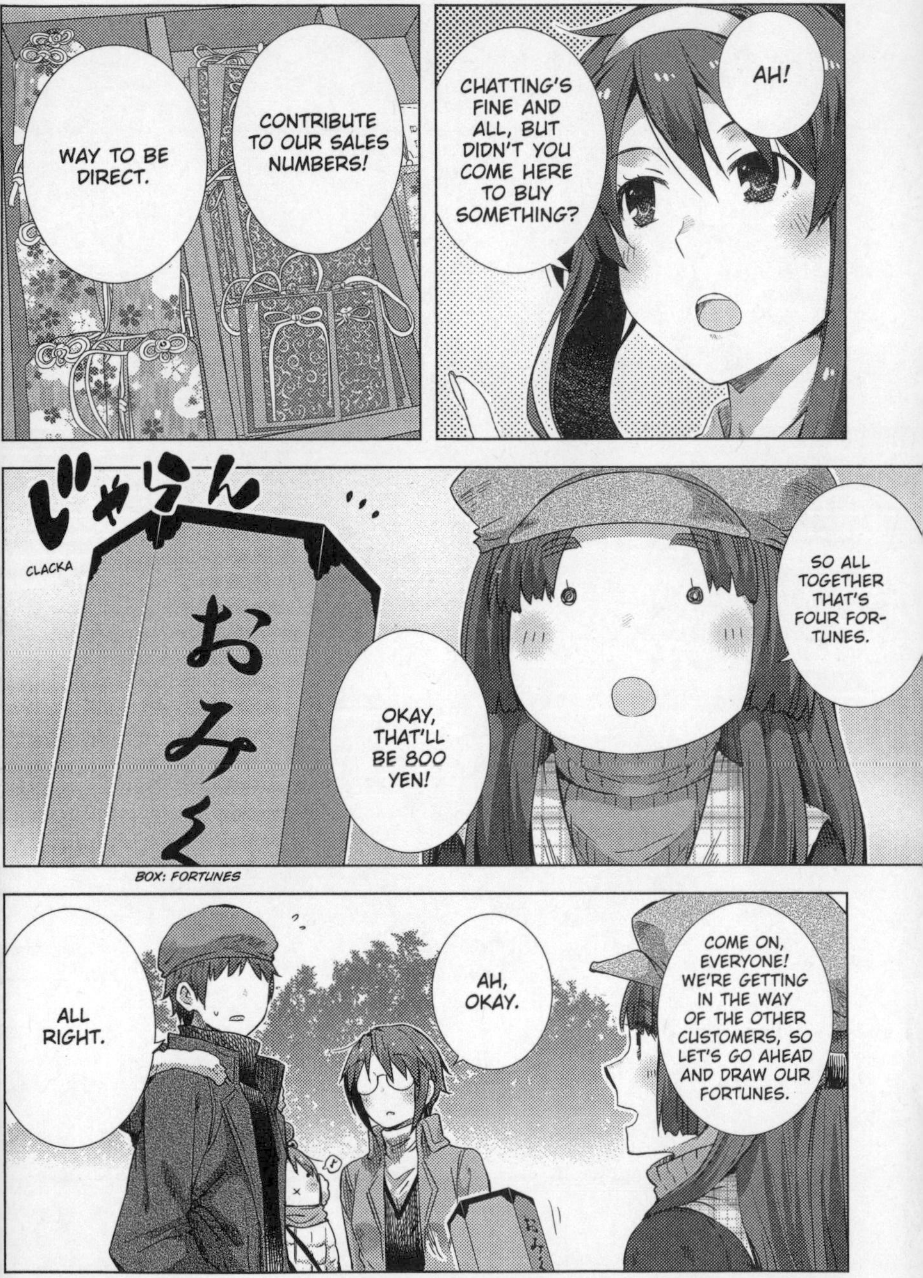
AH!
CHATTING'S FINE AND ALL, BUT DIDN'T YOU COME HERE TO BUY SOMETHING?
CONTRIBUTE TO OUR SALES NUMBERS!
WAY TO BE DIRECT.
SO ALL TOGETHER THAT'S FOUR FOR-TUNES.
...
OKAY, THAT'LL BE 800 YEN!
じゃらん
CLACKA
おみく
COME ON, EVERYONE! WE'RE GETTING IN THE WAY OF THE OTHER CUSTOMERS, SO LET'S GO AHEAD AND DRAW OUR FORTUNES.
AH, OKAY.
ALL RIGHT.
BOX: FORTUNES

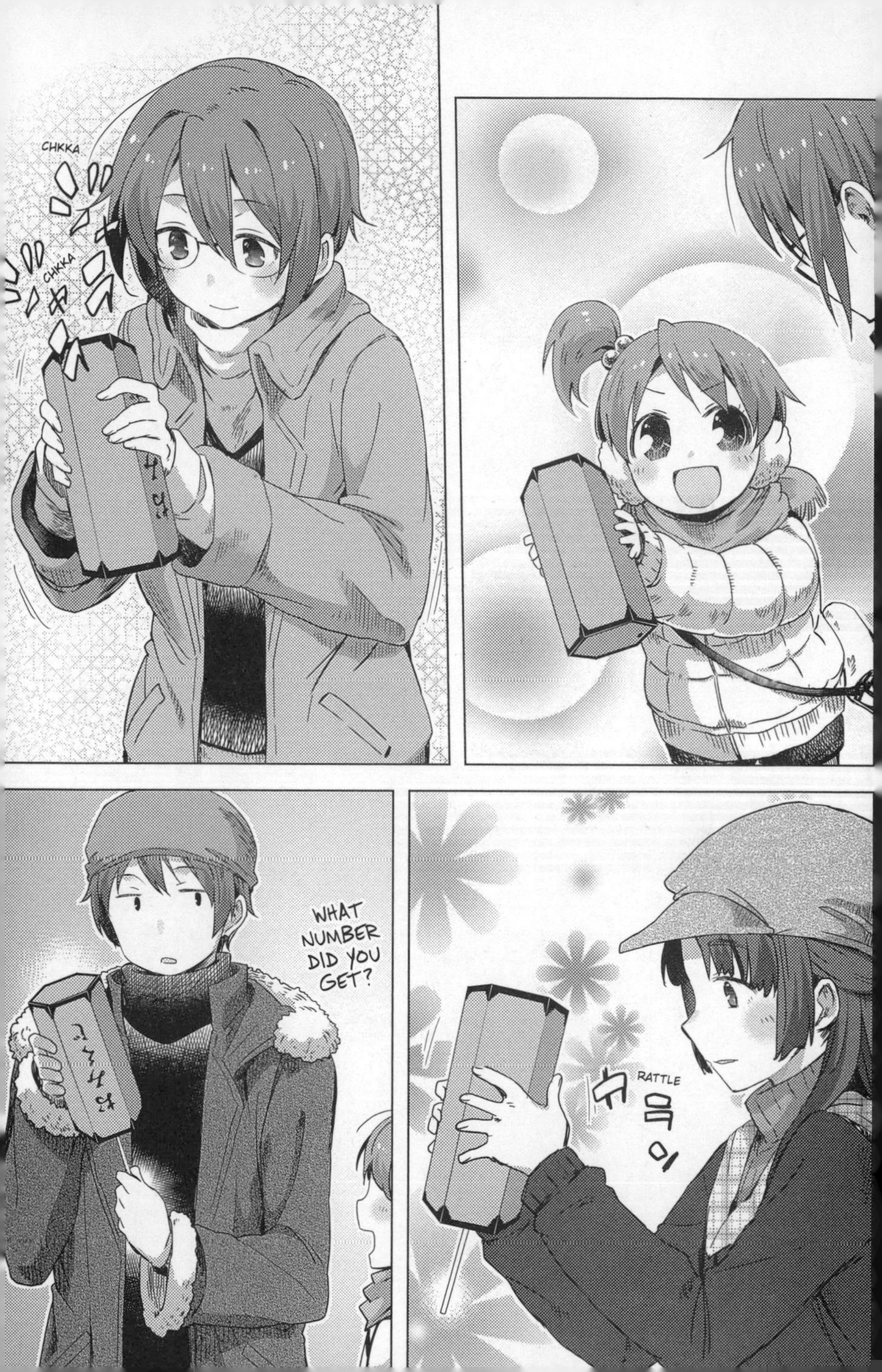
CHKKA
CHKKA
RATTLE
WHAT NUMBER DID YOU GET?

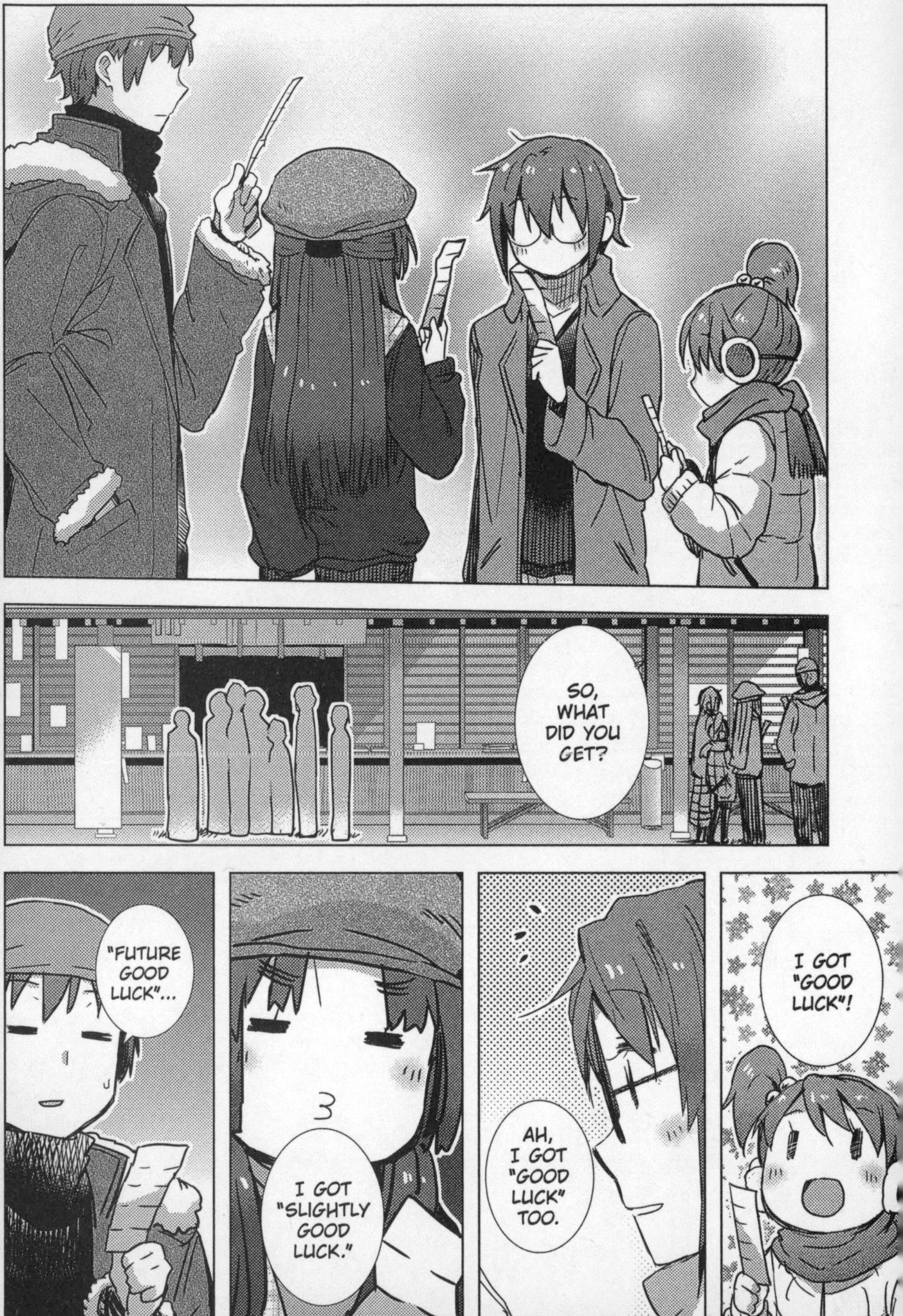
SO, WHAT DID YOU GET?
I GOT "GOOD LUCK"!
AH, I GOT "GOOD LUCK" TOO.
I GOT "SLIGHTLY GOOD LUCK."
"FUTURE GOOD LUCK"...

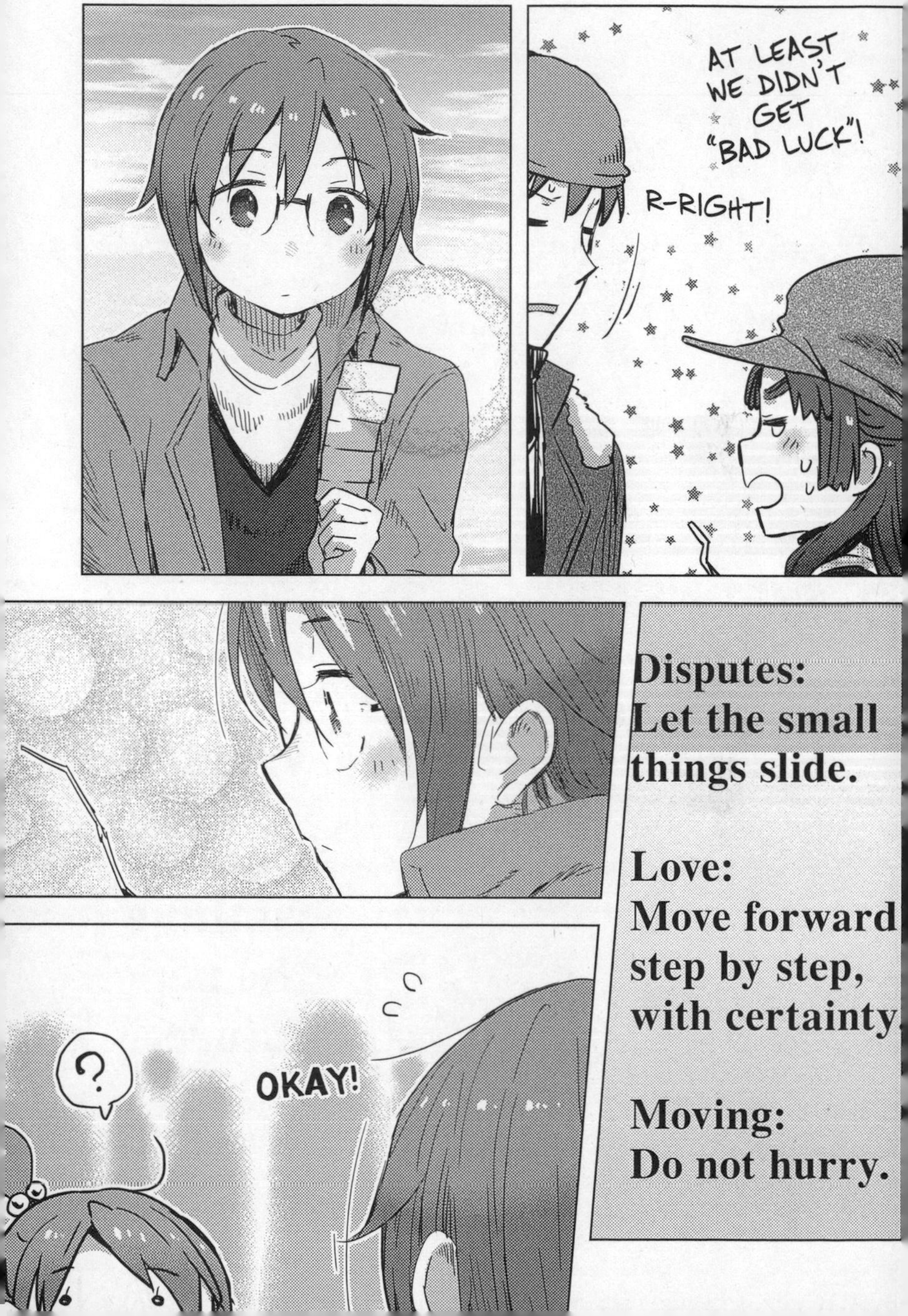
AT LEAST WE DIDN'T GET "BAD LUCK"!
R-RIGHT!
Disputes:
Let the small things slide.
Love:
Move forward step by step, with certainty.
Moving:
Do not hurry.
OKAY!
?

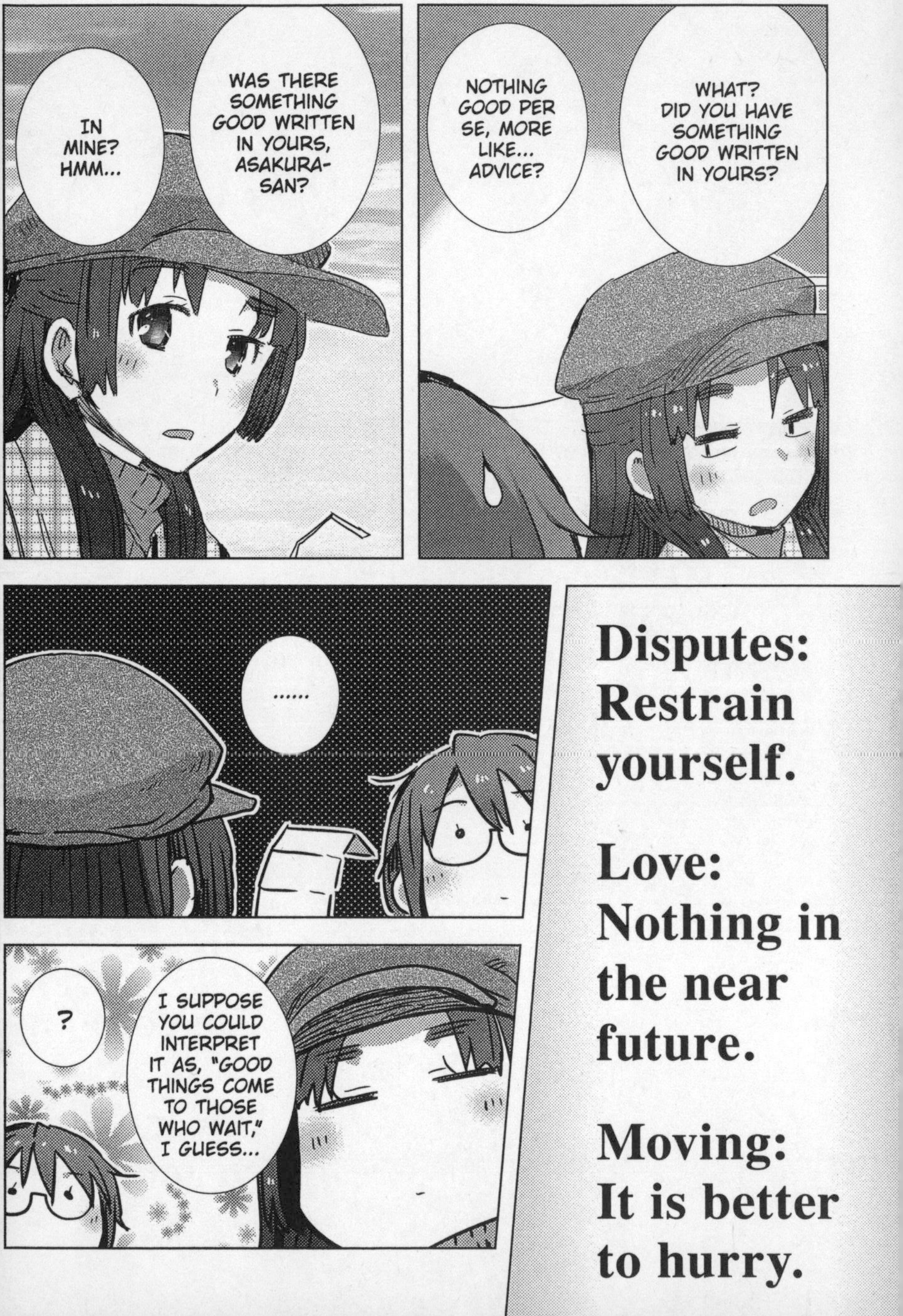
WHAT? DID YOU HAVE SOMETHING GOOD WRITTEN IN YOURS?
NOTHING GOOD PER SE, MORE LIKE... ADVICE?
WAS THERE SOMETHING GOOD WRITTEN IN YOURS, ASAKURA-SAN?
IN MINE? HMM...
Disputes: Restrain yourself.
Love: Nothing in the near future.
Moving: It is better to hurry.
......
I SUPPOSE YOU COULD INTERPRET IT AS, "GOOD THINGS COME TO THOSE WHO WAIT," I GUESS...
?

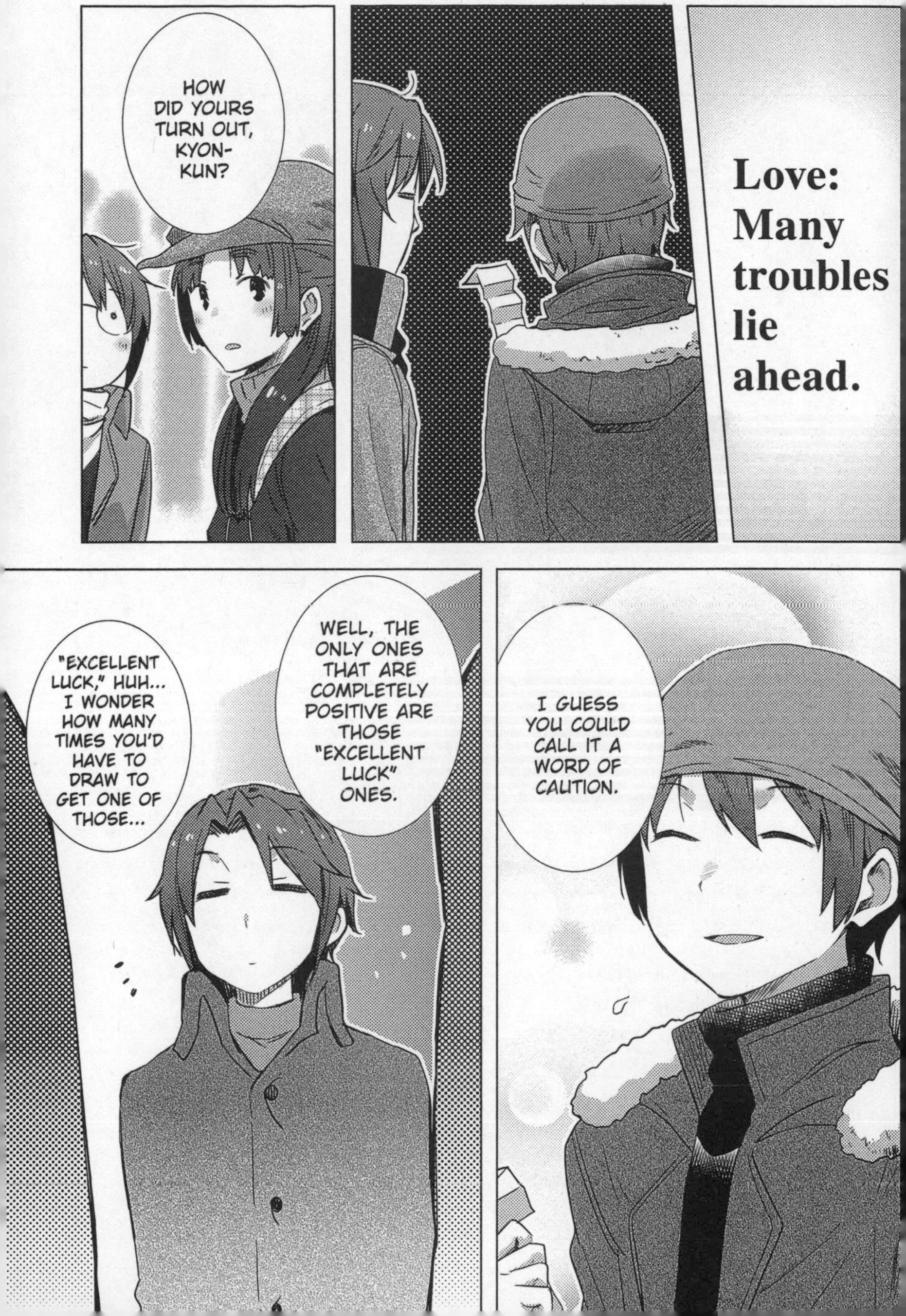
Love: Many troubles lie ahead.
HOW DID YOURS TURN OUT, KYON-KUN?
I GUESS YOU COULD CALL IT A WORD OF CAUTION.
WELL, THE ONLY ONES THAT ARE COMPLETELY POSITIVE ARE THOSE "EXCELLENT LUCK" ONES.
"EXCELLENT LUCK," HUH... I WONDER HOW MANY TIMES YOU'D HAVE TO DRAW TO GET ONE OF THOSE...

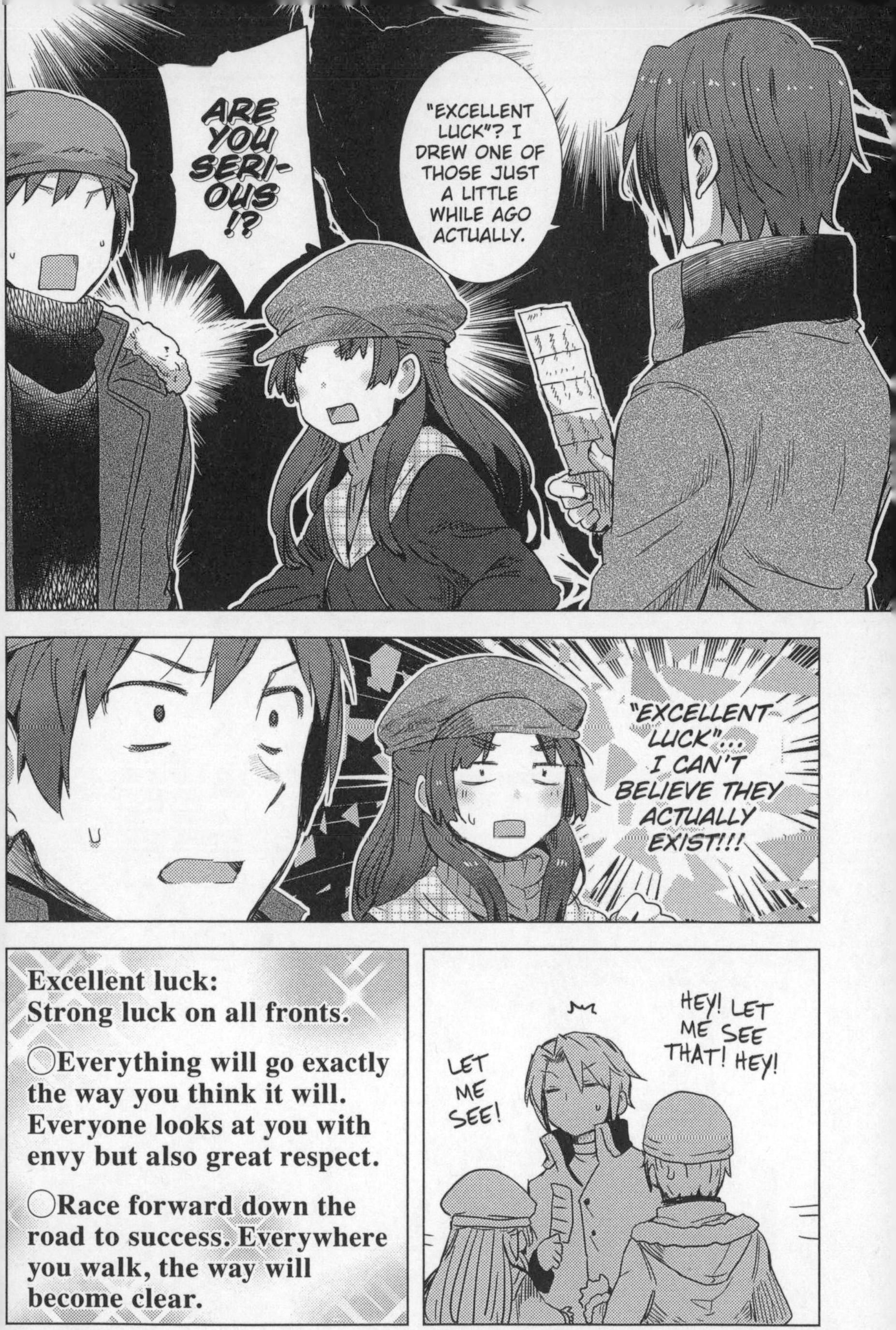
"EXCELLENT LUCK"? I DREW ONE OF THOSE JUST A LITTLE WHILE AGO ACTUALLY.
ARE YOU SERI-OUS!?
"EXCELLENT LUCK"... I CAN'T BELIEVE THEY ACTUALLY EXIST!!!
HEY! LET ME SEE THAT! HEY!
LET ME SEE!
Excellent luck: Strong luck on all fronts.
◯Everything will go exactly the way you think it will. Everyone looks at you with envy but also great respect.
◯Race forward down the road to success. Everywhere you walk, the way will become clear.

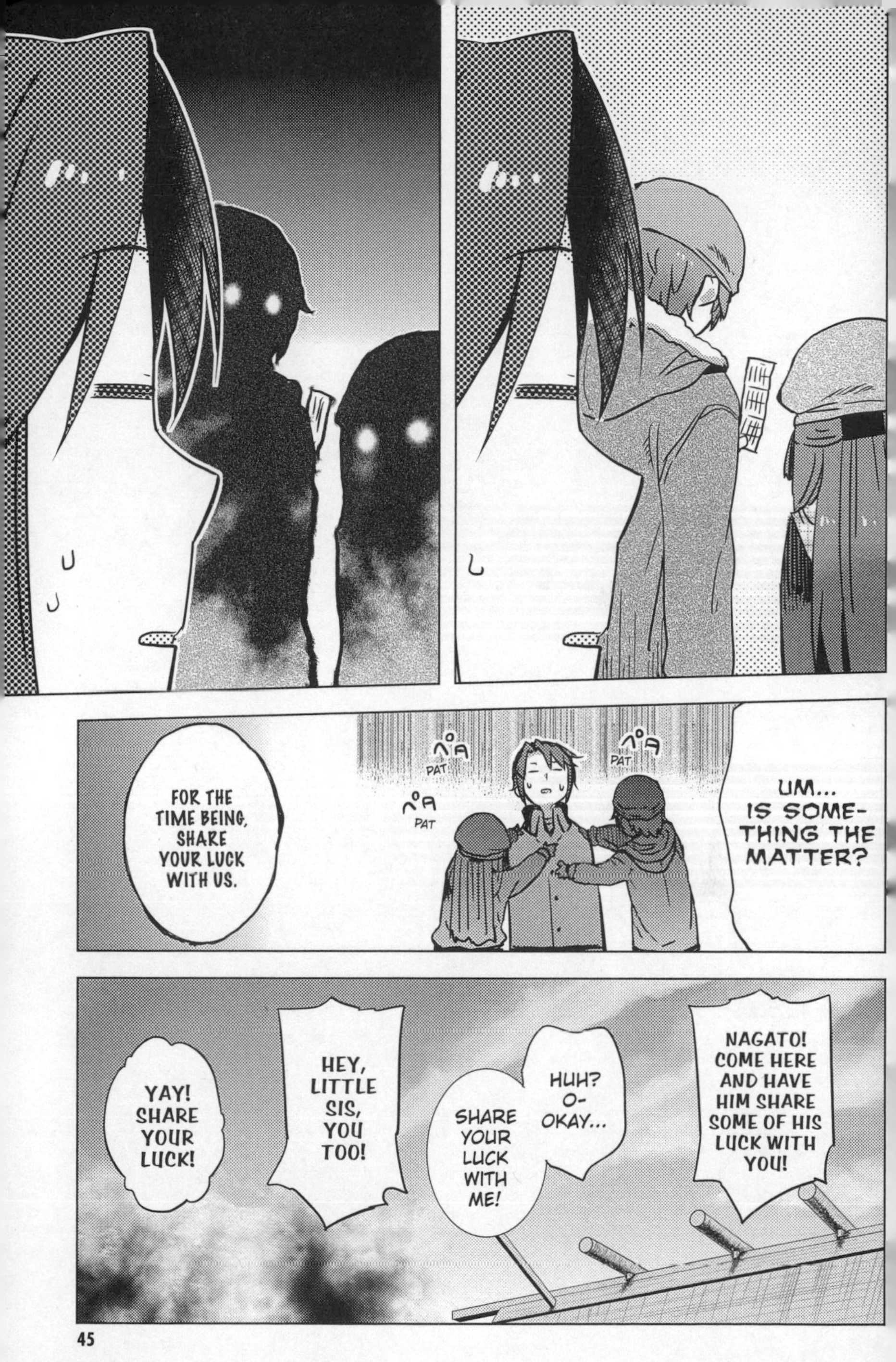
UM... IS SOME-THING THE MATTER?
PAT
PAT
PAT
FOR THE TIME BEING, SHARE YOUR LUCK WITH US.
NAGATO! COME HERE AND HAVE HIM SHARE SOME OF HIS LUCK WITH YOU!
HUH? O-OKAY...
SHARE YOUR LUCK WITH ME!
HEY, LITTLE SIS, YOU TOO!
YAY! SHARE YOUR LUCK!

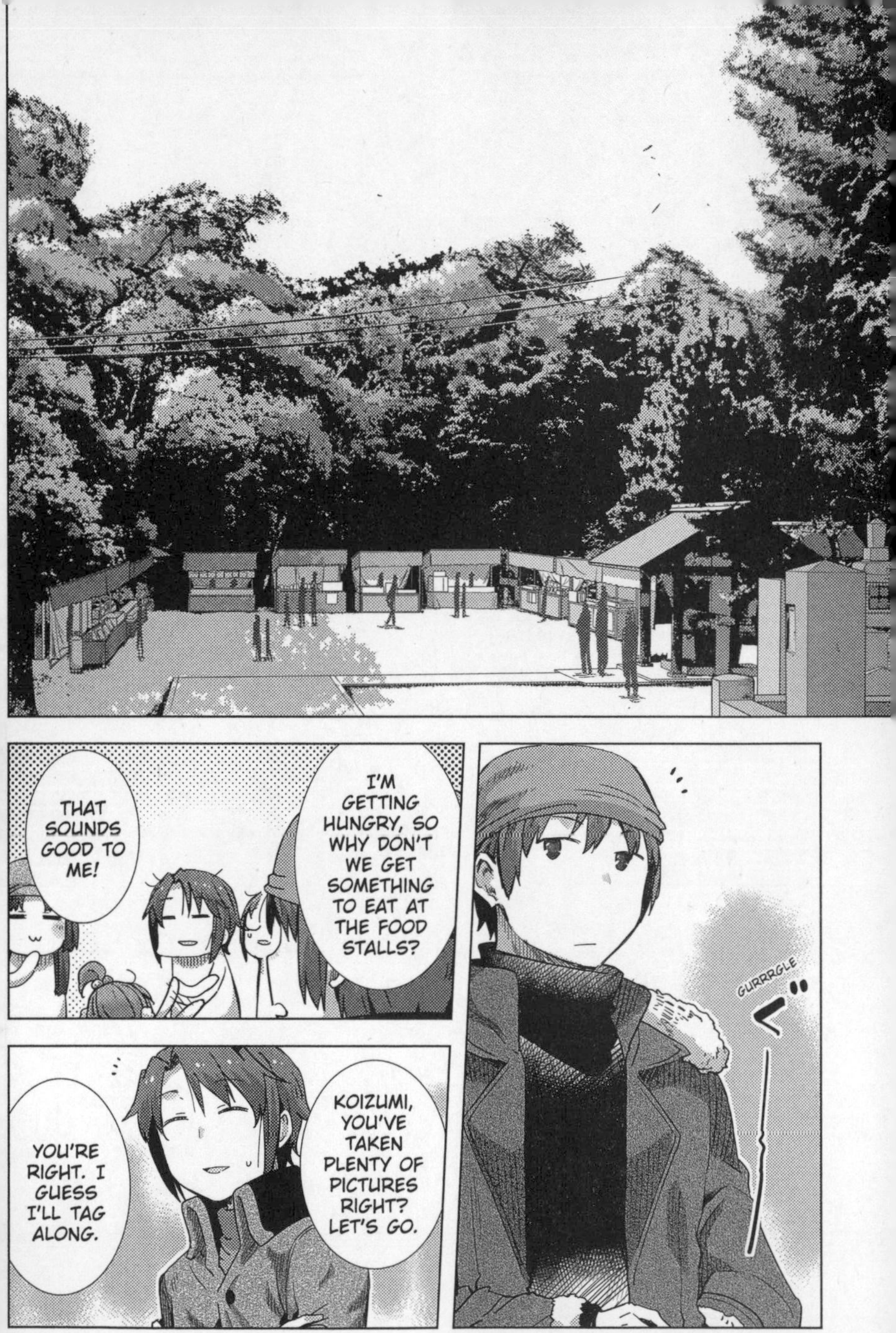
GURRRGLE
I'M GETTING HUNGRY, SO WHY DON'T WE GET SOMETHING TO EAT AT THE FOOD STALLS?
THAT SOUNDS GOOD TO ME!
KOIZUMI, YOU'VE TAKEN PLENTY OF PICTURES RIGHT? LET'S GO.
YOU'RE RIGHT. I GUESS I'LL TAG ALONG.

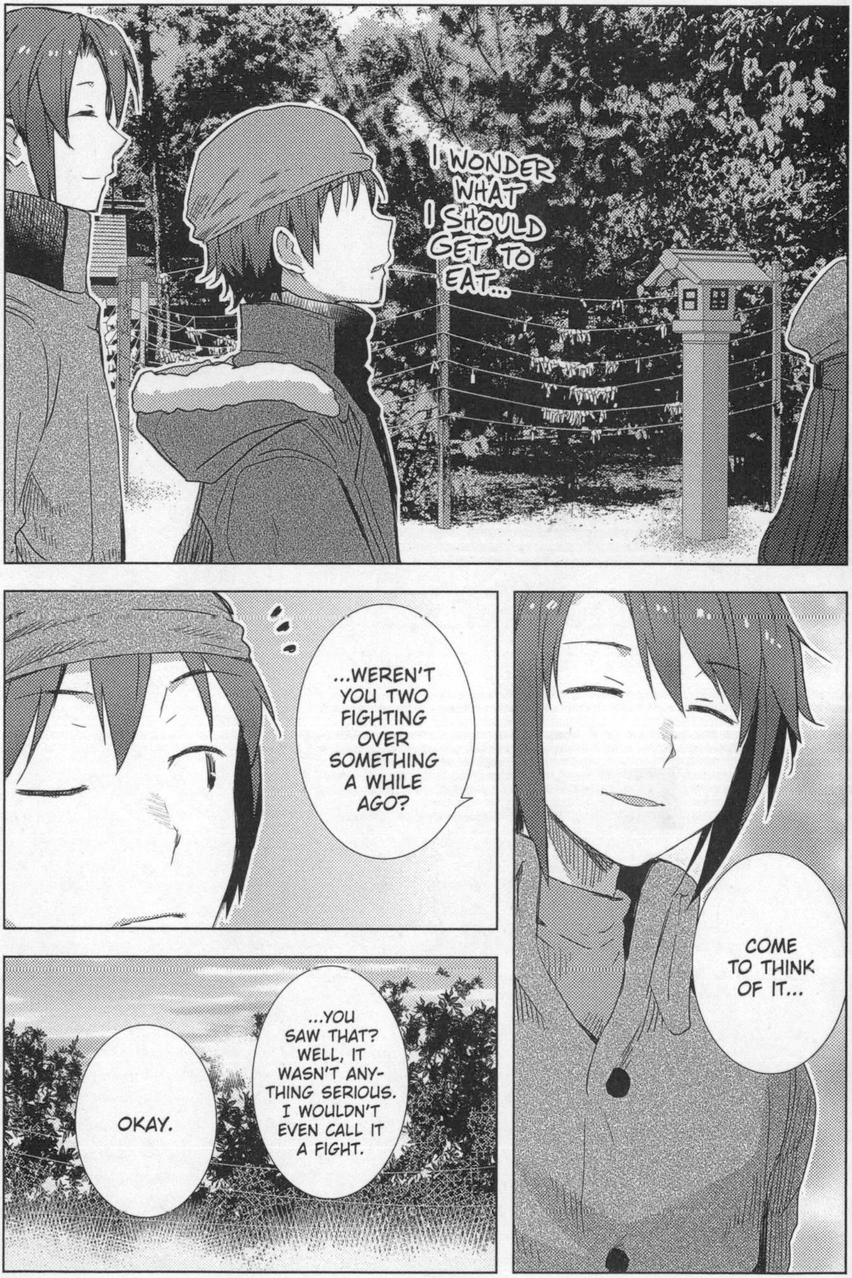
I WONDER WHAT I SHOULD GET TO EAT...
COME TO THINK OF IT...
...WEREN'T YOU TWO FIGHTING OVER SOMETHING A WHILE AGO?
...YOU SAW THAT? WELL, IT WASN'T ANY-THING SERIOUS. I WOULDN'T EVEN CALL IT A FIGHT.
OKAY.

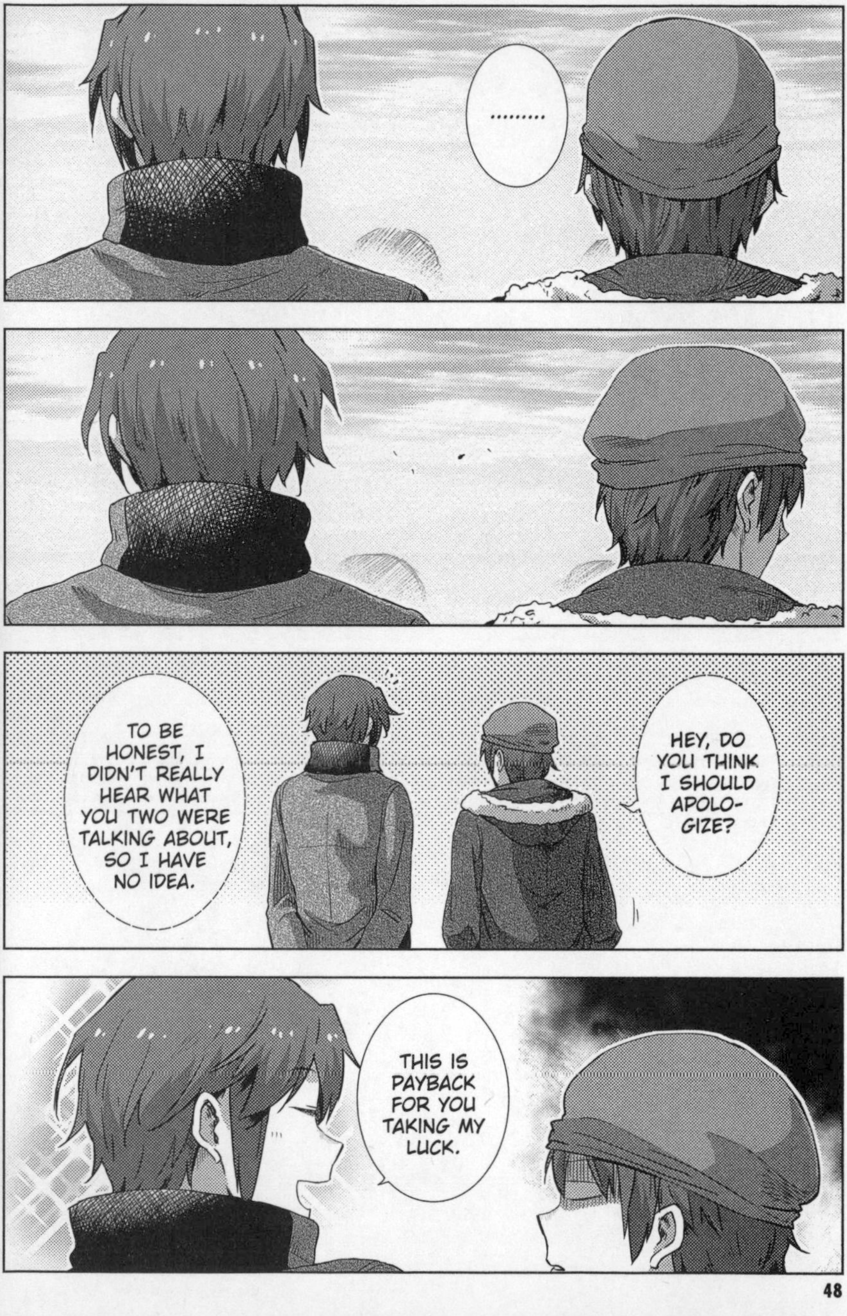
....
HEY, DO YOU THINK I SHOULD APOLO-GIZE?
TO BE HONEST, I DIDN'T REALLY HEAR WHAT YOU TWO WERE TALKING ABOUT, SO I HAVE NO IDEA.
THIS IS PAYBACK FOR YOU TAKING MY LUCK.

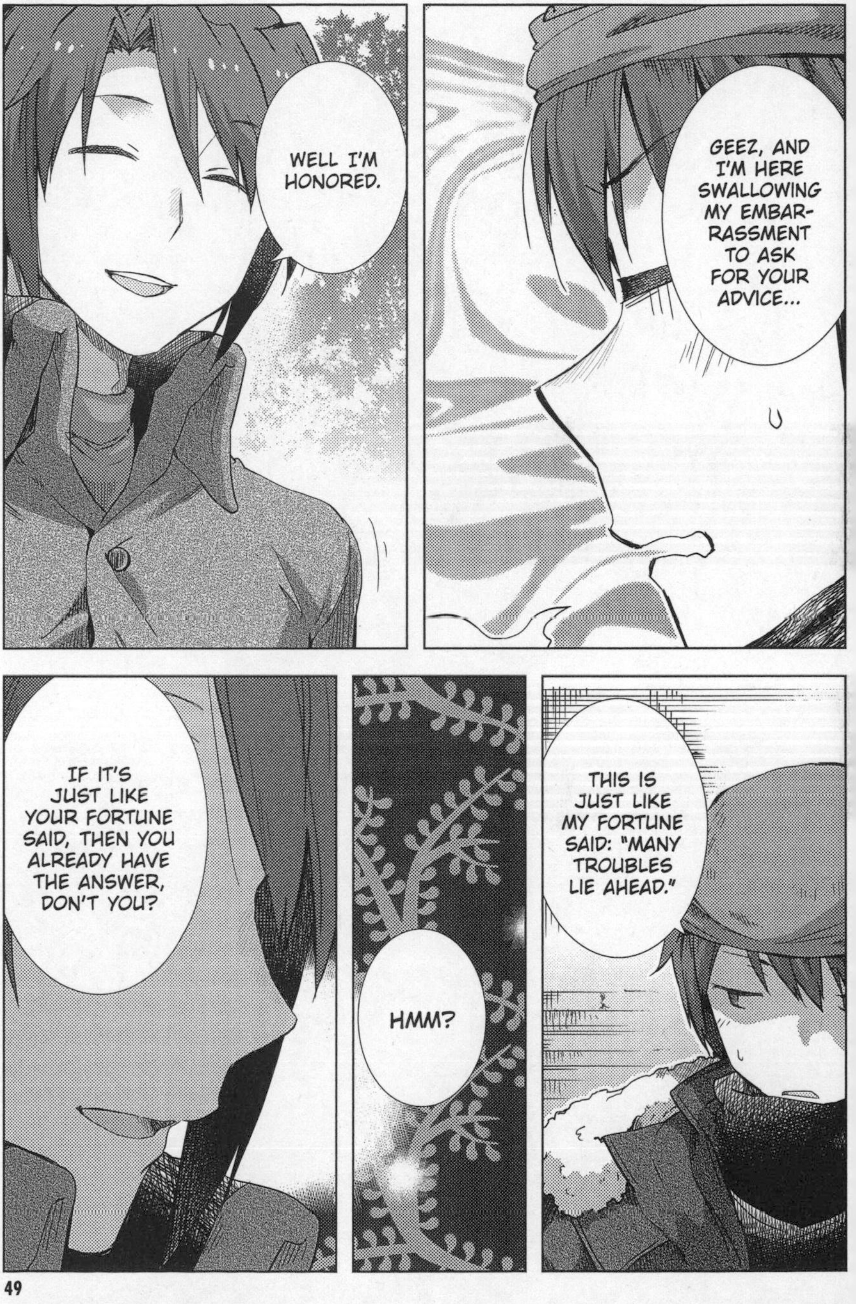
GEEZ, AND I'M HERE SWALLOWING MY EMBAR-RASSMENT TO ASK FOR YOUR ADVICE...
WELL I'M HONORED.
THIS IS JUST LIKE MY FORTUNE SAID: "MANY TROUBLES LIE AHEAD."
HMM?
IF IT'S JUST LIKE YOUR FORTUNE SAID, THEN YOU ALREADY HAVE THE ANSWER, DON'T YOU?

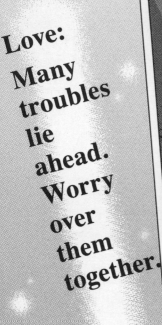

Love:

Many troubles lie ahead. Worry over them together.

"MANY TROUBLES LIE AHEAD. WORRY OVER THEM TOGETHER." THAT'S WHAT'S WRITTEN ON YOUR FORTUNE, IF I REMEMBER CORRECTLY.

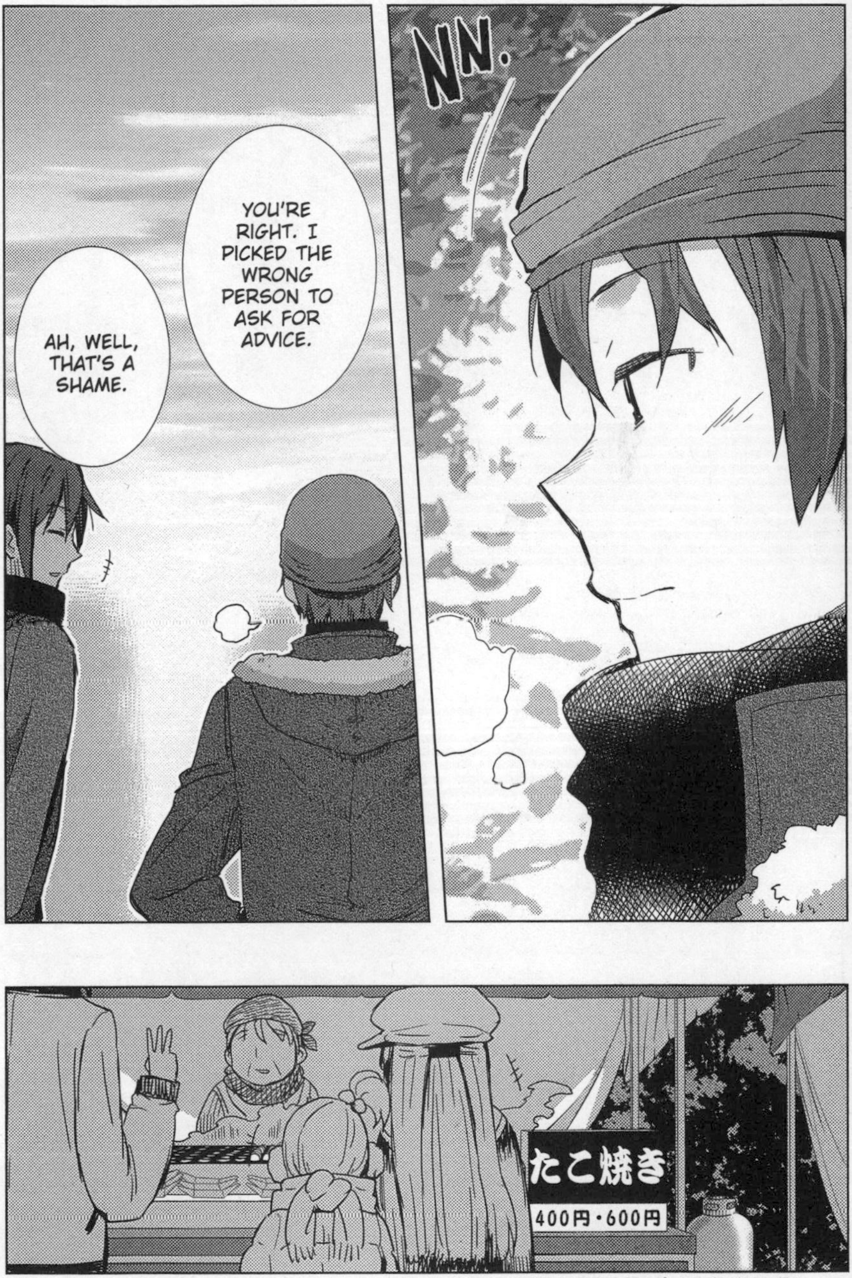
NN.
YOU'RE RIGHT. I PICKED THE WRONG PERSON TO ASK FOR ADVICE.
AH, WELL, THAT'S A SHAME.
たこ焼き
400円・600円

SIGN: TAKOYAKI (FRIED OCTOPUS BALLS), 400 YEN/600 YEN

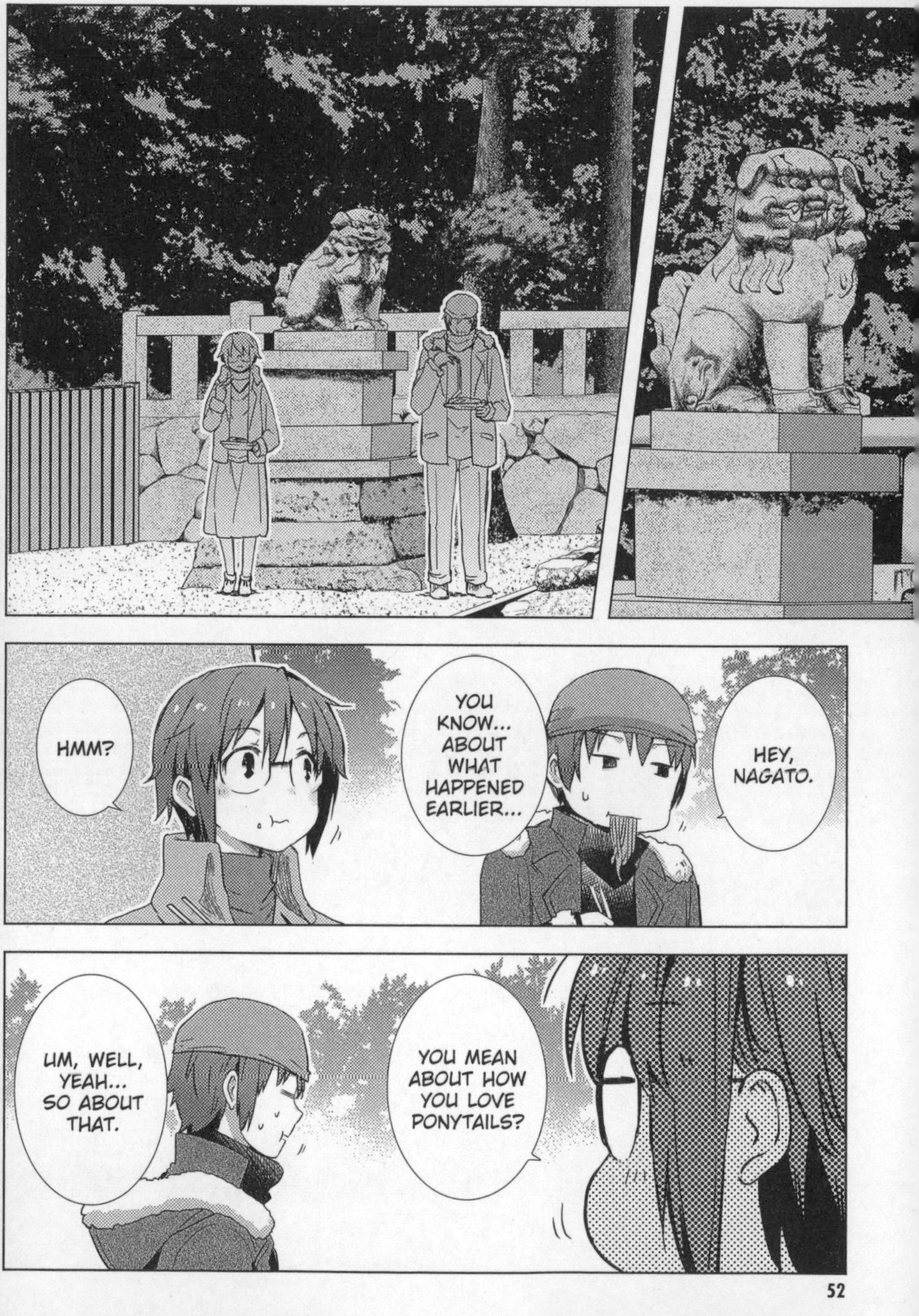
HEY, NAGATO.
YOU KNOW... ABOUT WHAT HAPPENED EARLIER...
HMM?
YOU MEAN ABOUT HOW YOU LOVE PONYTAILS?
UM, WELL, YEAH... SO ABOUT THAT.

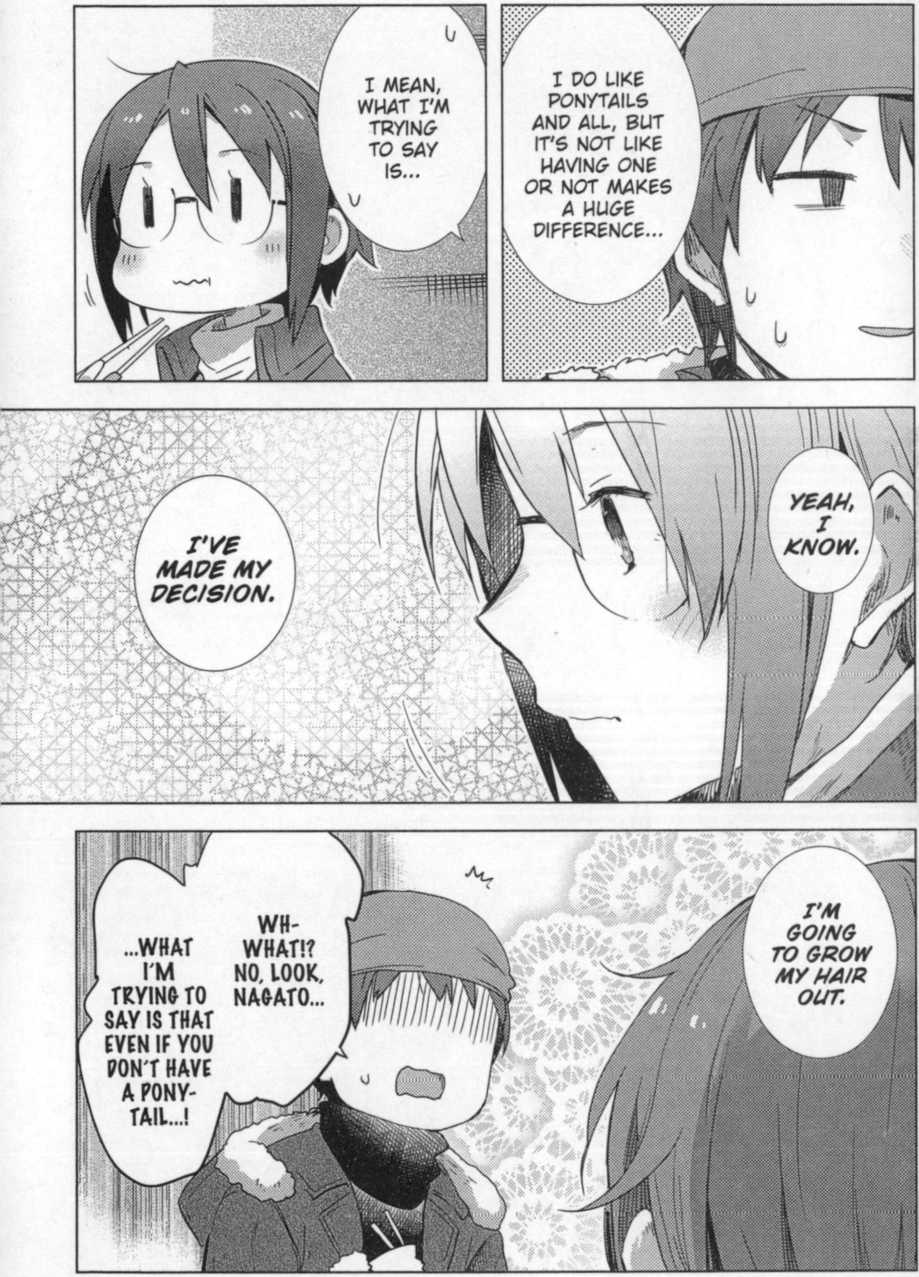
I DO LIKE PONYTAILS AND ALL, BUT IT'S NOT LIKE HAVING ONE OR NOT MAKES A HUGE DIFFERENCE...
I MEAN, WHAT I'M TRYING TO SAY IS...
YEAH, I KNOW.
I'VE MADE MY DECISION.
I'M GOING TO GROW MY HAIR OUT.
WH-WHAT!? NO, LOOK, NAGATO...
...WHAT I'M TRYING TO SAY IS THAT EVEN IF YOU DON'T HAVE A PONY-TAIL...!

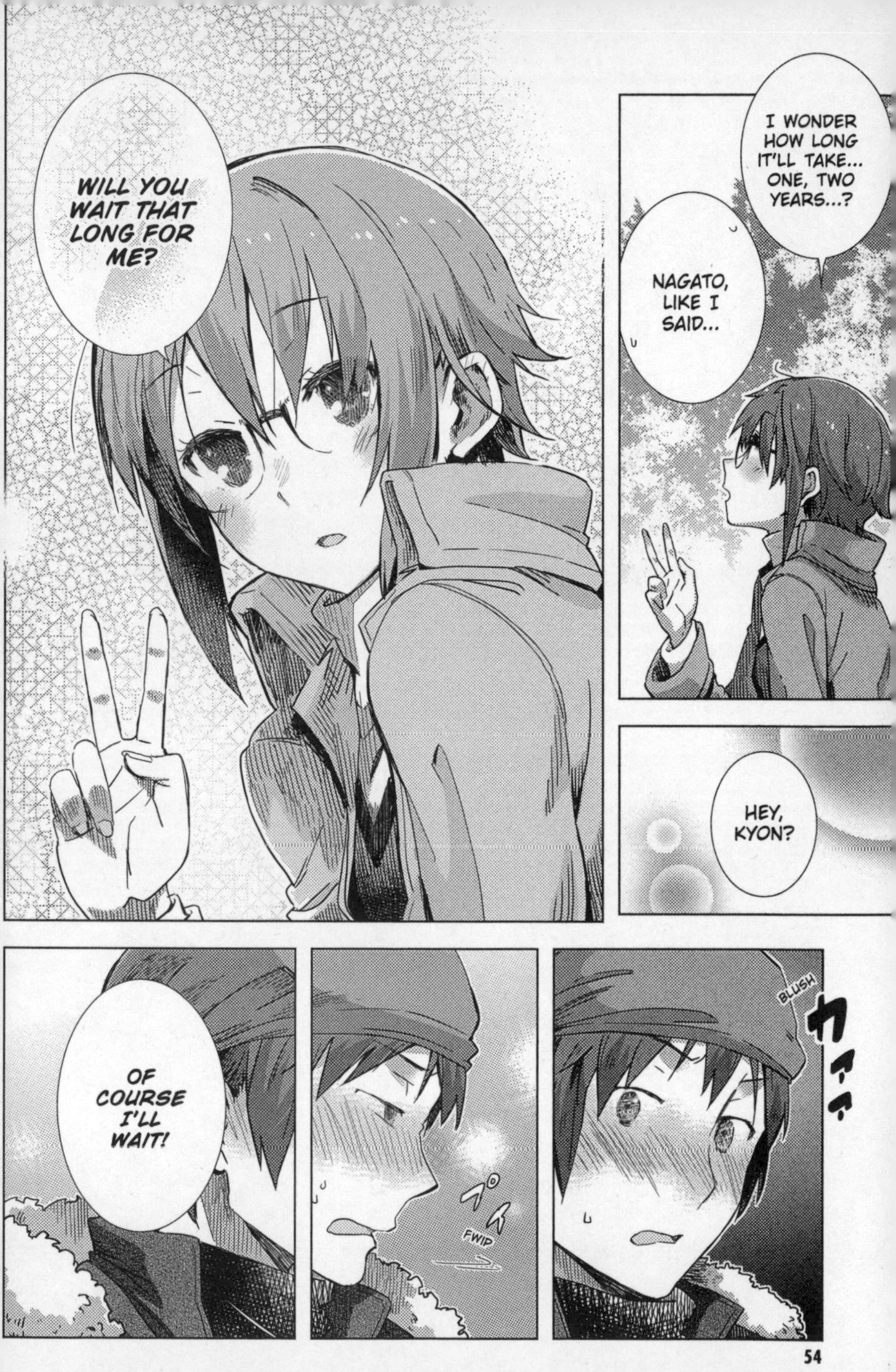
I WONDER HOW LONG IT'LL TAKE... ONE, TWO YEARS...?
NAGATO, LIKE I SAID...
HEY, KYON?
WILL YOU WAIT THAT LONG FOR ME?
BLUSH
FWIP
OF COURSE I'LL WAIT!

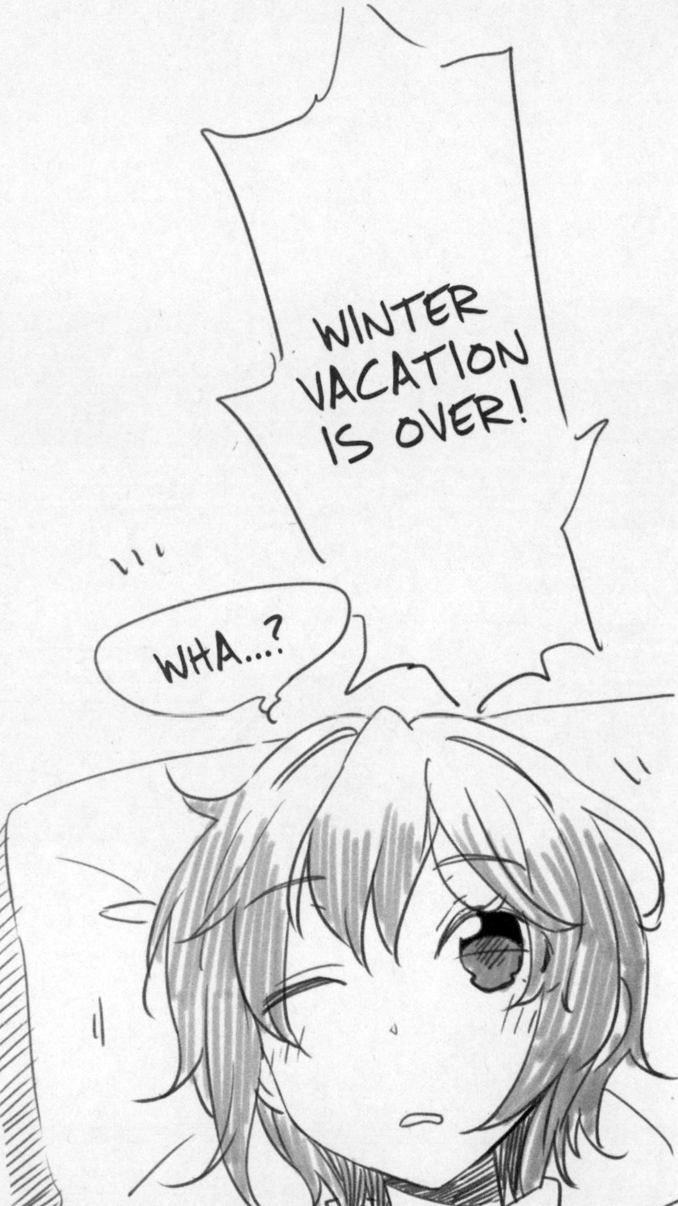
WINTER VACATION IS OVER!
WHA...?

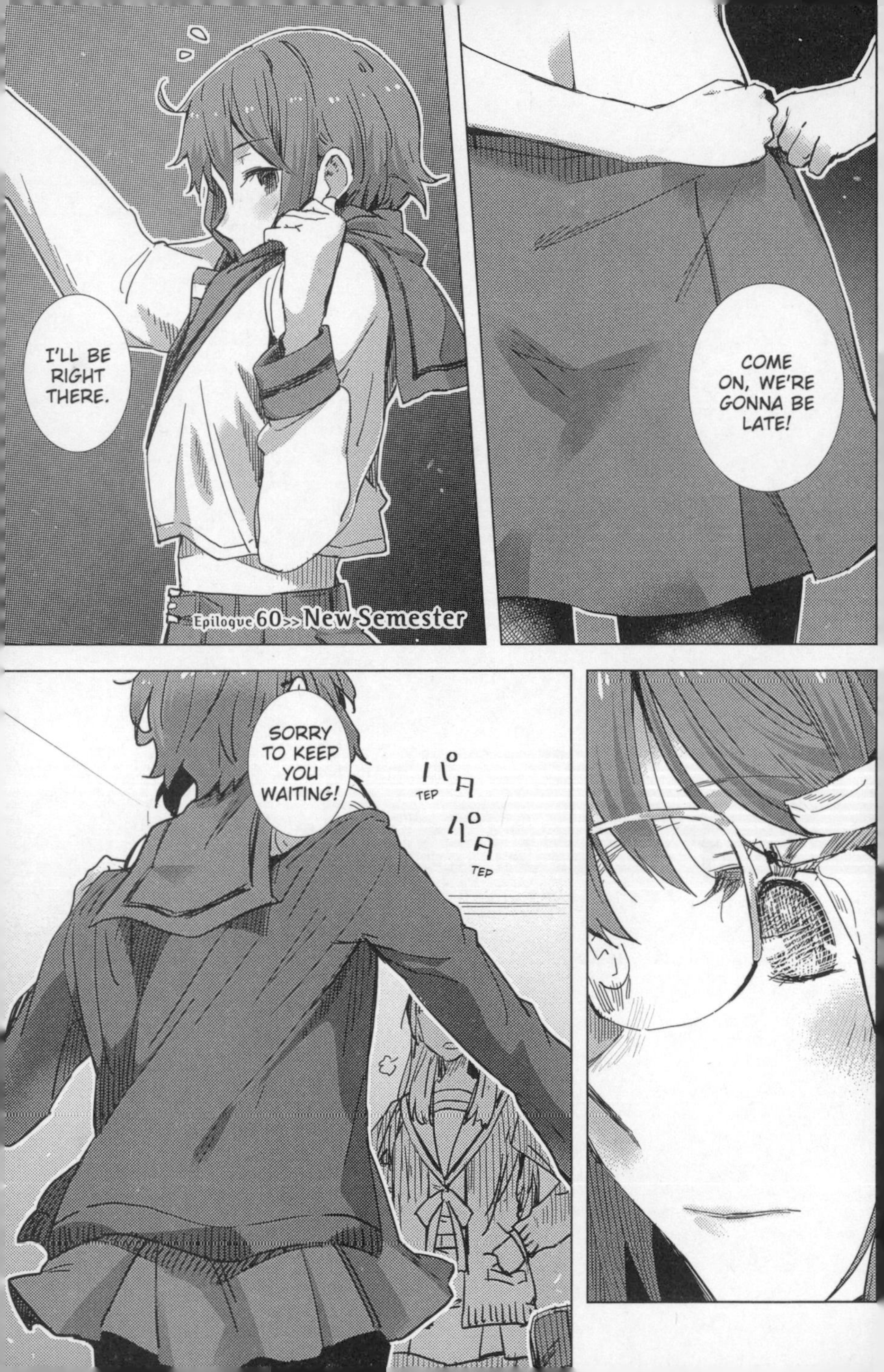
COME ON, WE'RE GONNA BE LATE!
I'LL BE RIGHT THERE.
Epilogue 60>> New Semester
SORRY TO KEEP YOU WAITING!
パタ
TEP
パタ
TEP

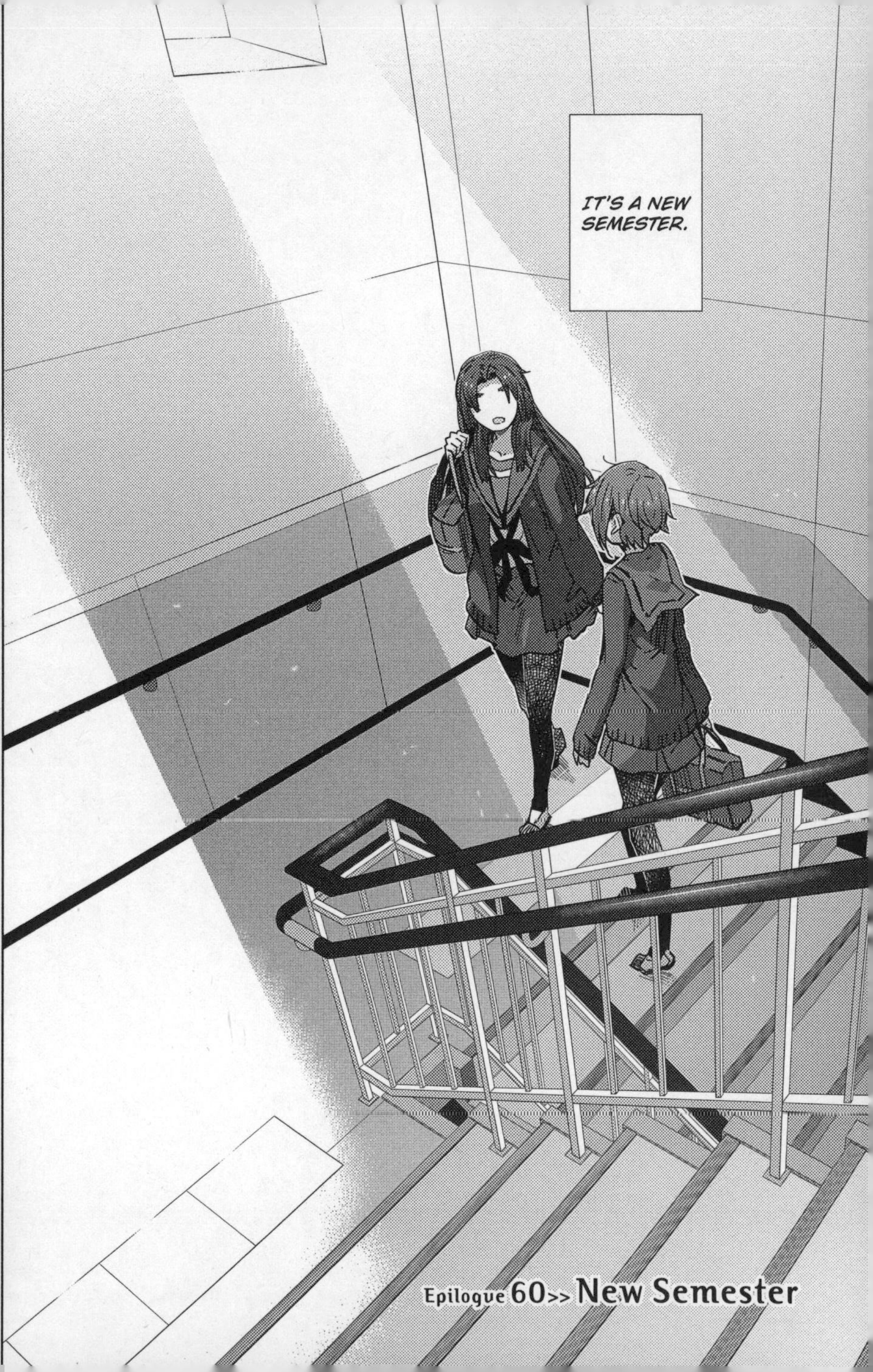
IT'S A NEW SEMESTER.
Epilogue 60>> New Semester

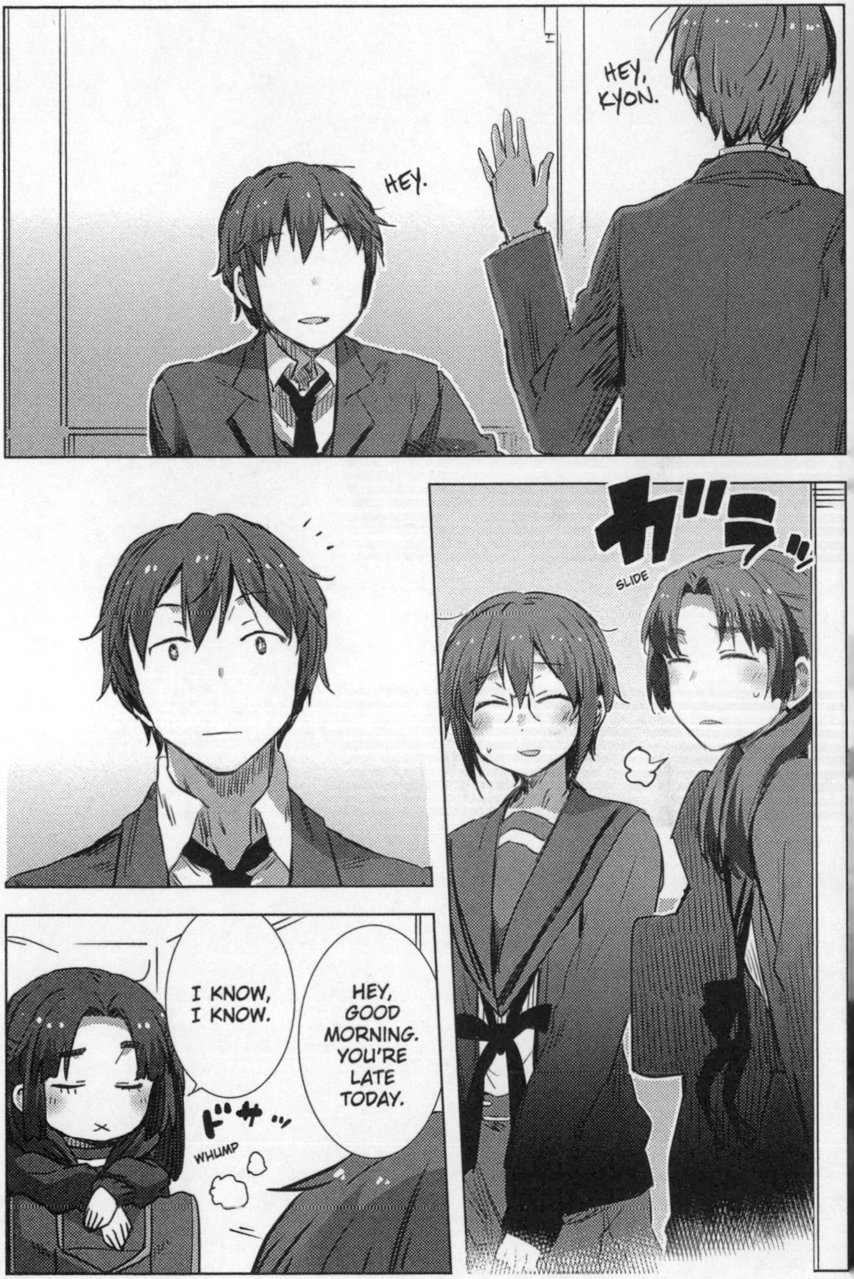
HEY, KYON.
HEY.
ガラッ
SLIDE
HEY, GOOD MORNING. YOU'RE LATE TODAY.
I KNOW, I KNOW.
ドサッ
WHUMP

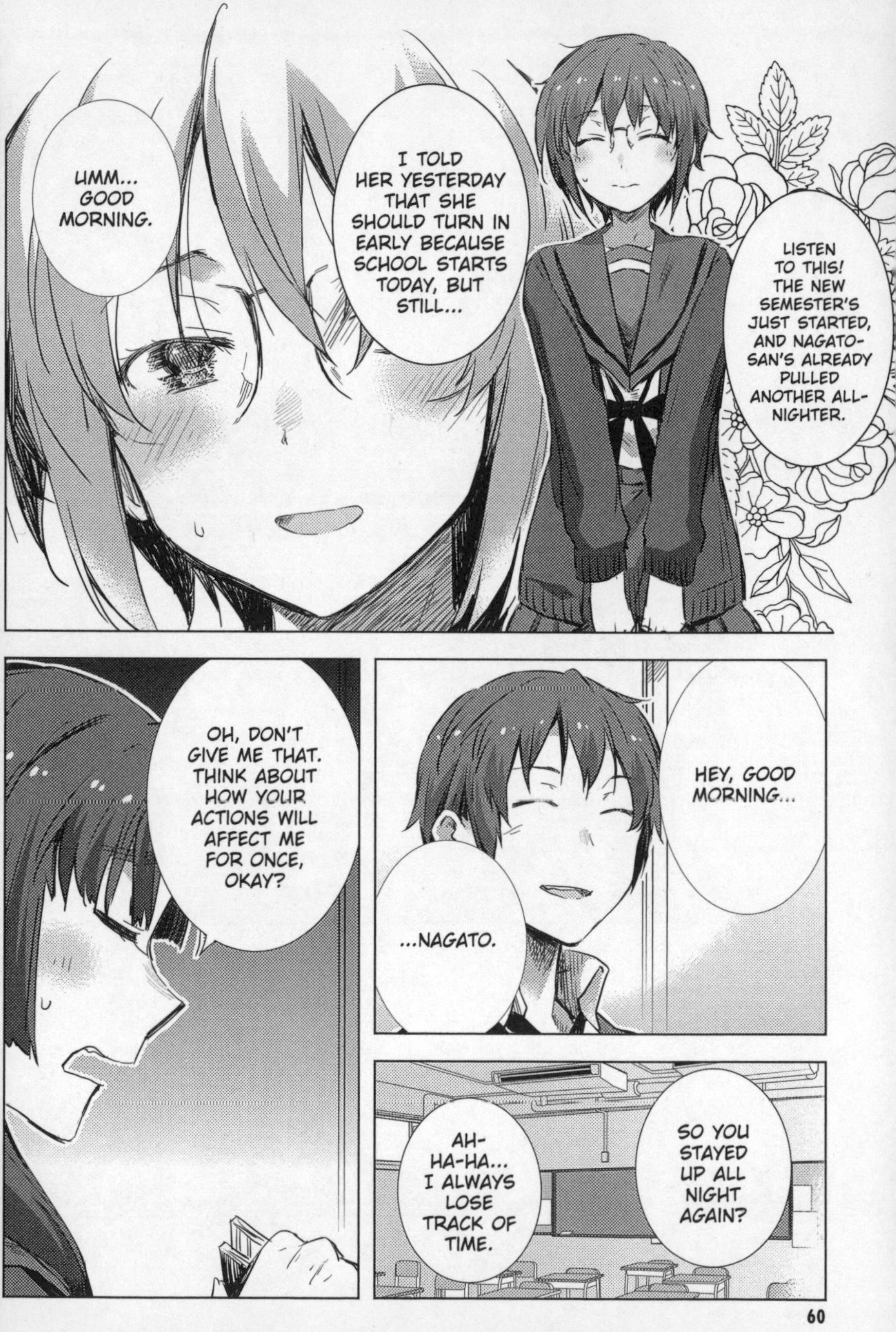
LISTEN TO THIS! THE NEW SEMESTER'S JUST STARTED, AND NAGATO-SAN'S ALREADY PULLED ANOTHER ALL-NIGHTER.
I TOLD HER YESTERDAY THAT SHE SHOULD TURN IN EARLY BECAUSE SCHOOL STARTS TODAY, BUT STILL...
UMM... GOOD MORNING.
HEY, GOOD MORNING...
...NAGATO.
SO YOU STAYED UP ALL NIGHT AGAIN?
AH-HA-HA... I ALWAYS LOSE TRACK OF TIME.
OH, DON'T GIVE ME THAT. THINK ABOUT HOW YOUR ACTIONS WILL AFFECT ME FOR ONCE, OKAY?

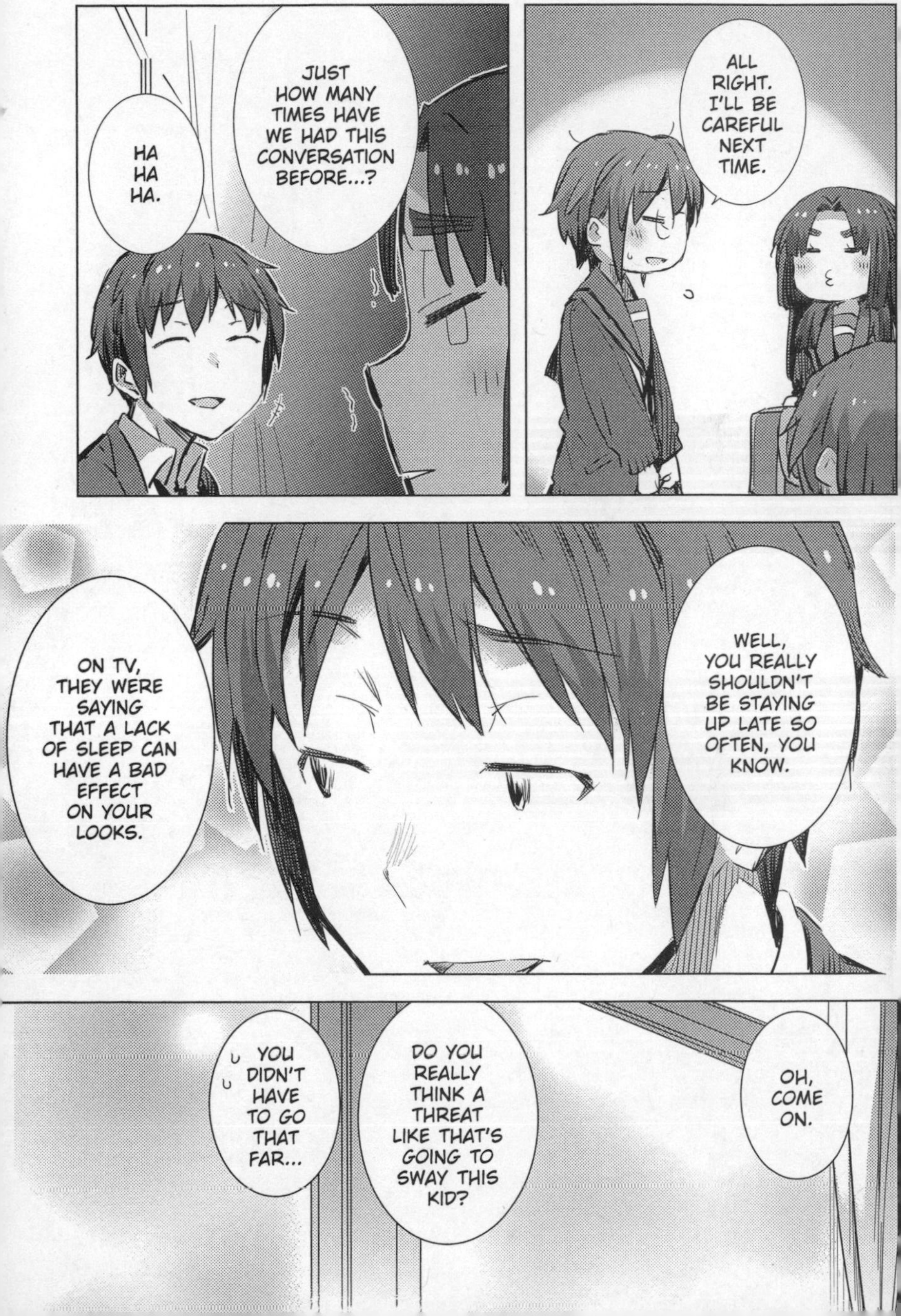
ALL RIGHT. I'LL BE CAREFUL NEXT TIME.
JUST HOW MANY TIMES HAVE WE HAD THIS CONVERSATION BEFORE...?
HA HA HA.
WELL, YOU REALLY SHOULDN'T BE STAYING UP LATE SO OFTEN, YOU KNOW.
ON TV, THEY WERE SAYING THAT A LACK OF SLEEP CAN HAVE A BAD EFFECT ON YOUR LOOKS.
OH, COME ON.
DO YOU REALLY THINK A THREAT LIKE THAT'S GOING TO SWAY THIS KID?
YOU DIDN'T HAVE TO GO THAT FAR...

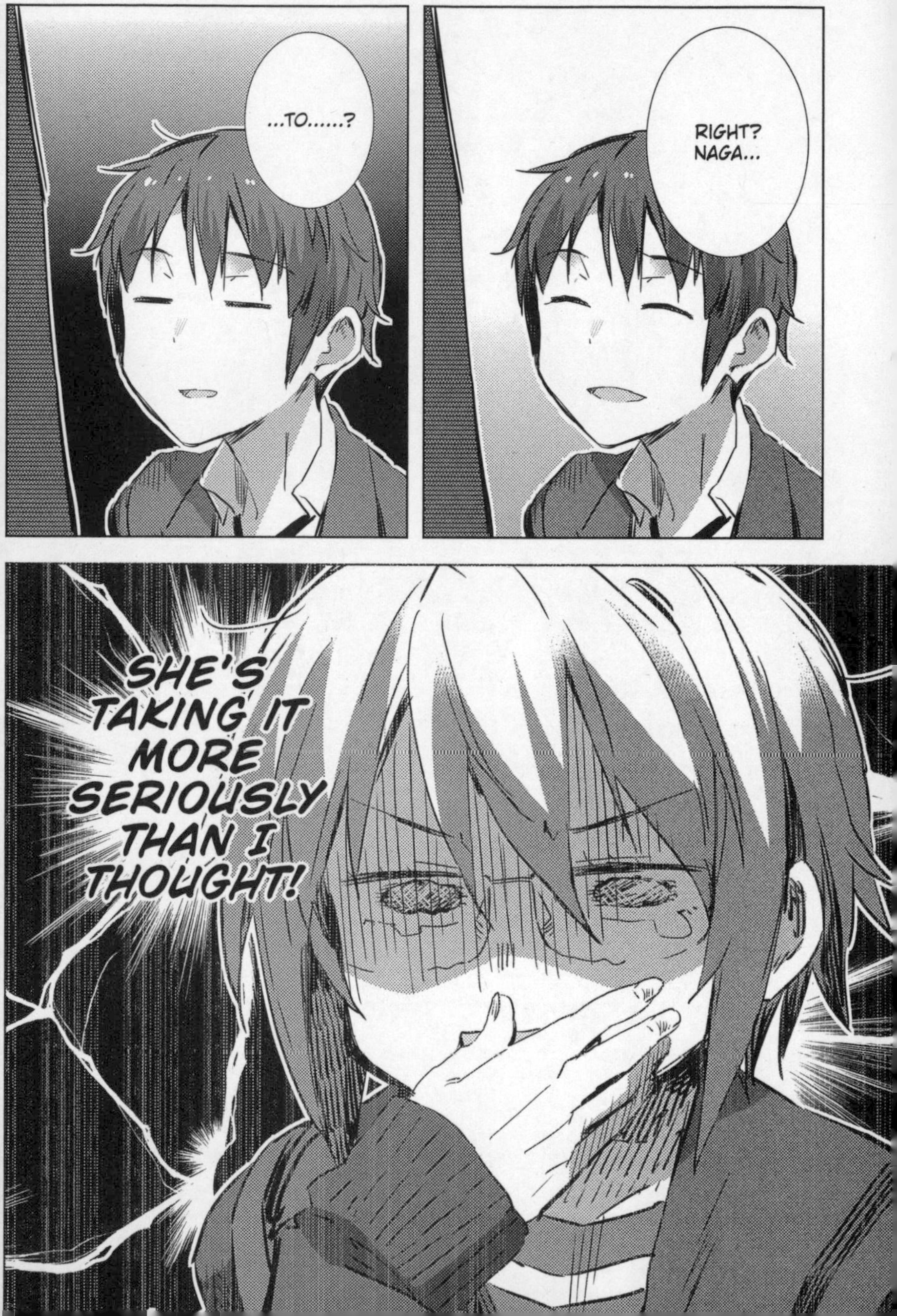
RIGHT? NAGA...
...TO......?
SHE'S TAKING IT MORE SERIOUSLY THAN I THOUGHT!

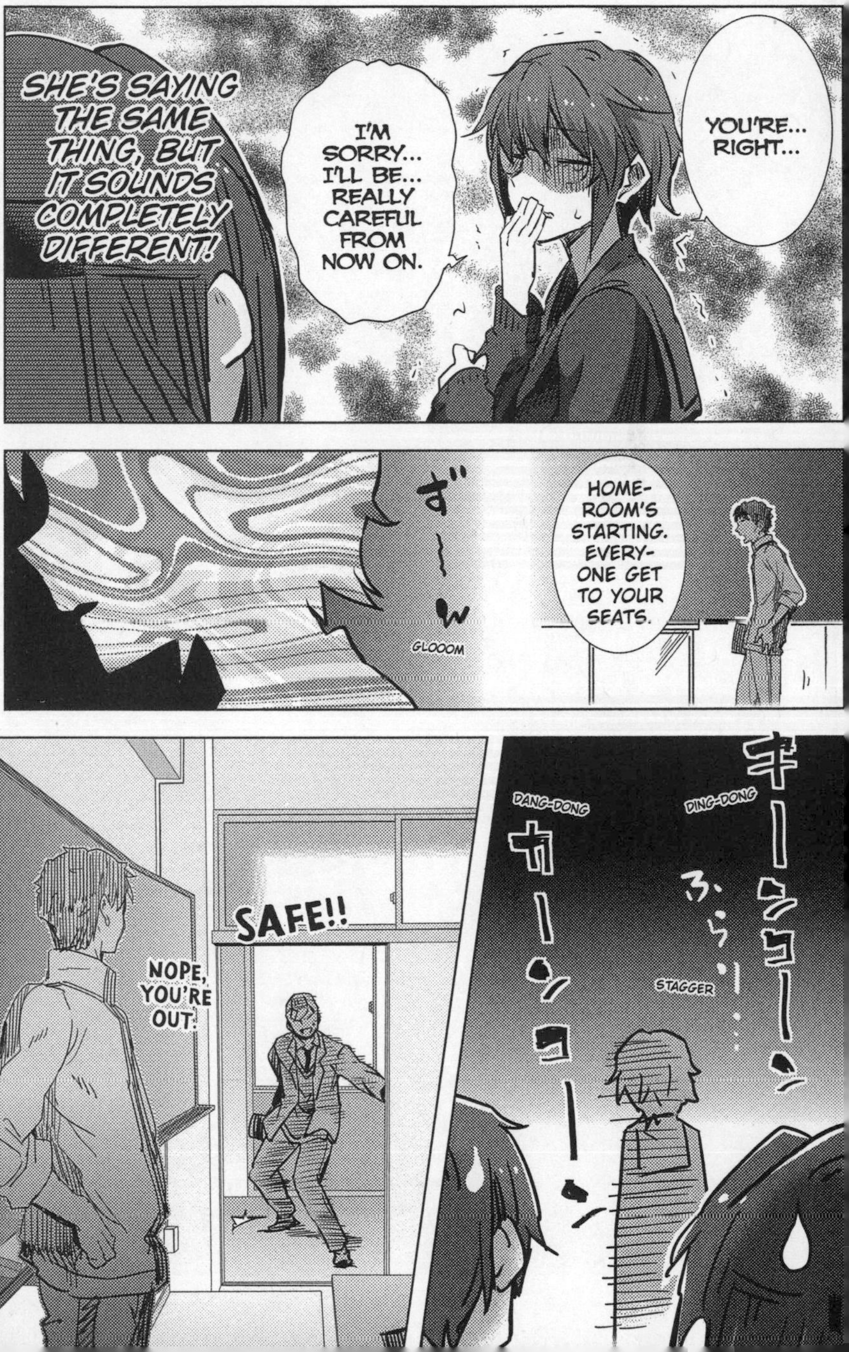
YOU'RE... RIGHT...
I'M SORRY... I'LL BE... REALLY CAREFUL FROM NOW ON.
SHE'S SAYING THE SAME THING, BUT IT SOUNDS COMPLETELY DIFFERENT!
HOME-ROOM'S STARTING. EVERY-ONE GET TO YOUR SEATS.
ず〜ん
GLOOOM
キーンコーン
DING-DONG
カーンコーン
DANG-DONG
ふら〜…
STAGGER
SAFE!!
NOPE, YOU'RE OUT.

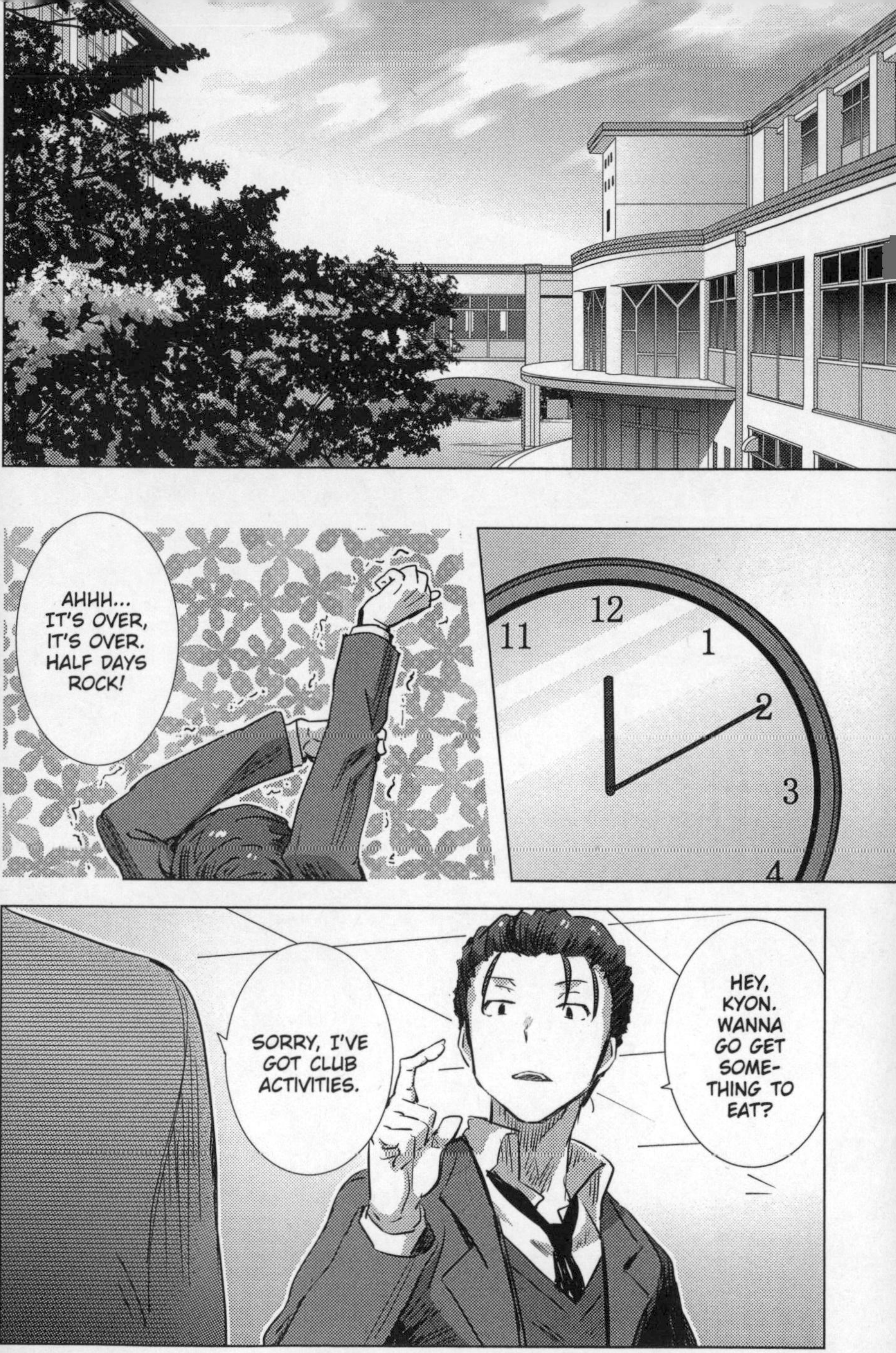
AHHH... IT'S OVER, IT'S OVER. HALF DAYS ROCK!
HEY, KYON. WANNA GO GET SOME-THING TO EAT?
SORRY, I'VE GOT CLUB ACTIVITIES.

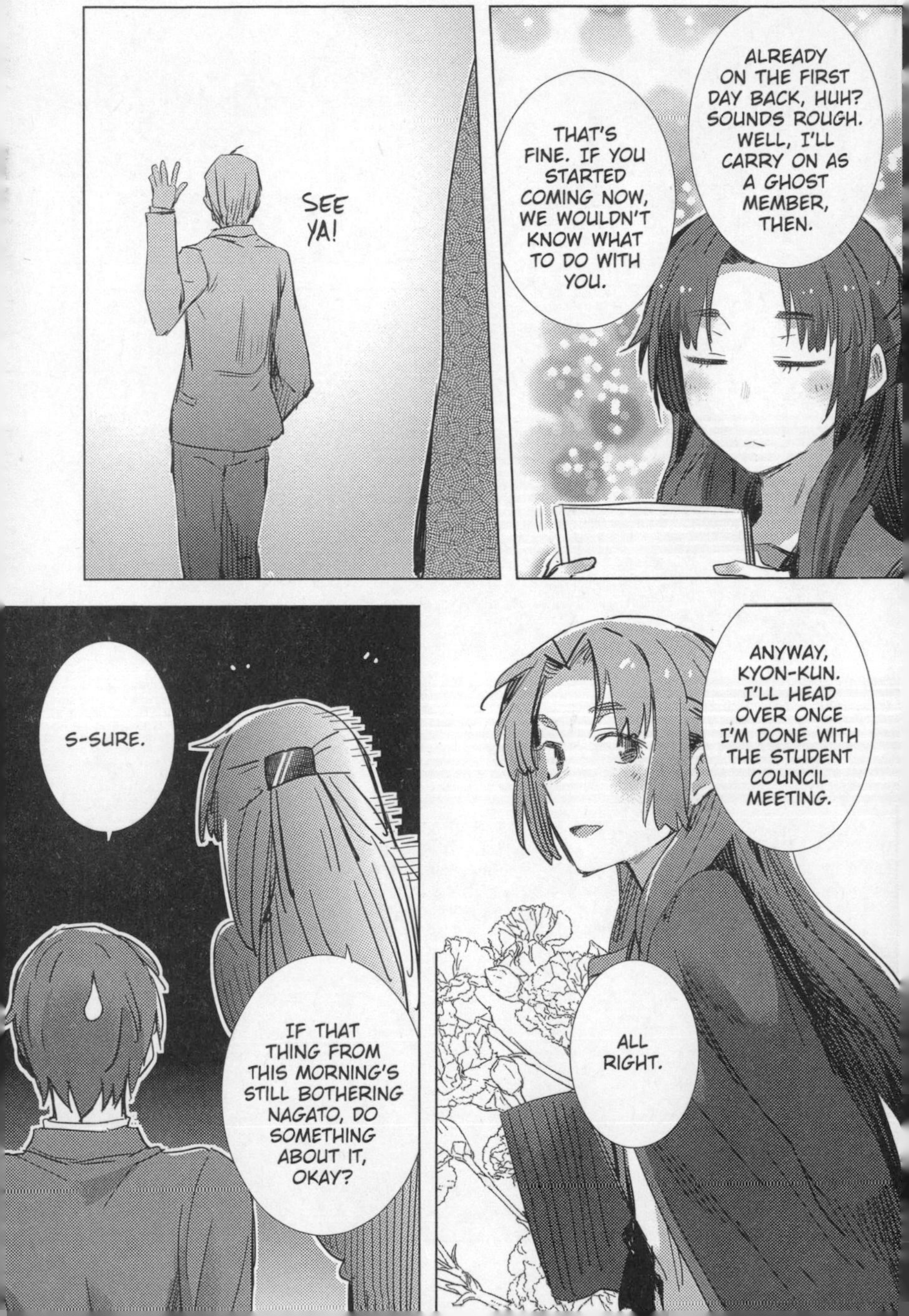
ALREADY ON THE FIRST DAY BACK, HUH? SOUNDS ROUGH. WELL, I'LL CARRY ON AS A GHOST MEMBER, THEN.
THAT'S FINE. IF YOU STARTED COMING NOW, WE WOULDN'T KNOW WHAT TO DO WITH YOU.
SEE YA!
ANYWAY, KYON-KUN. I'LL HEAD OVER ONCE I'M DONE WITH THE STUDENT COUNCIL MEETING.
ALL RIGHT.
S-SURE.
IF THAT THING FROM THIS MORNING'S STILL BOTHERING NAGATO, DO SOMETHING ABOUT IT, OKAY?

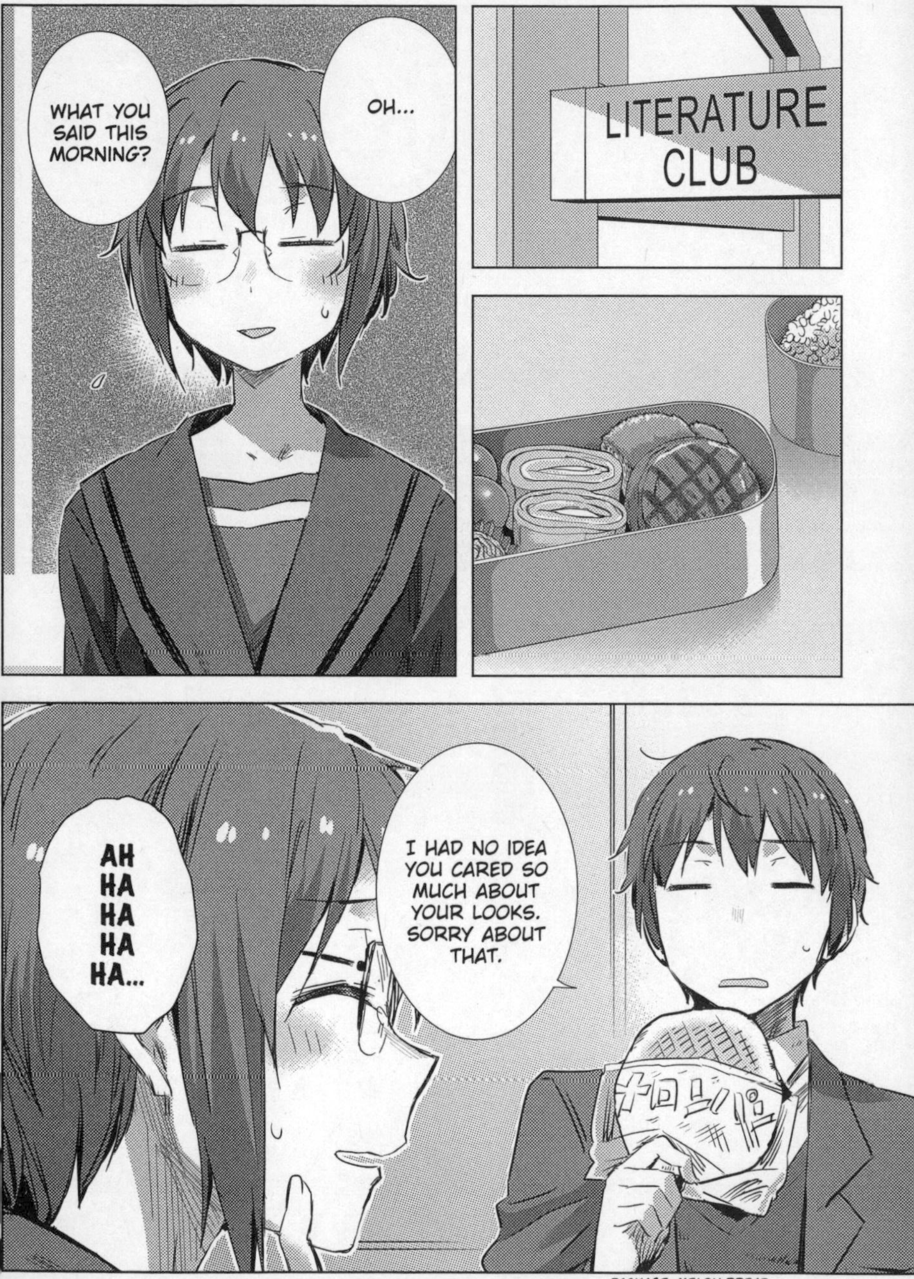
LITERATURE CLUB
OH...
WHAT YOU SAID THIS MORNING?
I HAD NO IDEA YOU CARED SO MUCH ABOUT YOUR LOOKS. SORRY ABOUT THAT.
AH HA HA HA HA...

PACKAGE: MELON BREAD

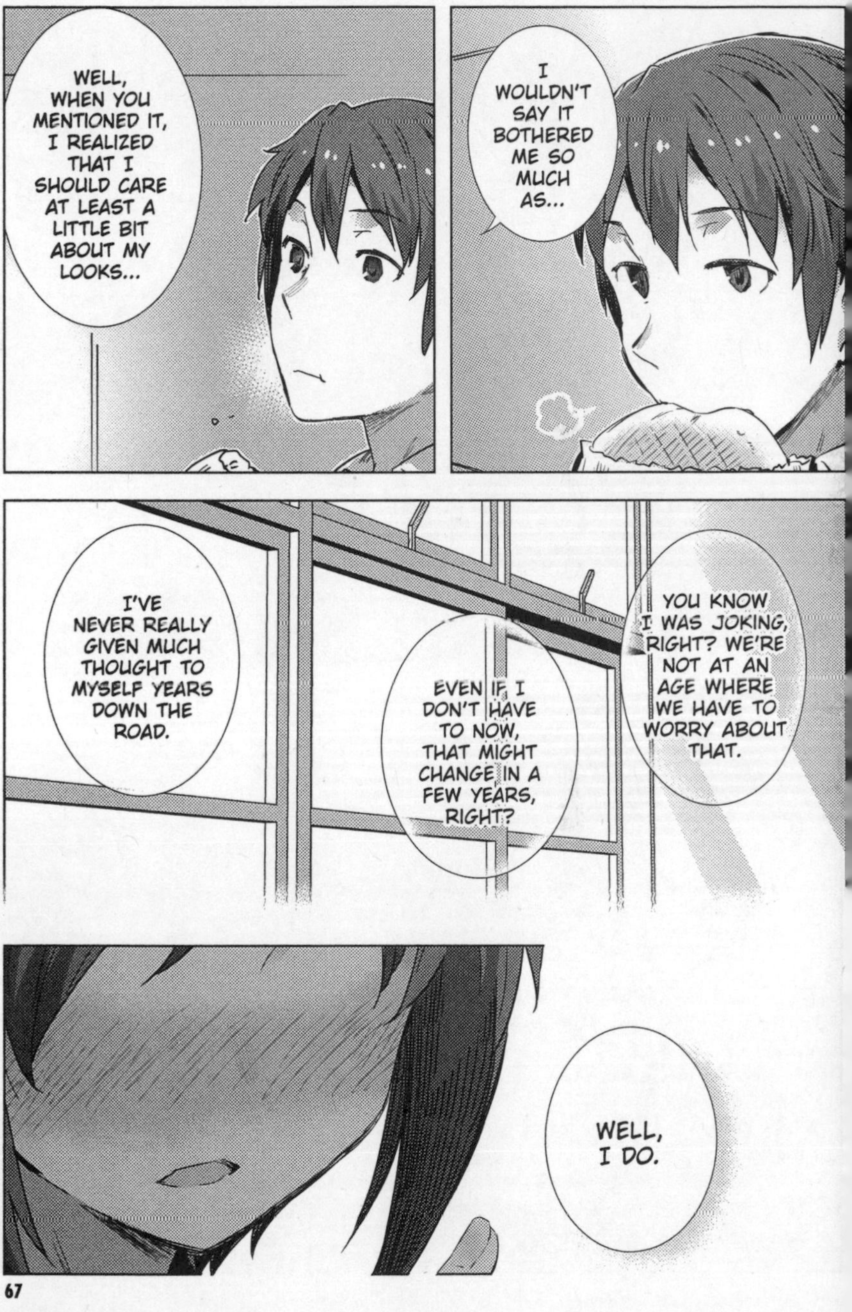
I WOULDN'T SAY IT BOTHERED ME SO MUCH AS...
WELL, WHEN YOU MENTIONED IT, I REALIZED THAT I SHOULD CARE AT LEAST A LITTLE BIT ABOUT MY LOOKS...
YOU KNOW I WAS JOKING, RIGHT? WE'RE NOT AT AN AGE WHERE WE HAVE TO WORRY ABOUT THAT.
EVEN IF I DON'T HAVE TO NOW, THAT MIGHT CHANGE IN A FEW YEARS, RIGHT?
I'VE NEVER REALLY GIVEN MUCH THOUGHT TO MYSELF YEARS DOWN THE ROAD.
WELL, I DO.

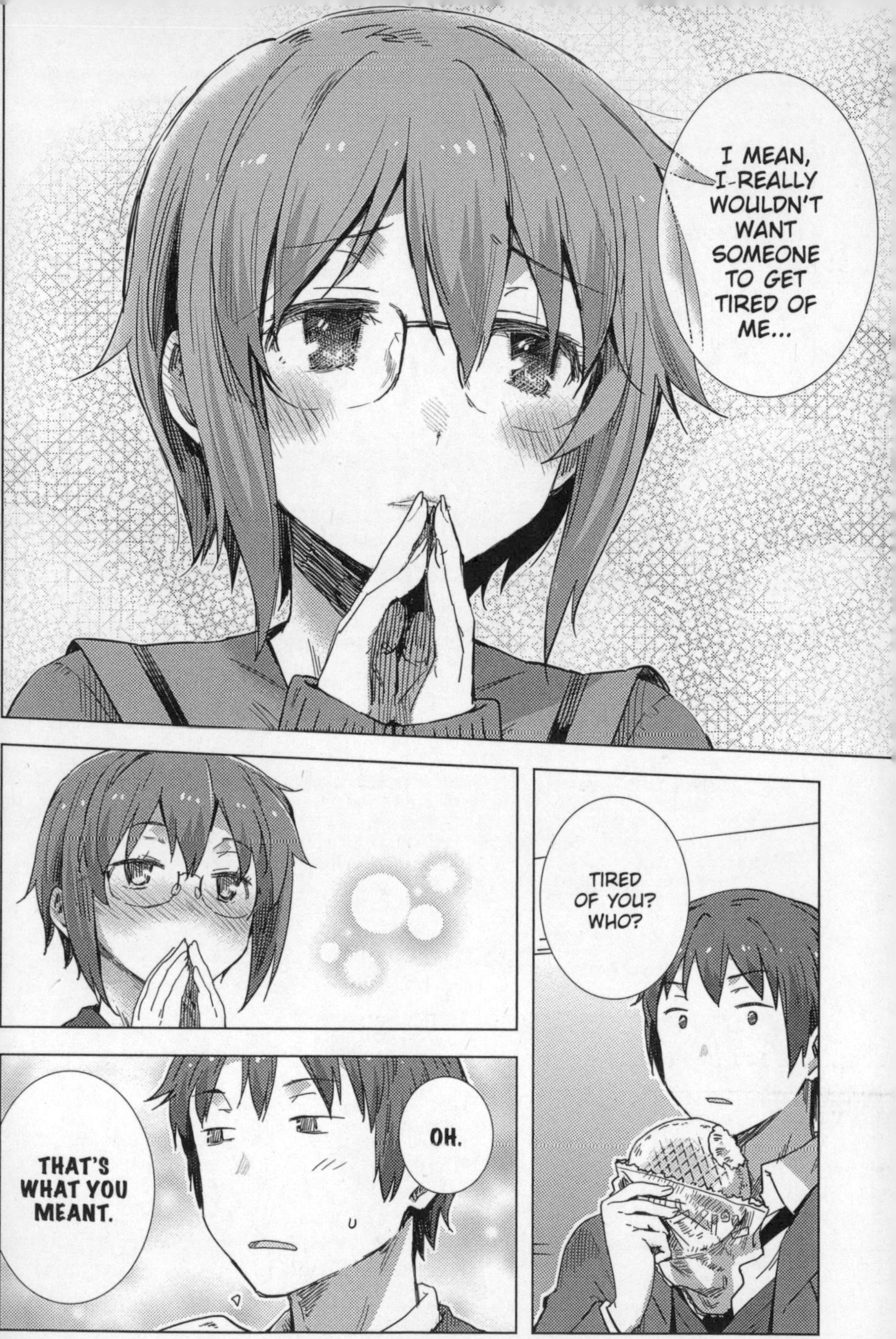
I MEAN, I-REALLY WOULDN'T WANT SOMEONE TO GET TIRED OF ME...
TIRED OF YOU? WHO?
OH.
THAT'S WHAT YOU MEANT.

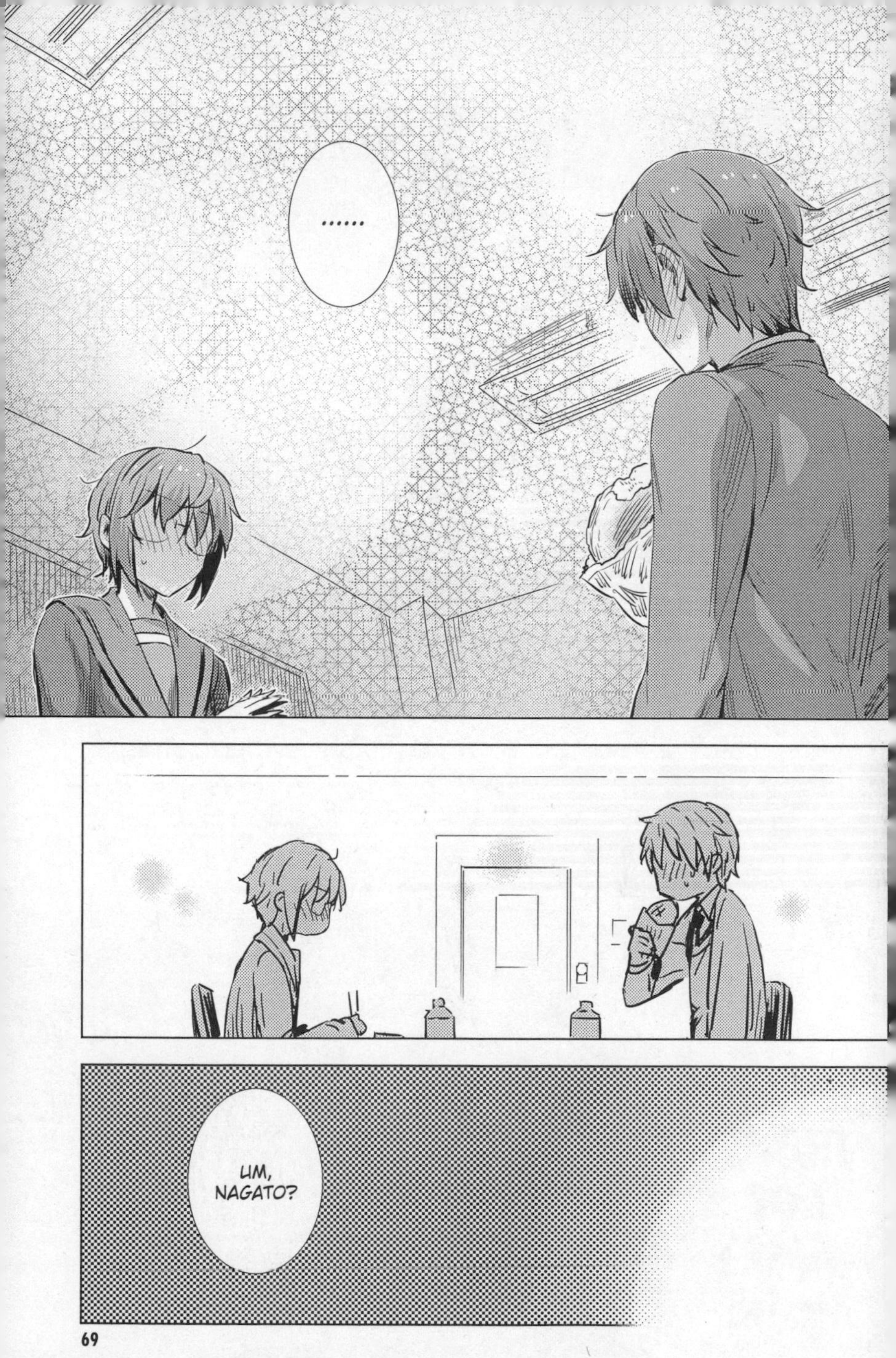
......
UM, NAGATO?

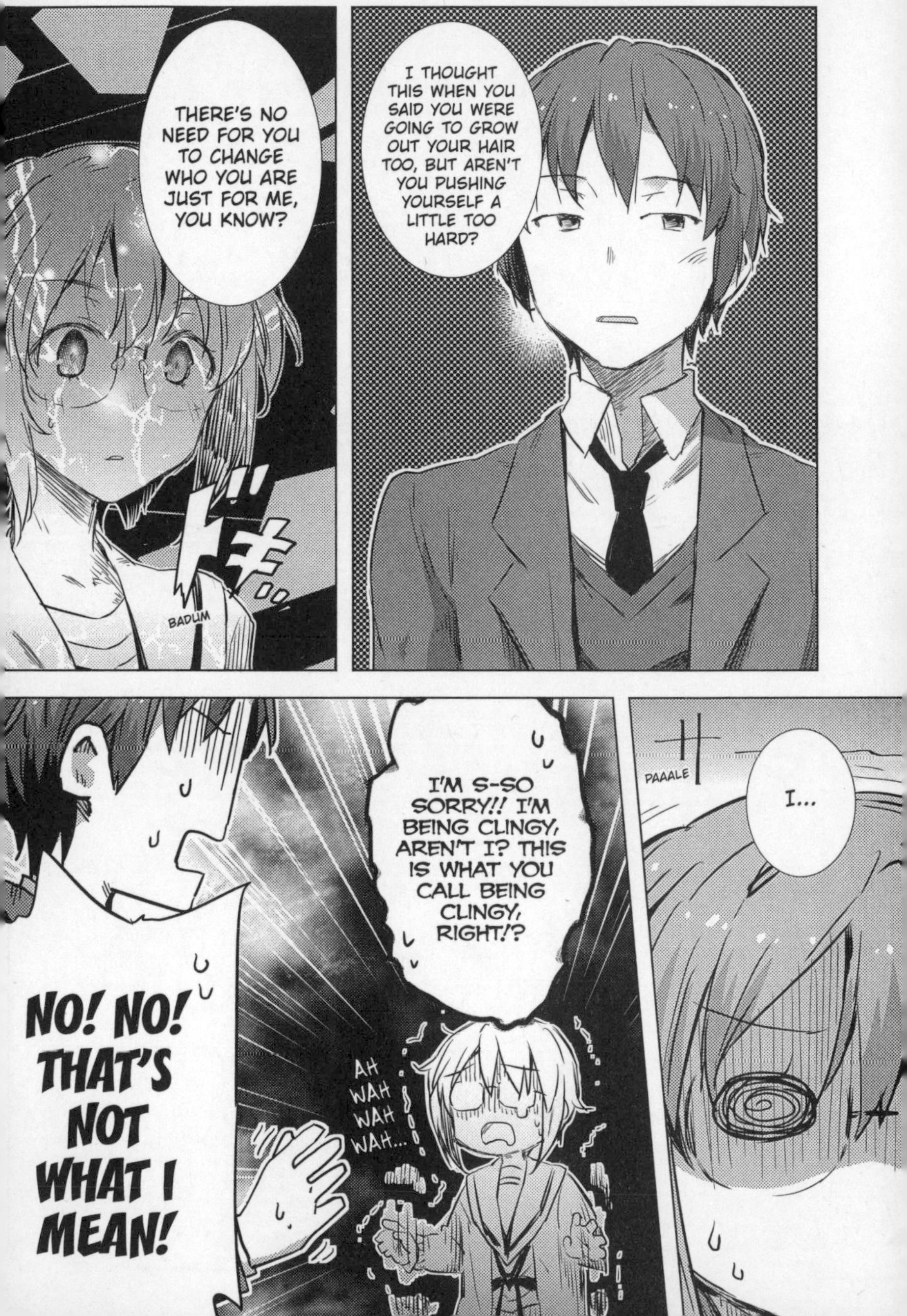
I THOUGHT THIS WHEN YOU SAID YOU WERE GOING TO GROW OUT YOUR HAIR TOO, BUT AREN'T YOU PUSHING YOURSELF A LITTLE TOO HARD?
THERE'S NO NEED FOR YOU TO CHANGE WHO YOU ARE JUST FOR ME, YOU KNOW?
BADUM
PAAALE
I...
I'M S-SO SORRY!! I'M BEING CLINGY, AREN'T I? THIS IS WHAT YOU CALL BEING CLINGY, RIGHT!?
AH WAH WAH WAH...
NO! NO! THAT'S NOT WHAT I MEAN!

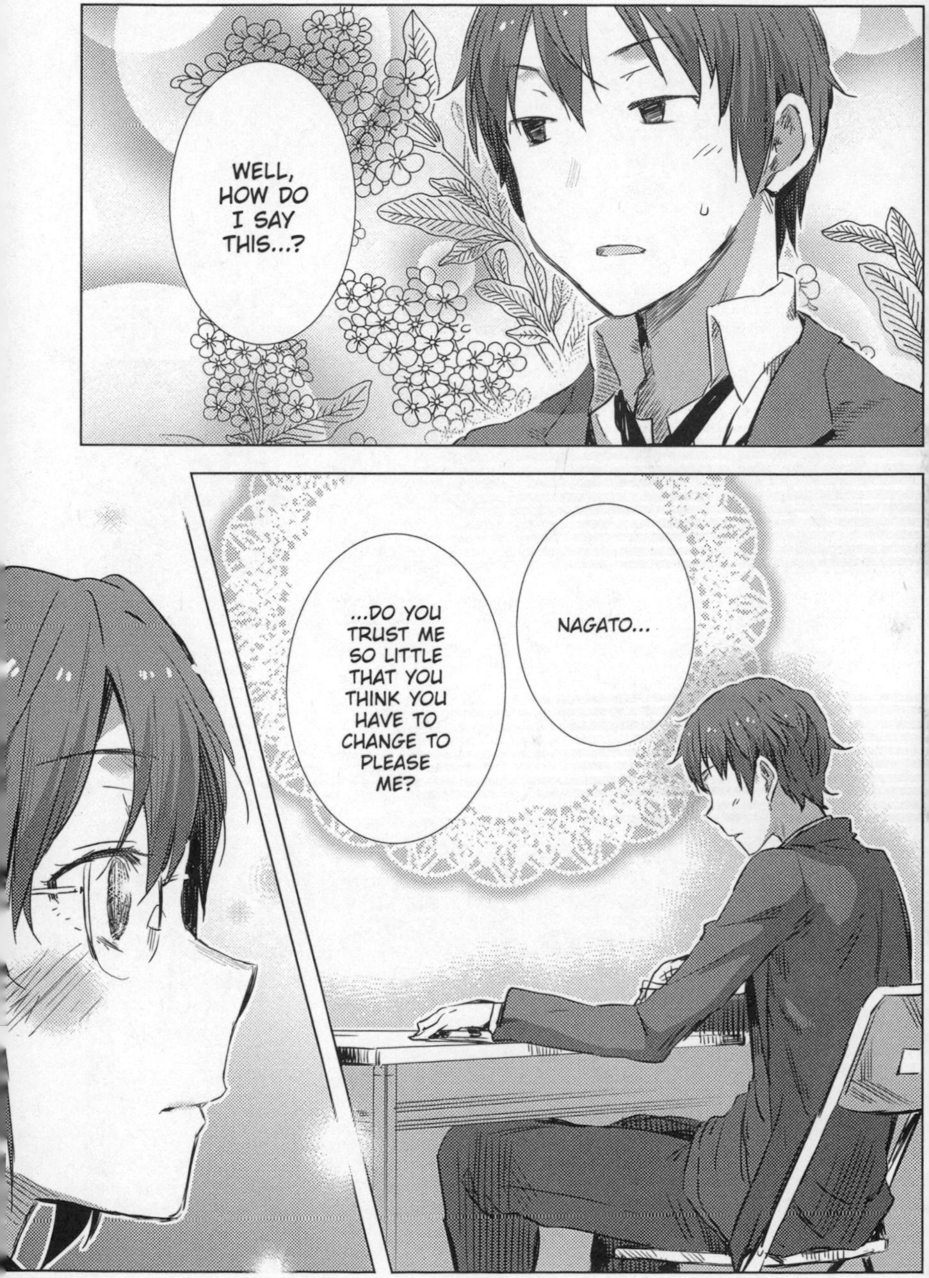
WELL, HOW DO I SAY THIS...?
NAGATO...
...DO YOU TRUST ME SO LITTLE THAT YOU THINK YOU HAVE TO CHANGE TO PLEASE ME?

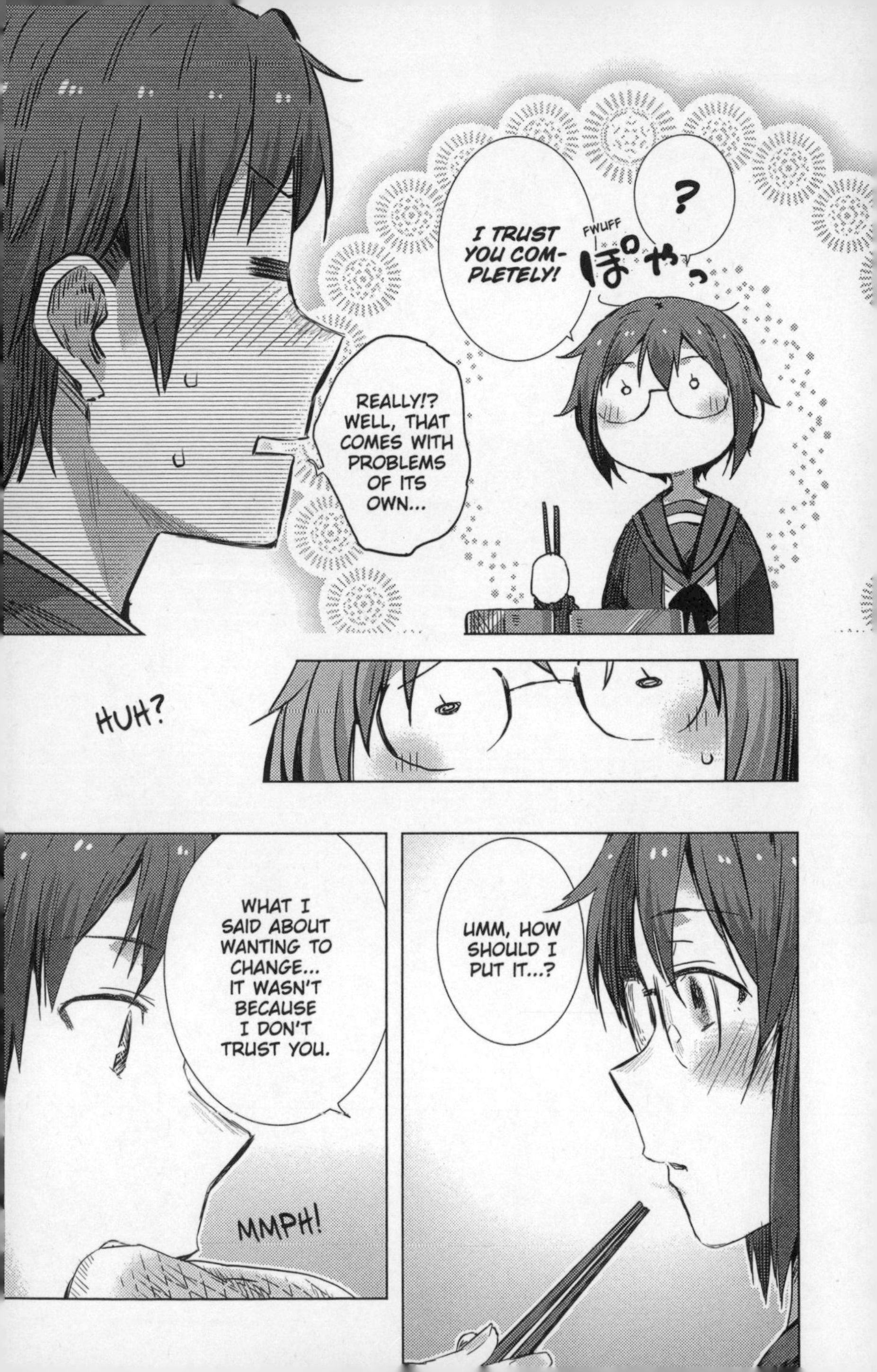
?
FWUFF
ぽやっ
I TRUST YOU COMPLETELY!
REALLY!? WELL, THAT COMES WITH PROBLEMS OF ITS OWN...
HUH?
UMM, HOW SHOULD I PUT IT...?
WHAT I SAID ABOUT WANTING TO CHANGE... IT WASN'T BECAUSE I DON'T TRUST YOU.
MMPH!

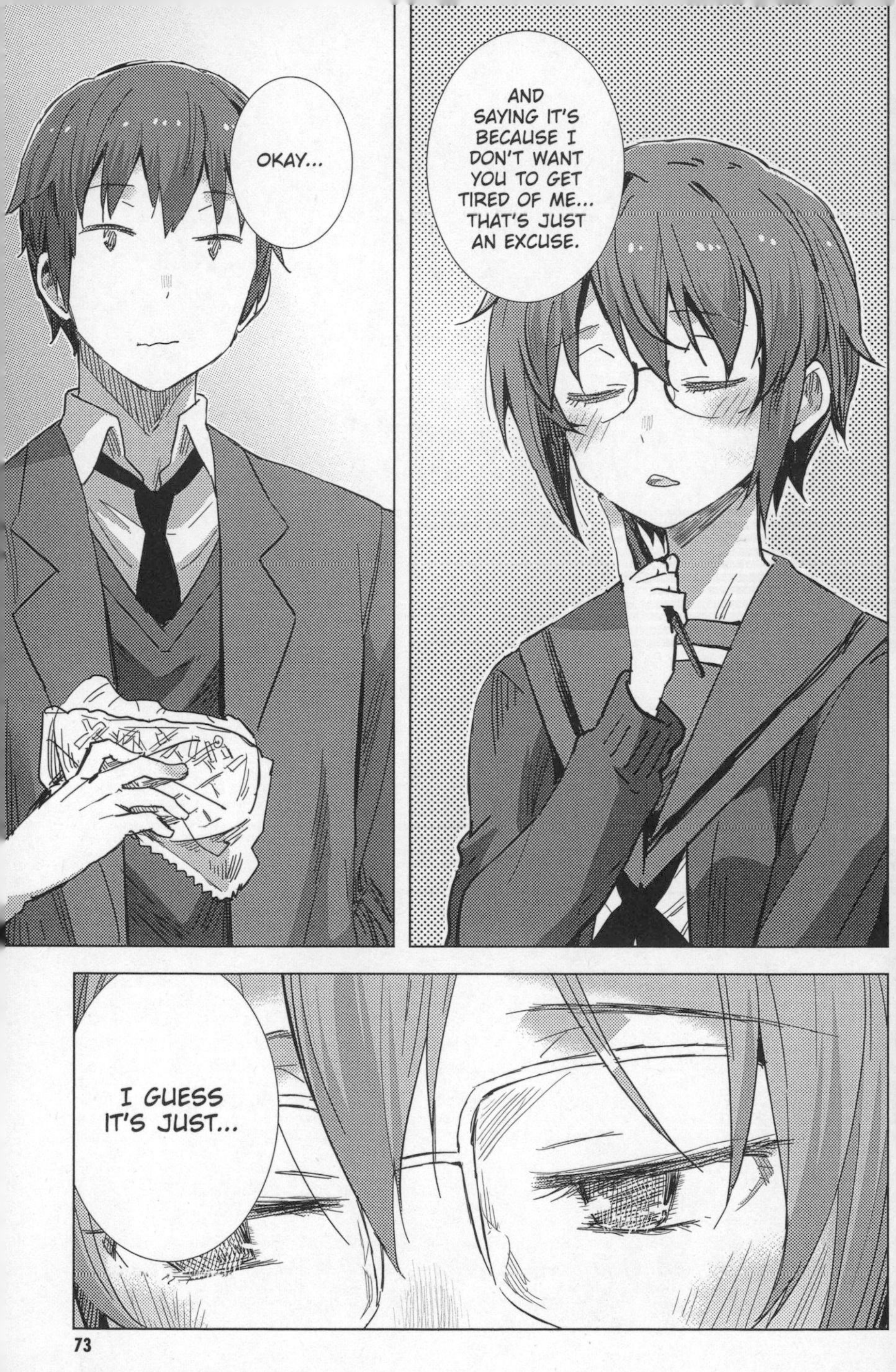
AND SAYING IT'S BECAUSE I DON'T WANT YOU TO GET TIRED OF ME... THAT'S JUST AN EXCUSE.
OKAY...
I GUESS IT'S JUST...

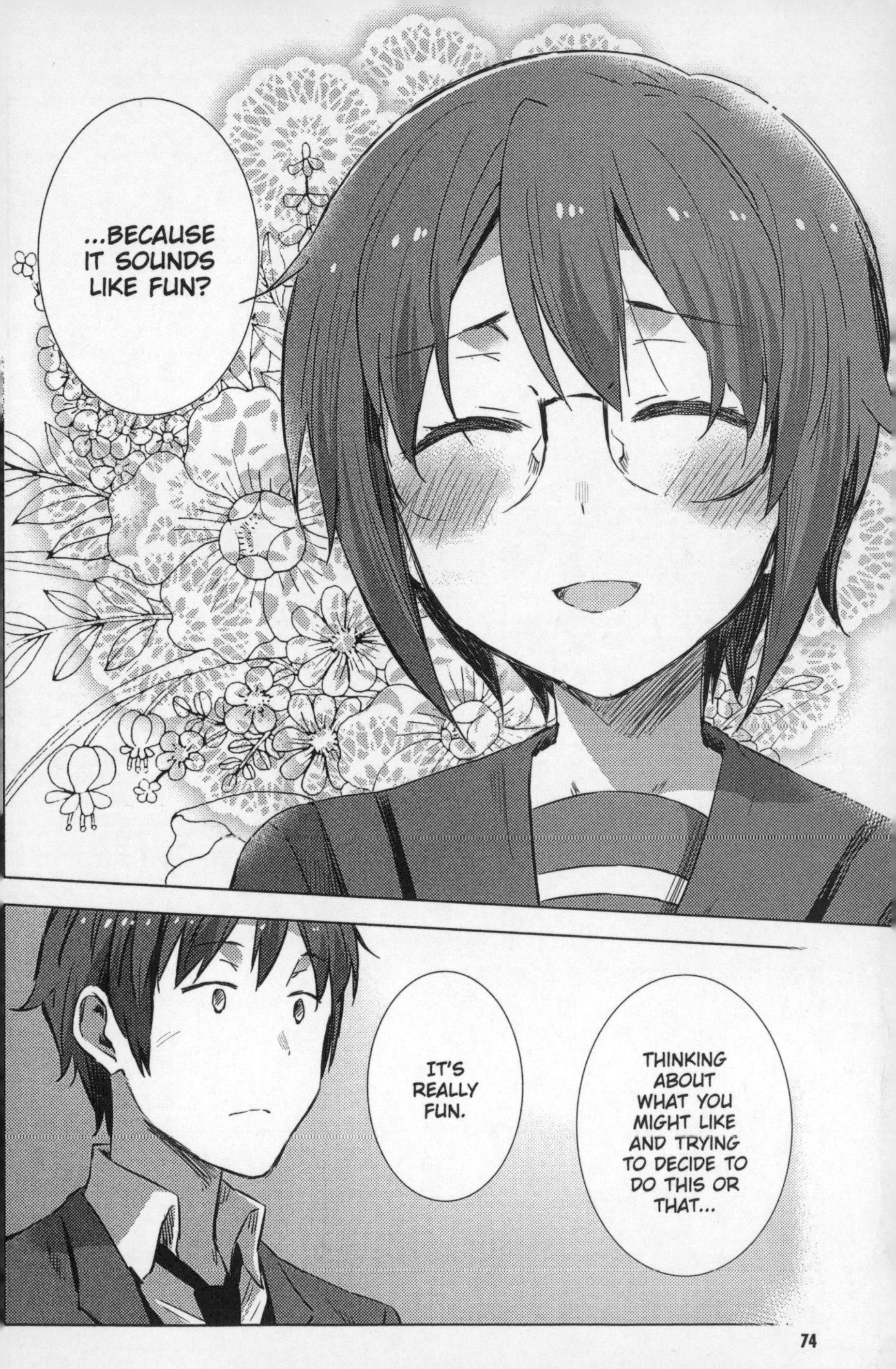
...BECAUSE IT SOUNDS LIKE FUN?
THINKING ABOUT WHAT YOU MIGHT LIKE AND TRYING TO DECIDE TO DO THIS OR THAT...
IT'S REALLY FUN.

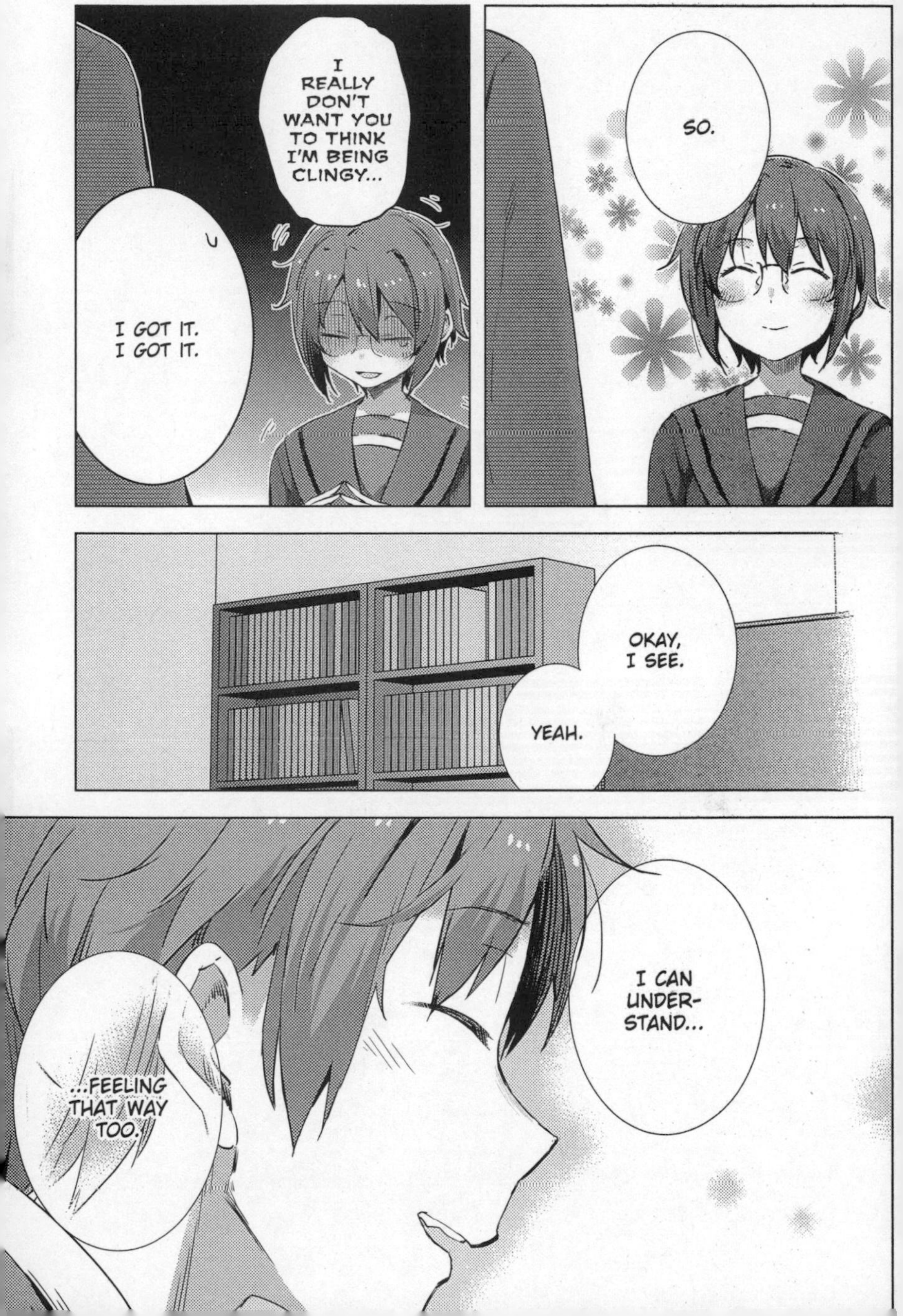
SO.
I REALLY DON'T WANT YOU TO THINK I'M BEING CLINGY...
I GOT IT. I GOT IT.
OKAY, I SEE.
YEAH.
I CAN UNDER-STAND...
...FEELING THAT WAY TOO.

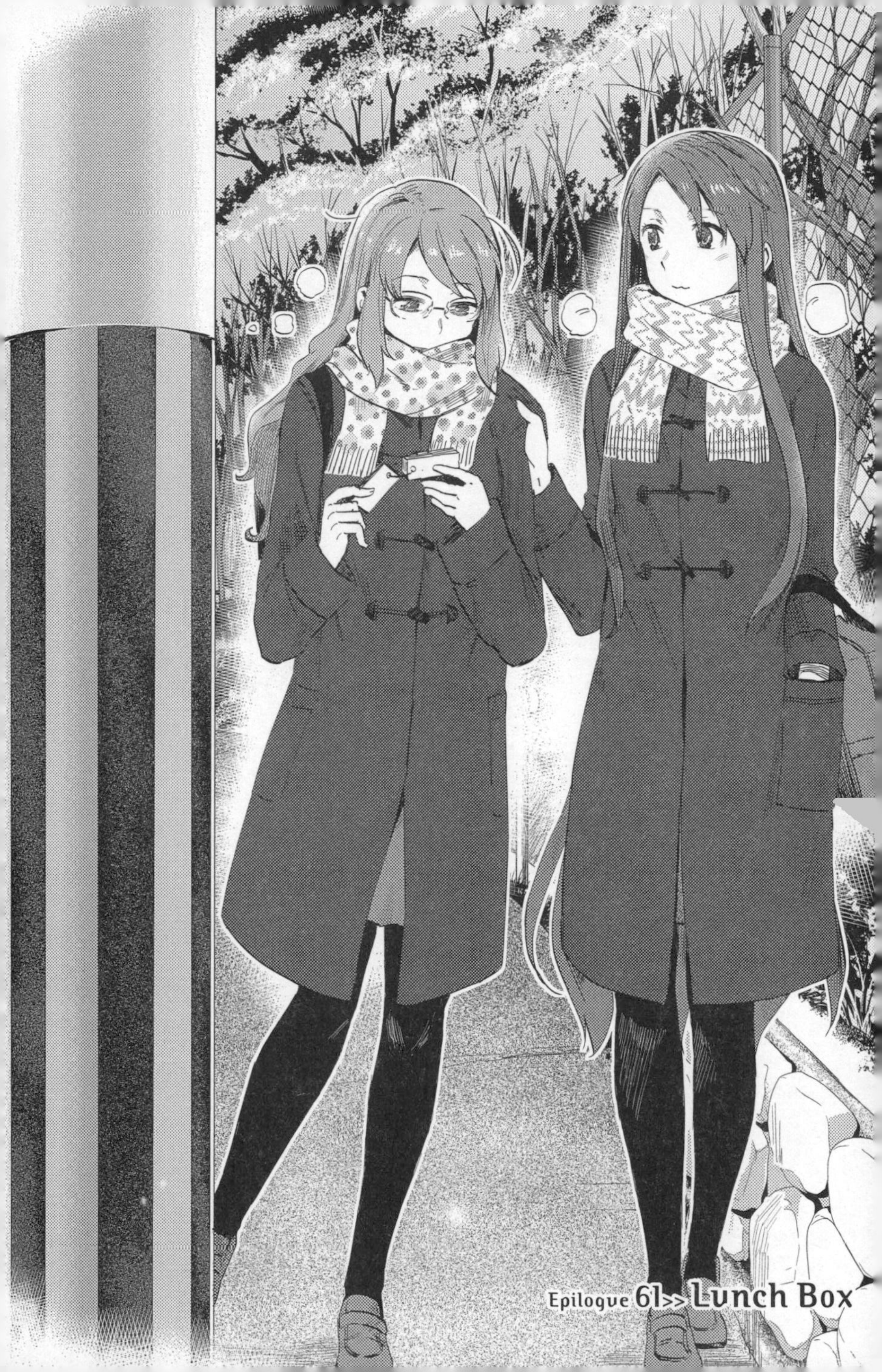
Epilogue 61>> Lunch Box

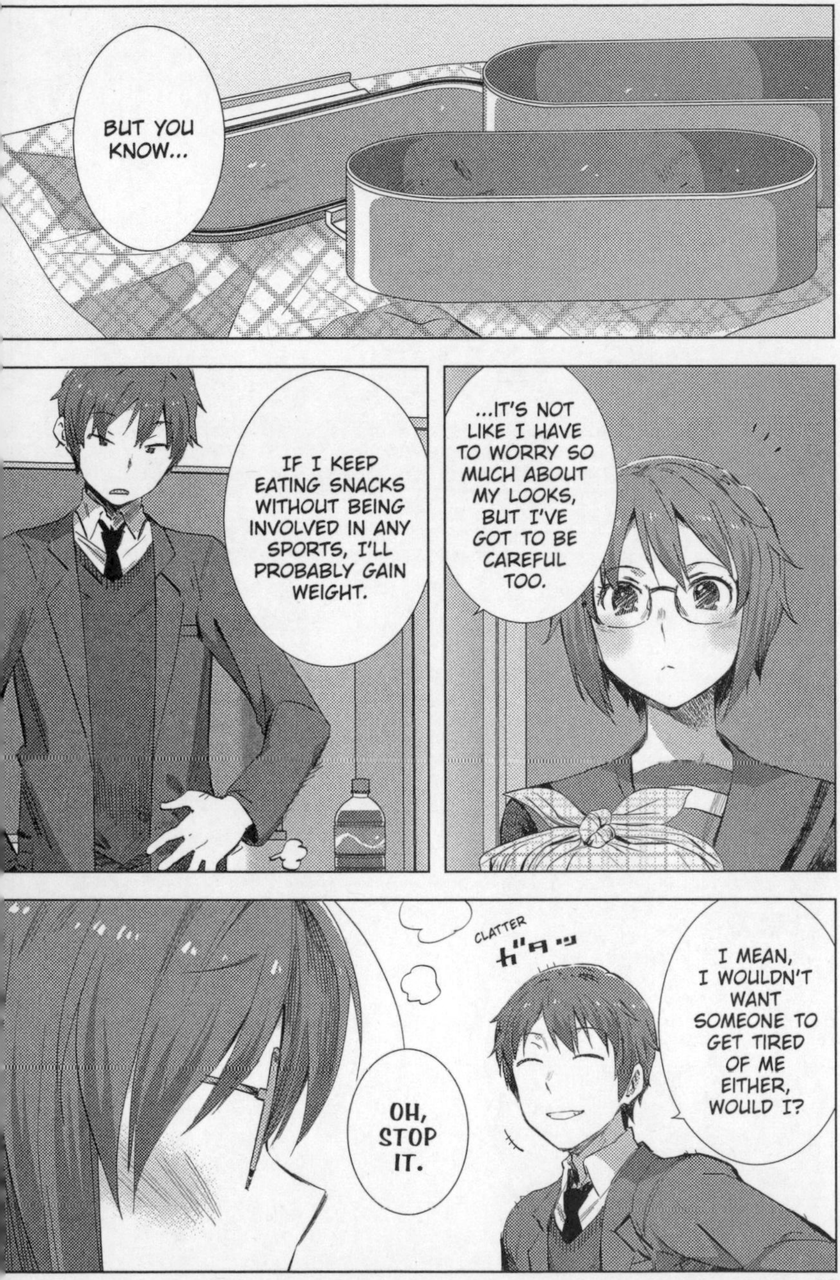
BUT YOU KNOW...
...IT'S NOT LIKE I HAVE TO WORRY SO MUCH ABOUT MY LOOKS, BUT I'VE GOT TO BE CAREFUL TOO.
IF I KEEP EATING SNACKS WITHOUT BEING INVOLVED IN ANY SPORTS, I'LL PROBABLY GAIN WEIGHT.
I MEAN, I WOULDN'T WANT SOMEONE TO GET TIRED OF ME EITHER, WOULD I?
CLATTER
ガタッ
OH, STOP IT.

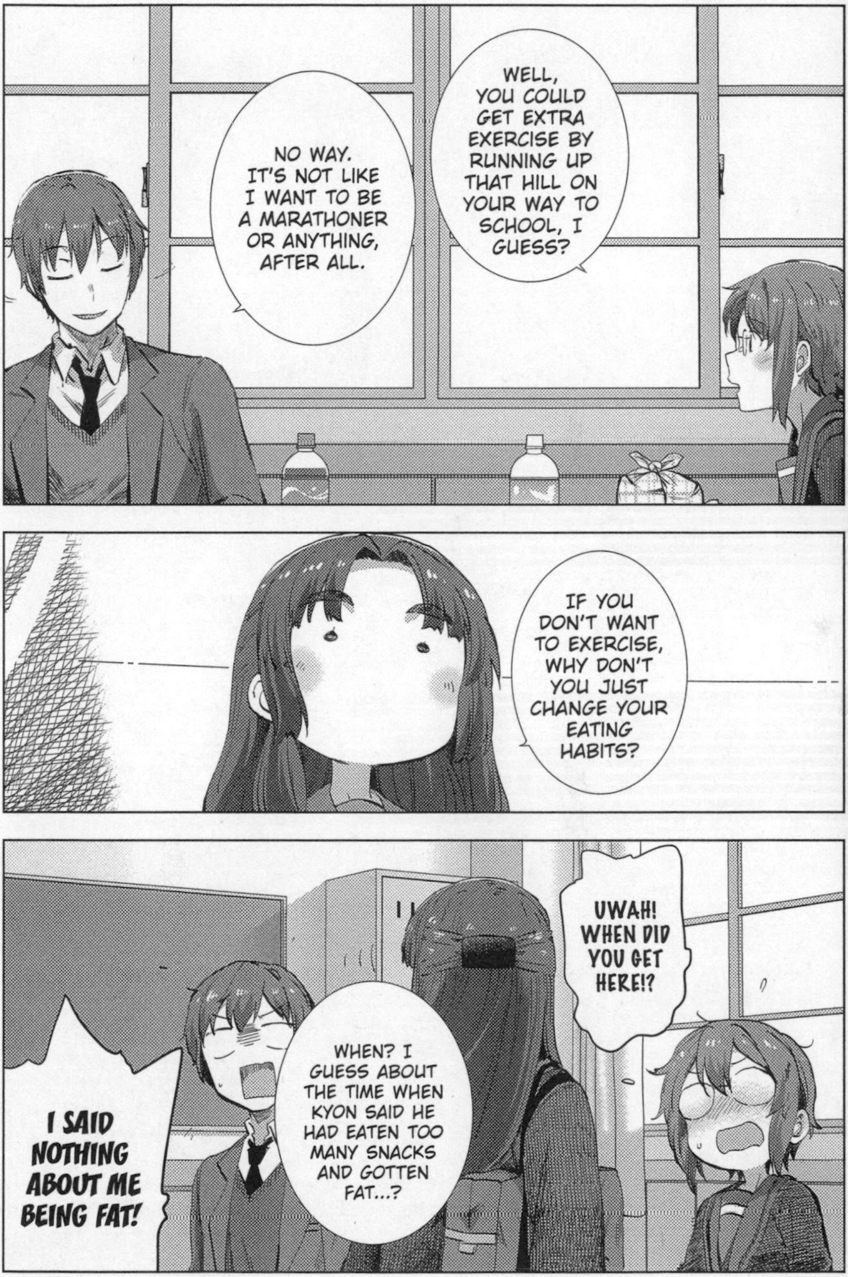
WELL, YOU COULD GET EXTRA EXERCISE BY RUNNING UP THAT HILL ON YOUR WAY TO SCHOOL, I GUESS?
NO WAY. IT'S NOT LIKE I WANT TO BE A MARATHONER OR ANYTHING, AFTER ALL.
IF YOU DON'T WANT TO EXERCISE, WHY DON'T YOU JUST CHANGE YOUR EATING HABITS?
UWAH! WHEN DID YOU GET HERE!?
WHEN? I GUESS ABOUT THE TIME WHEN KYON SAID HE HAD EATEN TOO MANY SNACKS AND GOTTEN FAT...?
I SAID NOTHING ABOUT ME BEING FAT!

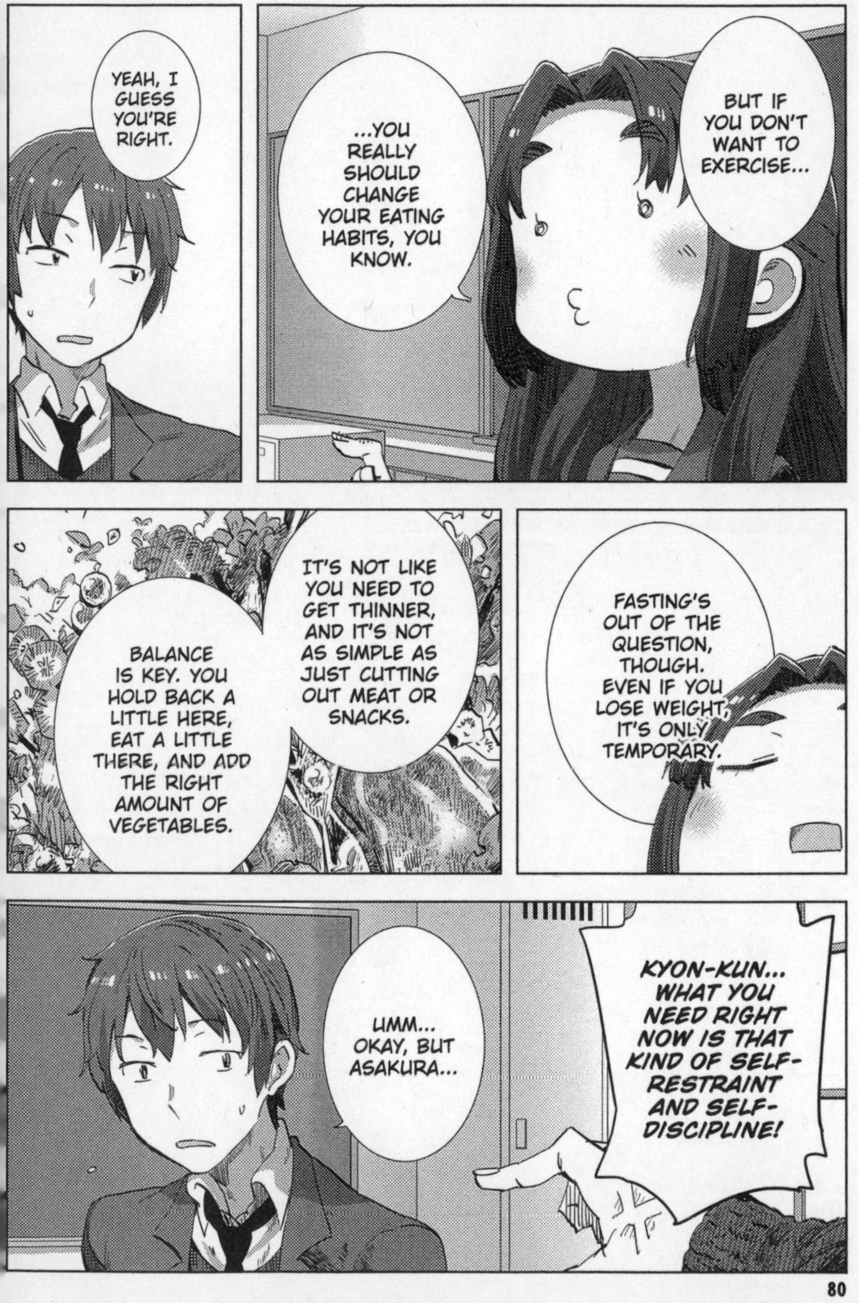
BUT IF YOU DON'T WANT TO EXERCISE...
...YOU REALLY SHOULD CHANGE YOUR EATING HABITS, YOU KNOW.
YEAH, I GUESS YOU'RE RIGHT.
FASTING'S OUT OF THE QUESTION, THOUGH. EVEN IF YOU LOSE WEIGHT, IT'S ONLY TEMPORARY.
IT'S NOT LIKE YOU NEED TO GET THINNER, AND IT'S NOT AS SIMPLE AS JUST CUTTING OUT MEAT OR SNACKS.
BALANCE IS KEY. YOU HOLD BACK A LITTLE HERE, EAT A LITTLE THERE, AND ADD THE RIGHT AMOUNT OF VEGETABLES.
KYON-KUN... WHAT YOU NEED RIGHT NOW IS THAT KIND OF SELF-RESTRAINT AND SELF-DISCIPLINE!
UMM... OKAY, BUT ASAKURA...

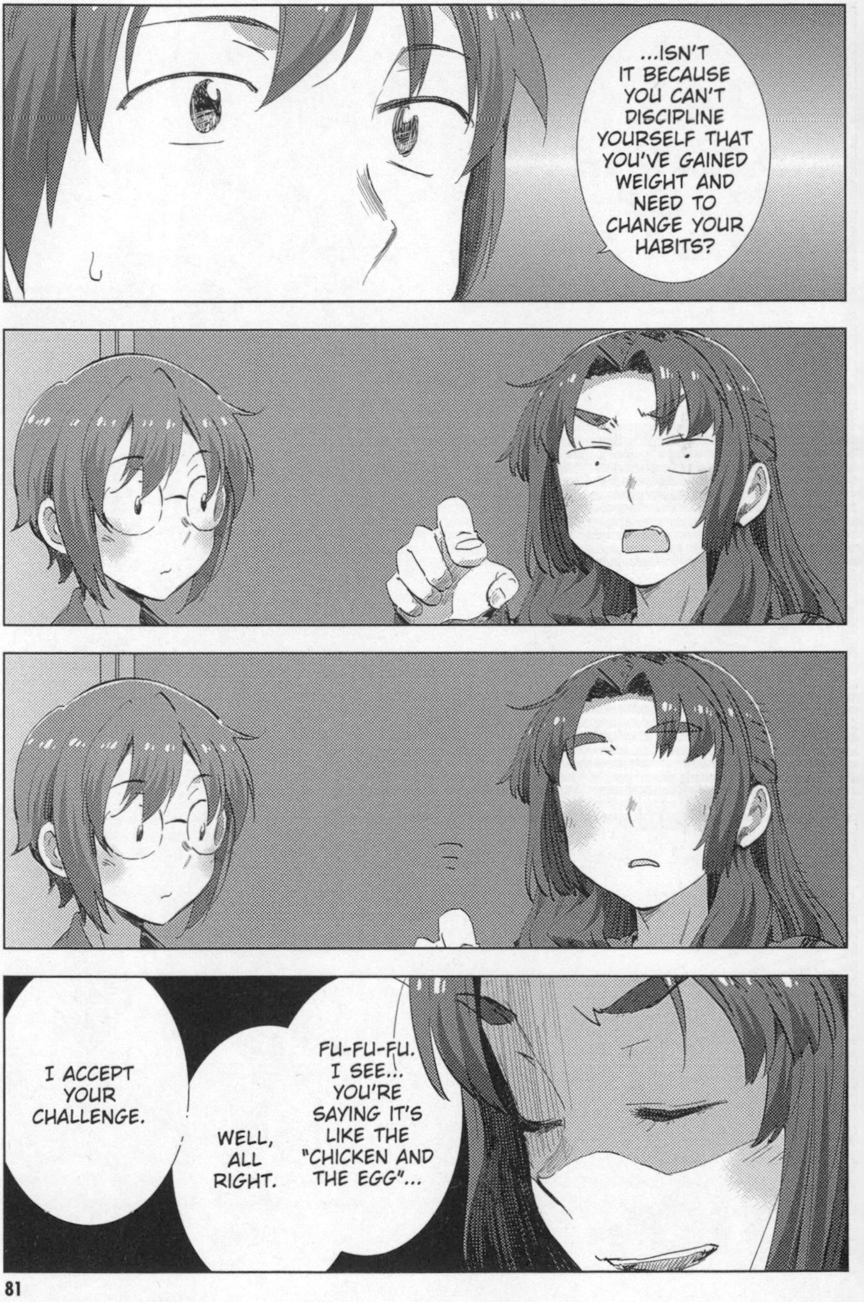
...ISN'T IT BECAUSE YOU CAN'T DISCIPLINE YOURSELF THAT YOU'VE GAINED WEIGHT AND NEED TO CHANGE YOUR HABITS?
FU-FU-FU. I SEE... YOU'RE SAYING IT'S LIKE THE "CHICKEN AND THE EGG"...
WELL, ALL RIGHT.
I ACCEPT YOUR CHALLENGE.

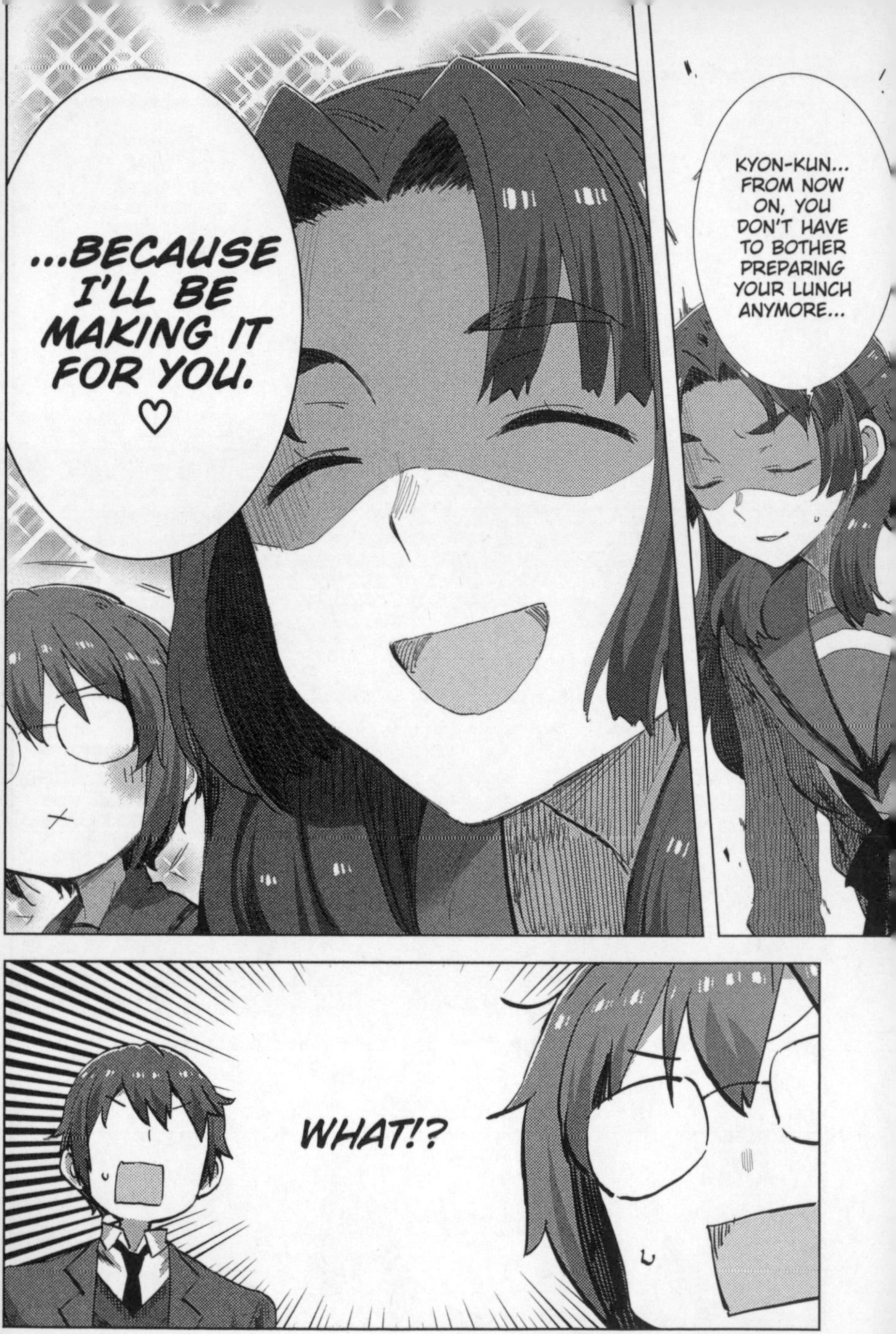
KYON-KUN... FROM NOW ON, YOU DON'T HAVE TO BOTHER PREPARING YOUR LUNCH ANYMORE...
...BECAUSE I'LL BE MAKING IT FOR YOU. ♡
WHAT!?

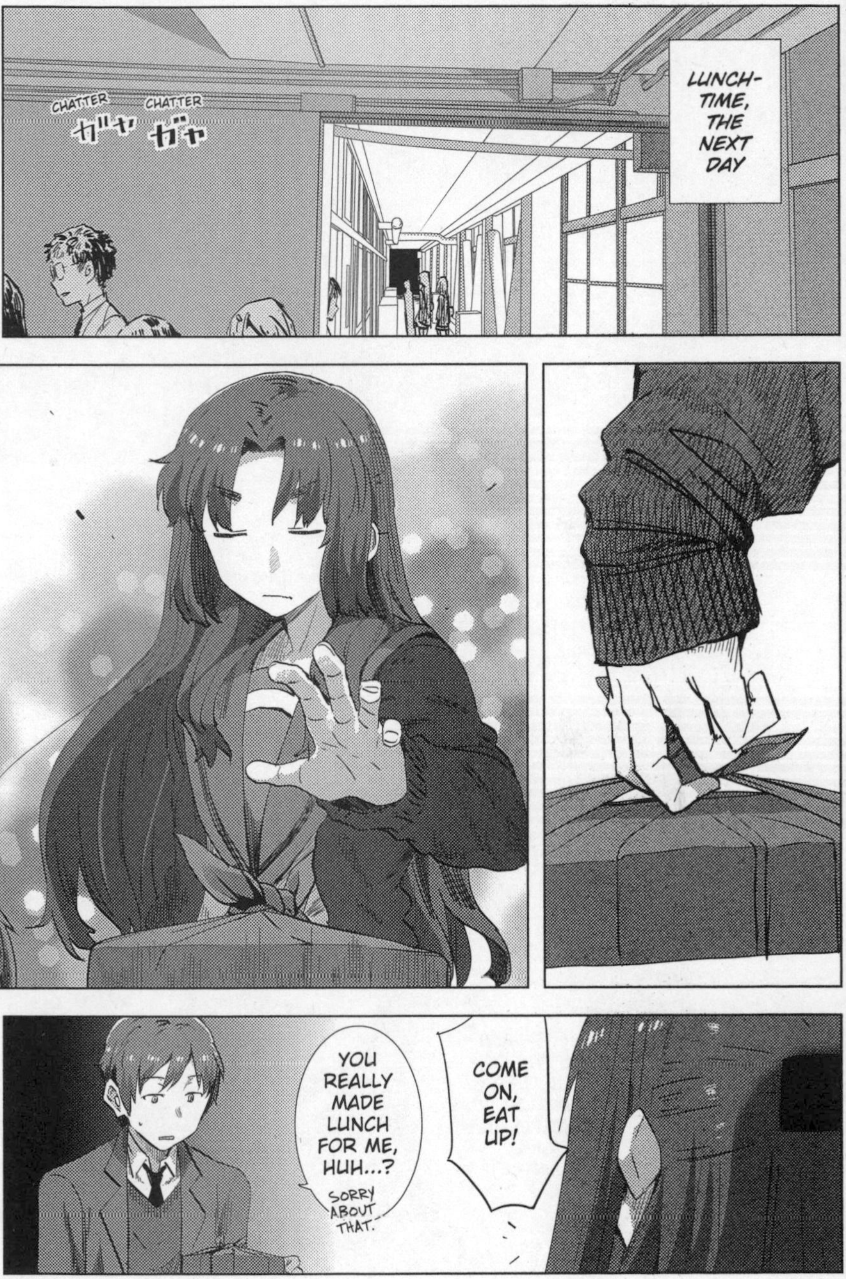
LUNCH-TIME, THE NEXT DAY
CHATTER ガヤ
CHATTER ガヤ
COME ON, EAT UP!
YOU REALLY MADE LUNCH FOR ME, HUH...?
SORRY ABOUT THAT.

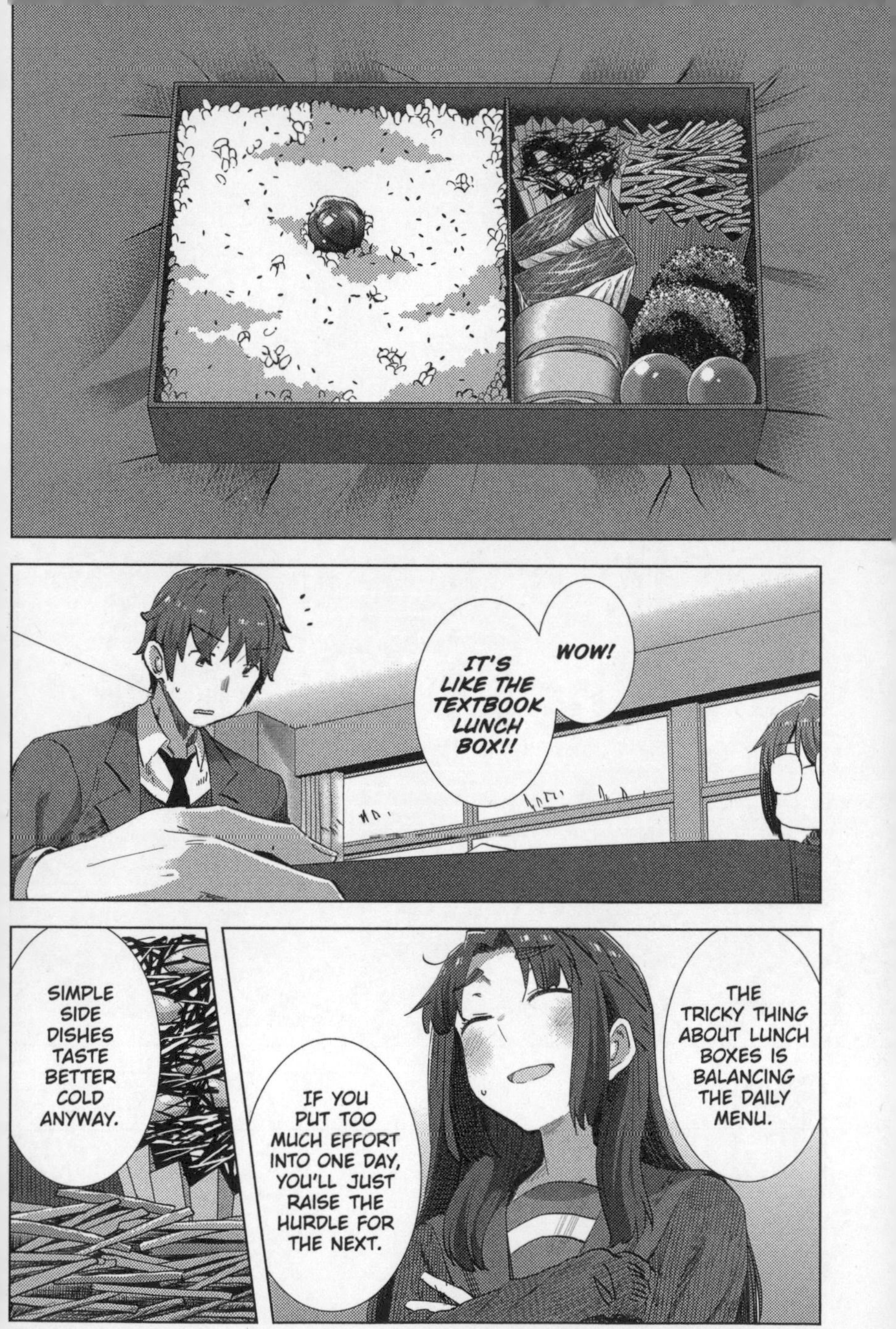
WOW! IT'S LIKE THE TEXTBOOK LUNCH BOX!!
THE TRICKY THING ABOUT LUNCH BOXES IS BALANCING THE DAILY MENU.
IF YOU PUT TOO MUCH EFFORT INTO ONE DAY, YOU'LL JUST RAISE THE HURDLE FOR THE NEXT.
SIMPLE SIDE DISHES TASTE BETTER COLD ANYWAY.

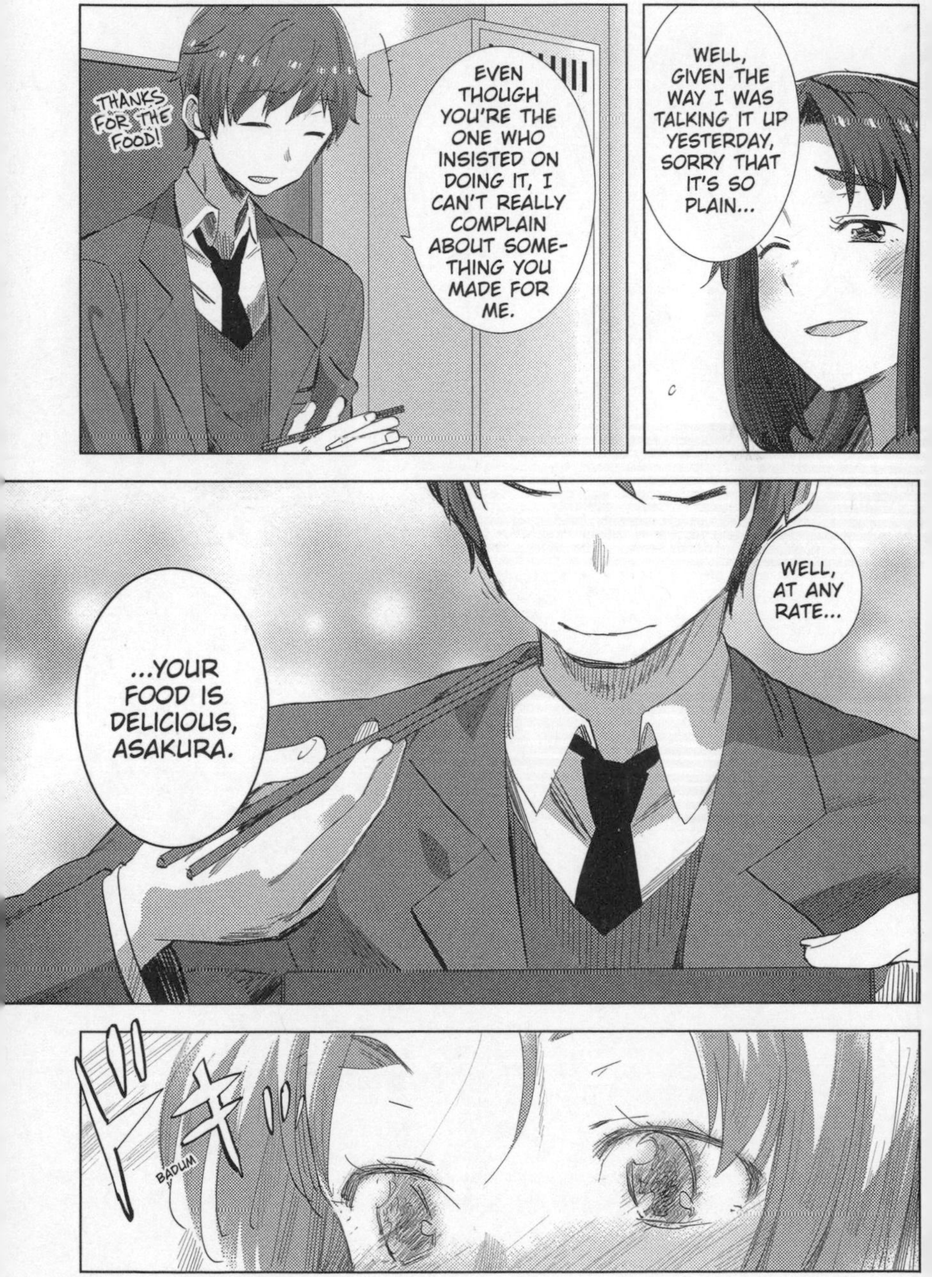
WELL, GIVEN THE WAY I WAS TALKING IT UP YESTERDAY, SORRY THAT IT'S SO PLAIN...
EVEN THOUGH YOU'RE THE ONE WHO INSISTED ON DOING IT, I CAN'T REALLY COMPLAIN ABOUT SOME-THING YOU MADE FOR ME.
THANKS FOR THE FOOD!
WELL, AT ANY RATE...
...YOUR FOOD IS DELICIOUS, ASAKURA.
ドキッ
BADUM

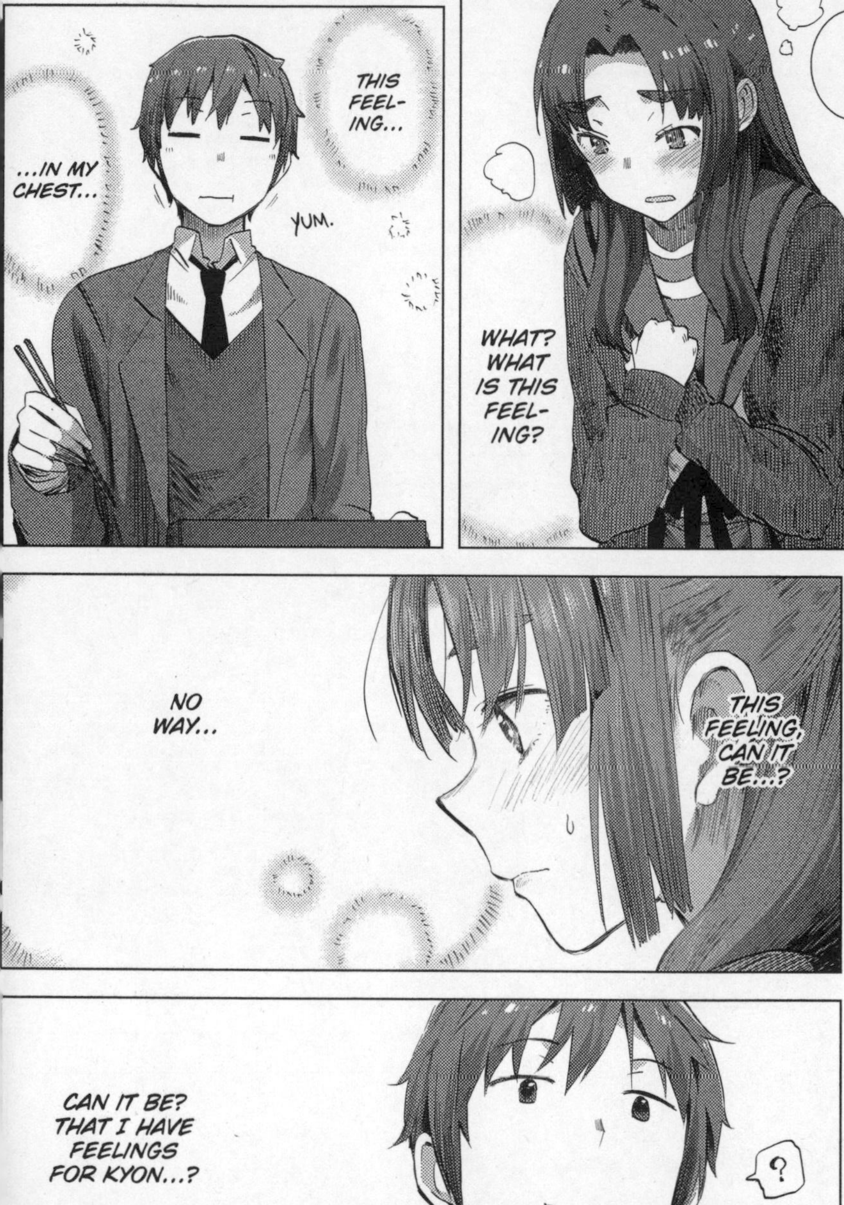
?
WHAT? WHAT IS THIS FEELING?
THIS FEELING...
...IN MY CHEST...
YUM.
THIS FEELING, CAN IT BE...?
NO WAY...
CAN IT BE? THAT I HAVE FEELINGS FOR KYON...?
?

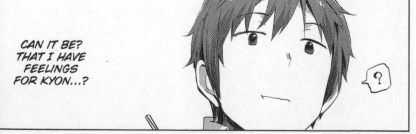

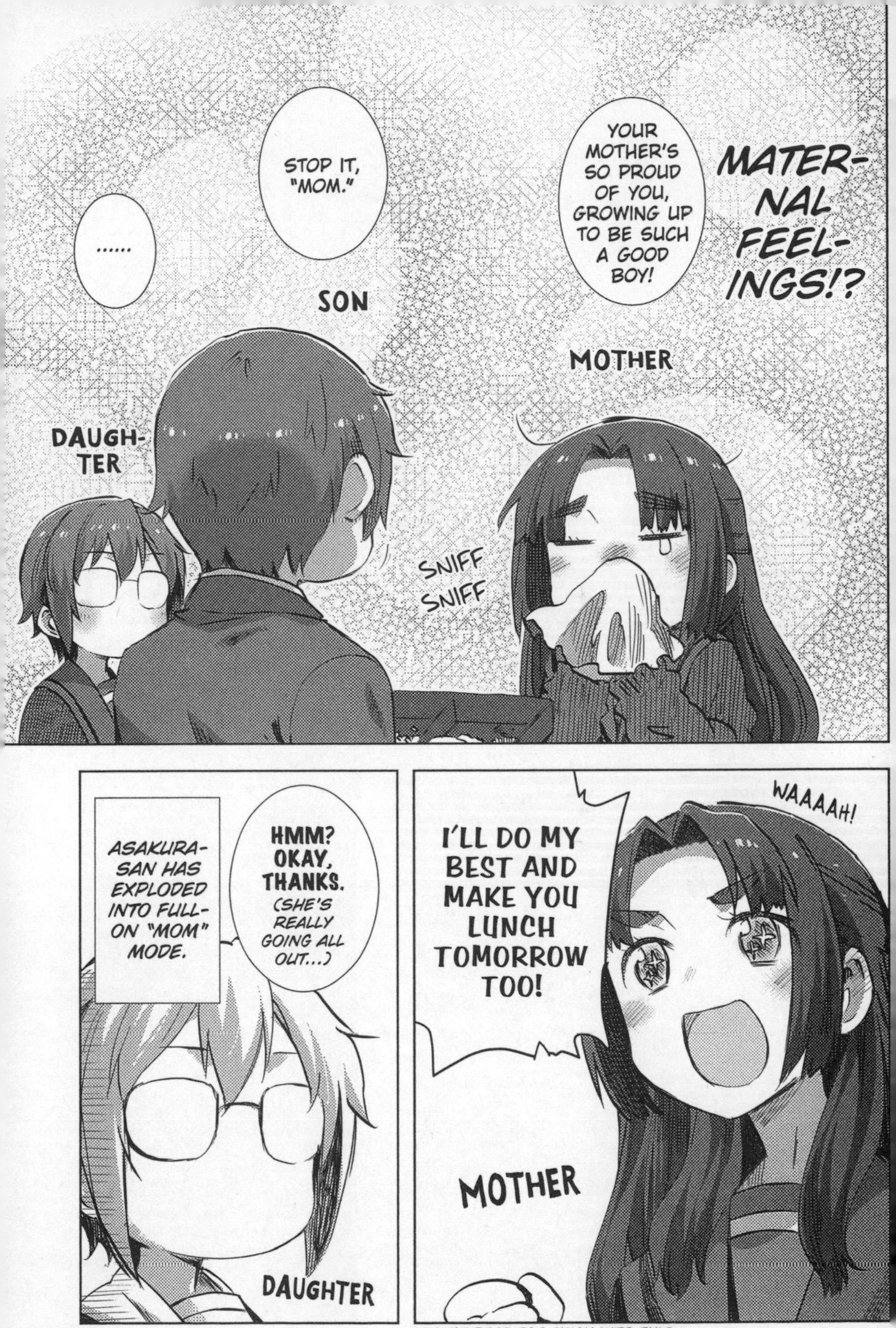
MATER-NAL FEEL-INGS!?
YOUR MOTHER'S SO PROUD OF YOU, GROWING UP TO BE SUCH A GOOD BOY!
MOTHER
STOP IT, "MOM."
SON
......
SNIFF SNIFF
DAUGH-TER
WAAAAH!
I'LL DO MY BEST AND MAKE YOU LUNCH TOMORROW TOO!
MOTHER
HMM? OKAY, THANKS. (SHE'S REALLY GOING ALL OUT...)
ASAKURA-SAN HAS EXPLODED INTO FULL-ON "MOM" MODE.
DAUGHTER

*DON'T READ TOO MUCH INTO THIS.

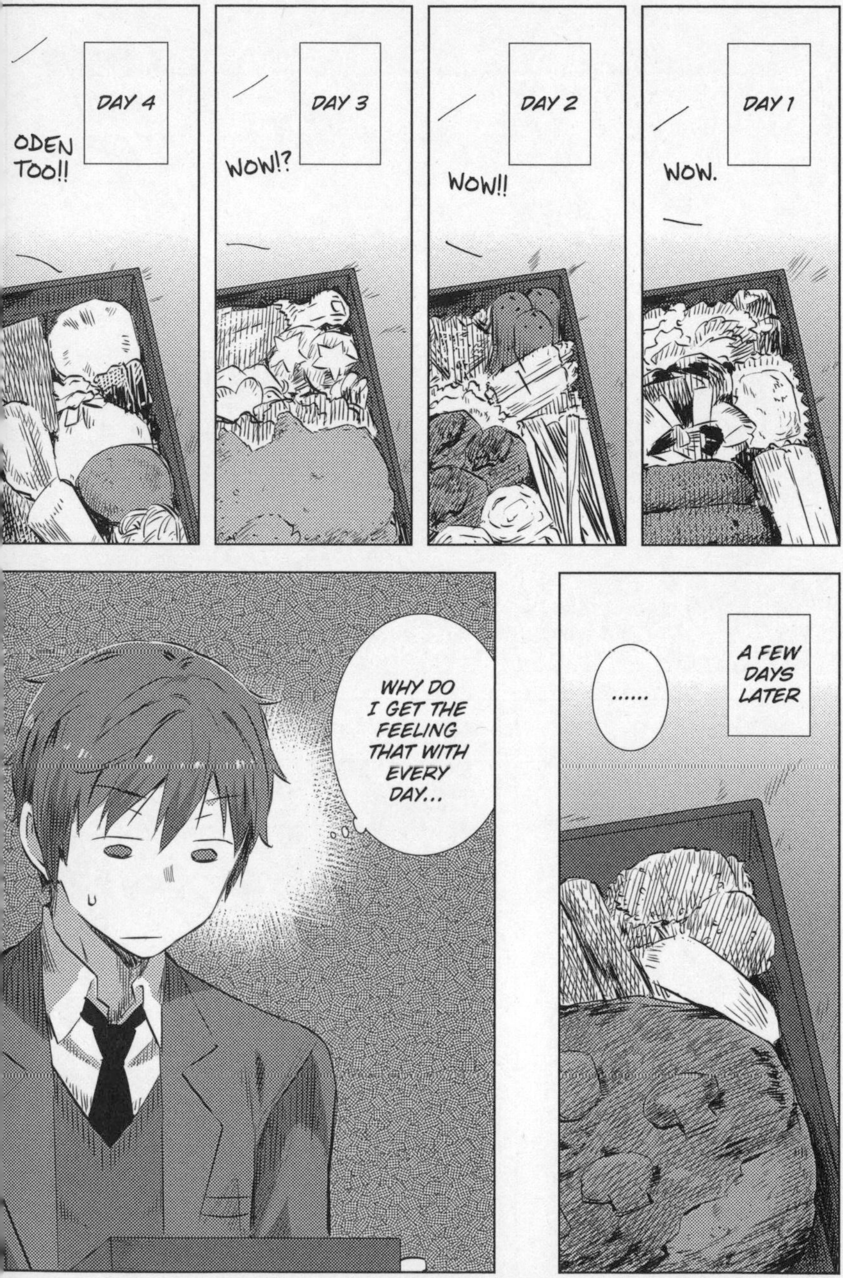
DAY 1
WOW.
DAY 2
WOW!!
DAY 3
WOW!?
DAY 4
ODEN TOO!!
A FEW DAYS LATER
......
WHY DO I GET THE FEELING THAT WITH EVERY DAY...

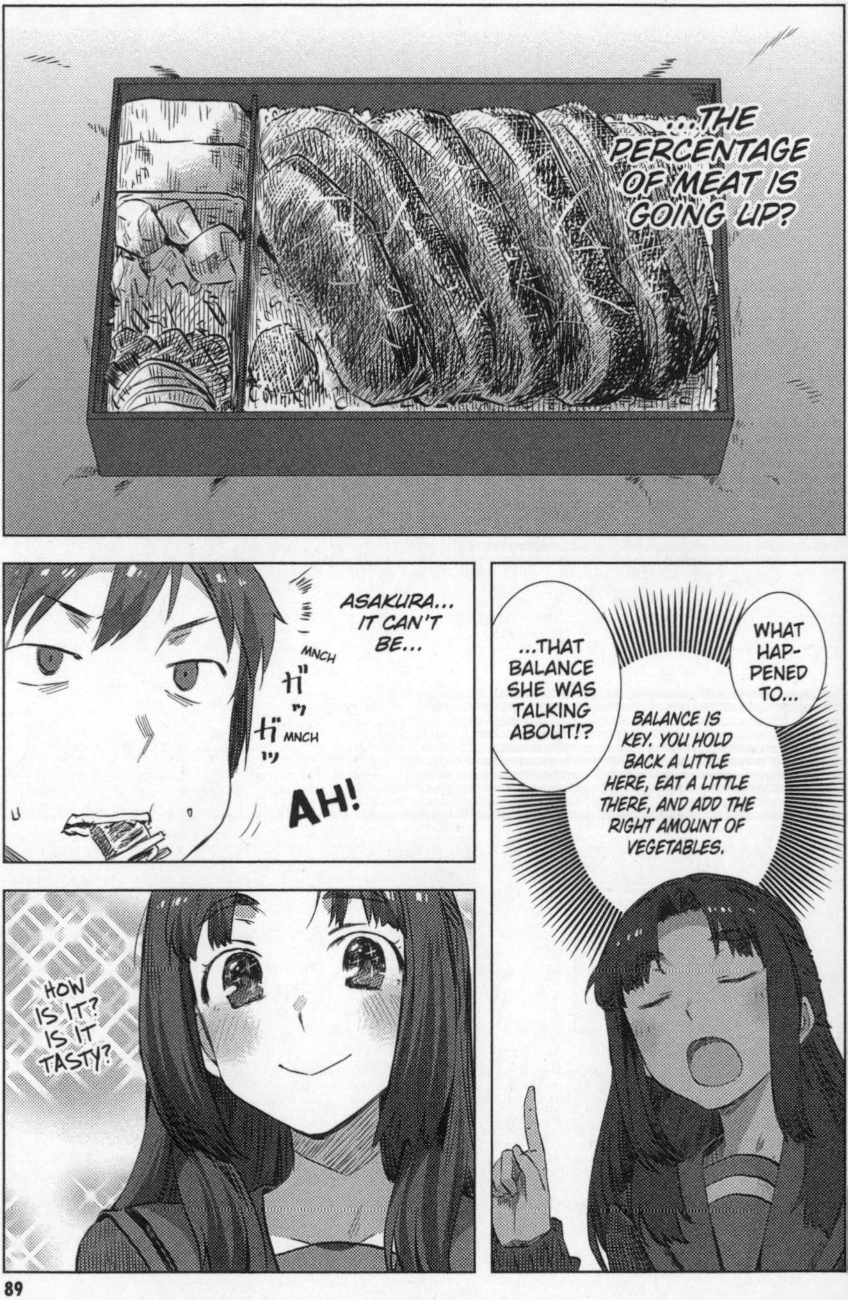

...THE PERCENTAGE OF MEAT IS GOING UP?
WHAT HAP-PENED TO...
...THAT BALANCE SHE WAS TALKING ABOUT!?
BALANCE IS KEY. YOU HOLD BACK A LITTLE HERE, EAT A LITTLE THERE, AND ADD THE RIGHT AMOUNT OF VEGETABLES.
ASAKURA... IT CAN'T BE...
ガッ MNCH
ガッ MNCH
AH!
HOW IS IT? IS IT TASTY?

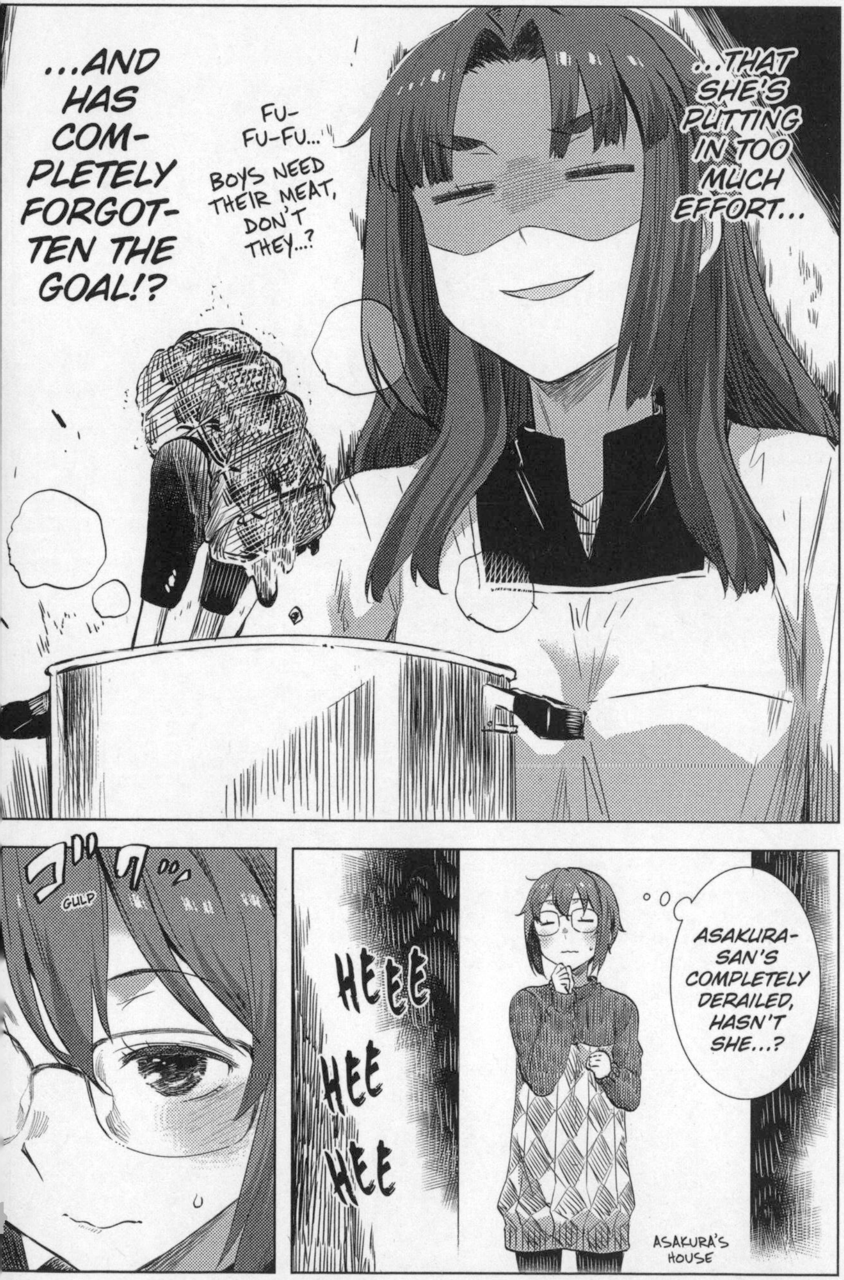
...THAT SHE'S PUTTING IN TOO MUCH EFFORT...
FU-FU-FU...
BOYS NEED THEIR MEAT, DON'T THEY...?
...AND HAS COM-PLETELY FORGOT-TEN THE GOAL!?
ASAKURA-SAN'S COMPLETELY DERAILED, HASN'T SHE...?
ASAKURA'S HOUSE
HEEE HEE HEE
GULP

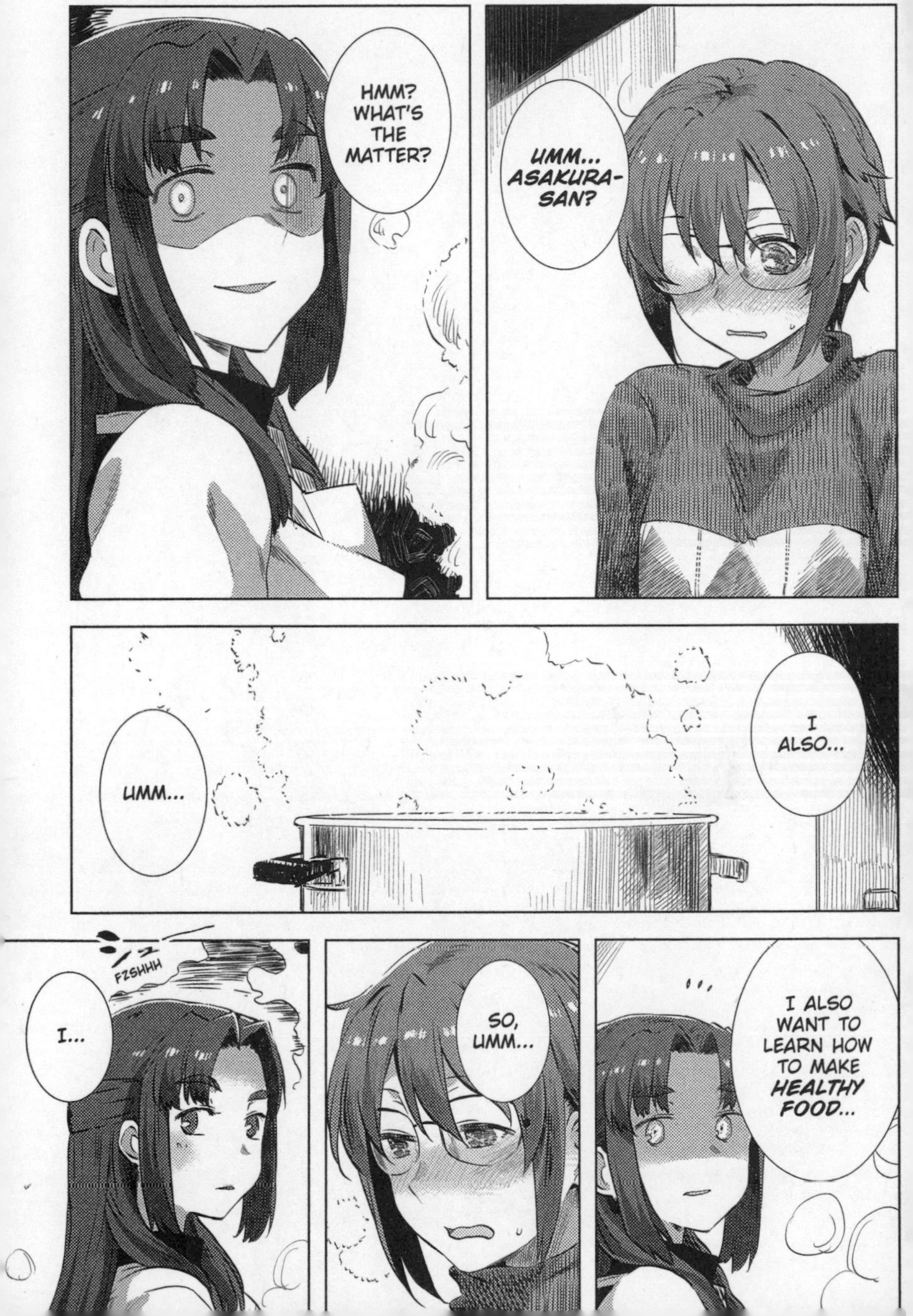
UMM... ASAKURA-SAN?
HMM? WHAT'S THE MATTER?
I ALSO...
UMM...
...
I ALSO WANT TO LEARN HOW TO MAKE HEALTHY FOOD...
SO, UMM...
FZSHHH
I...

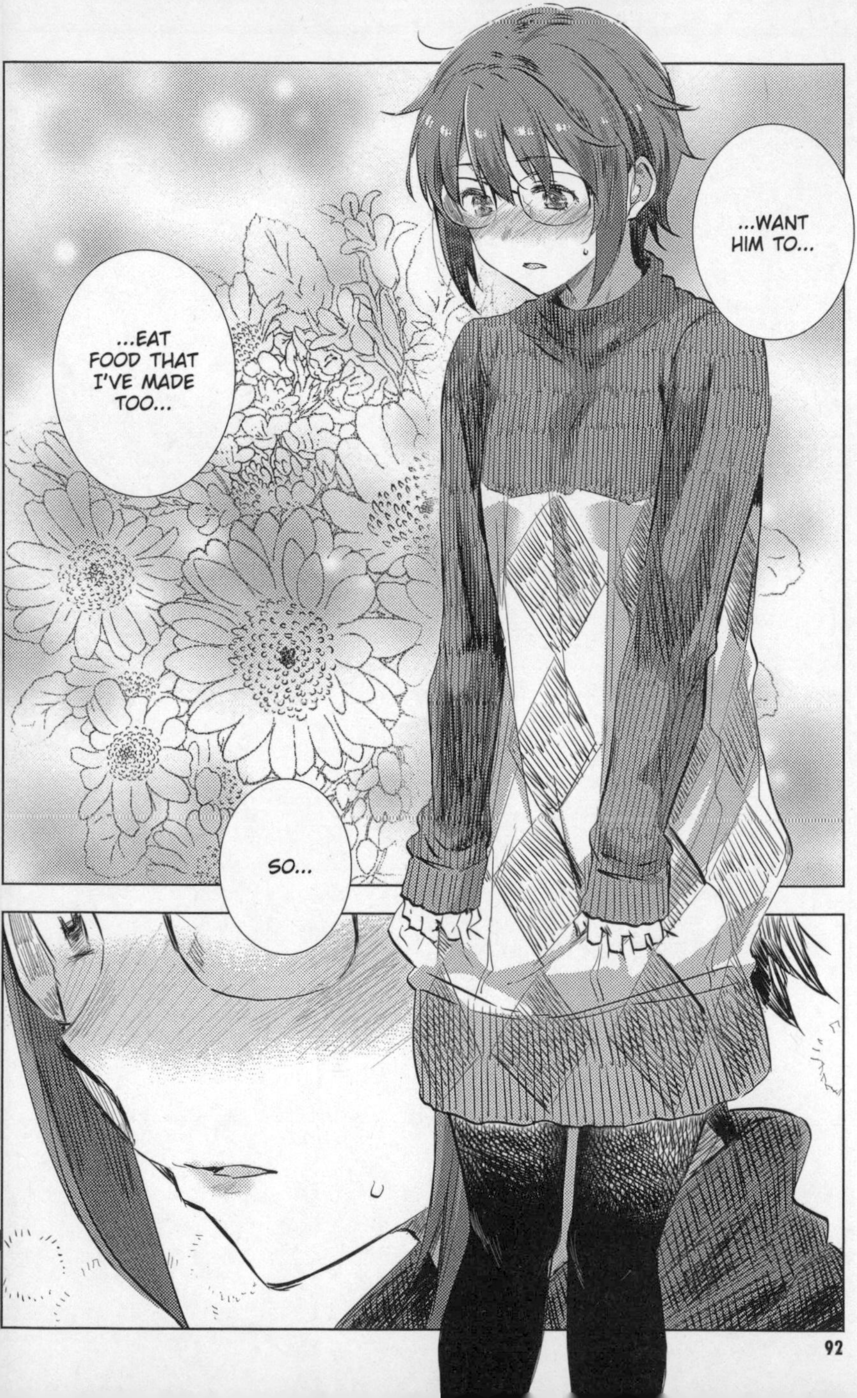
...WANT HIM TO...
...EAT FOOD THAT I'VE MADE TOO...
SO...

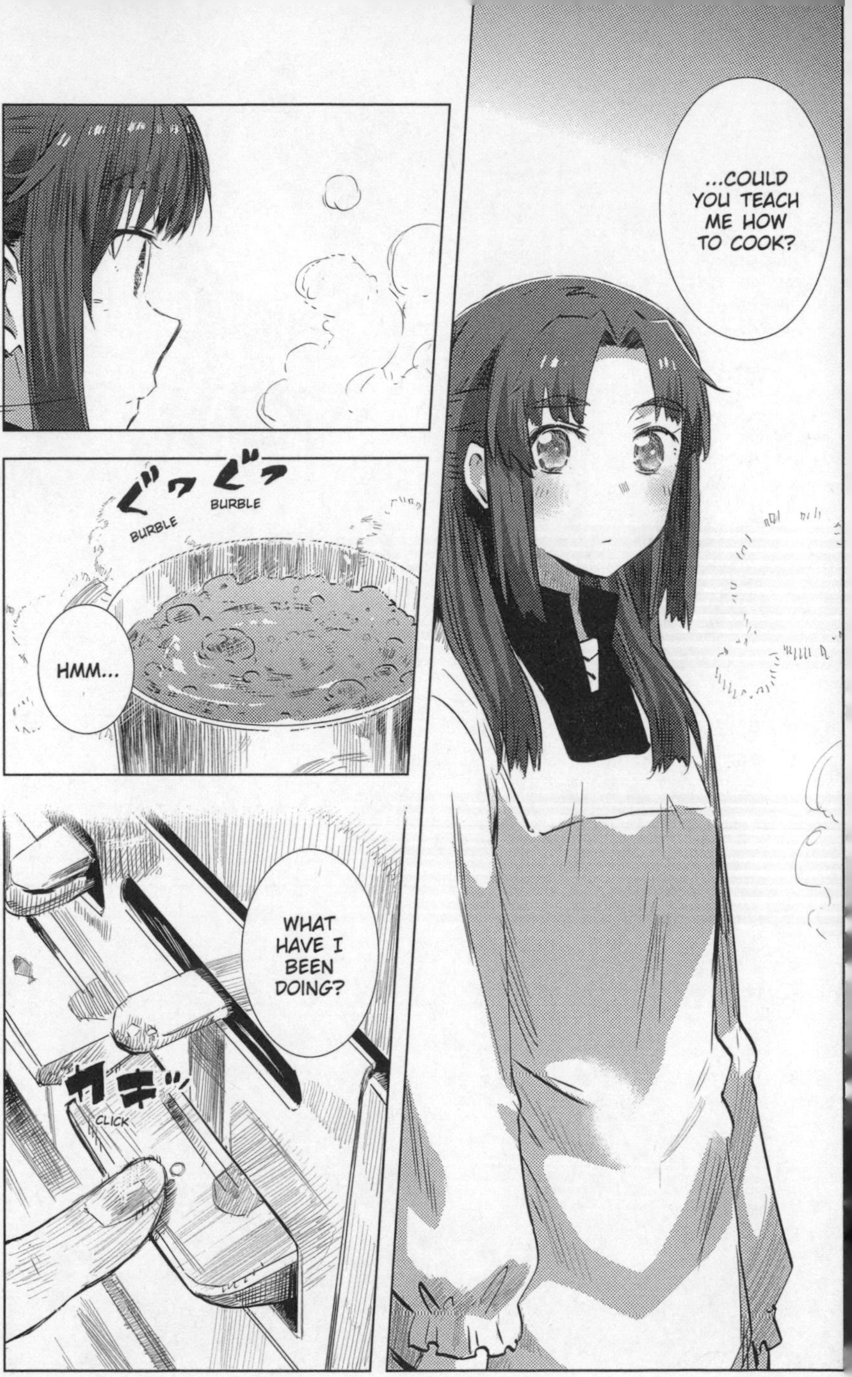
...COULD YOU TEACH ME HOW TO COOK?
BURBLE
BURBLE
HMM...
WHAT HAVE I BEEN DOING?
CLICK

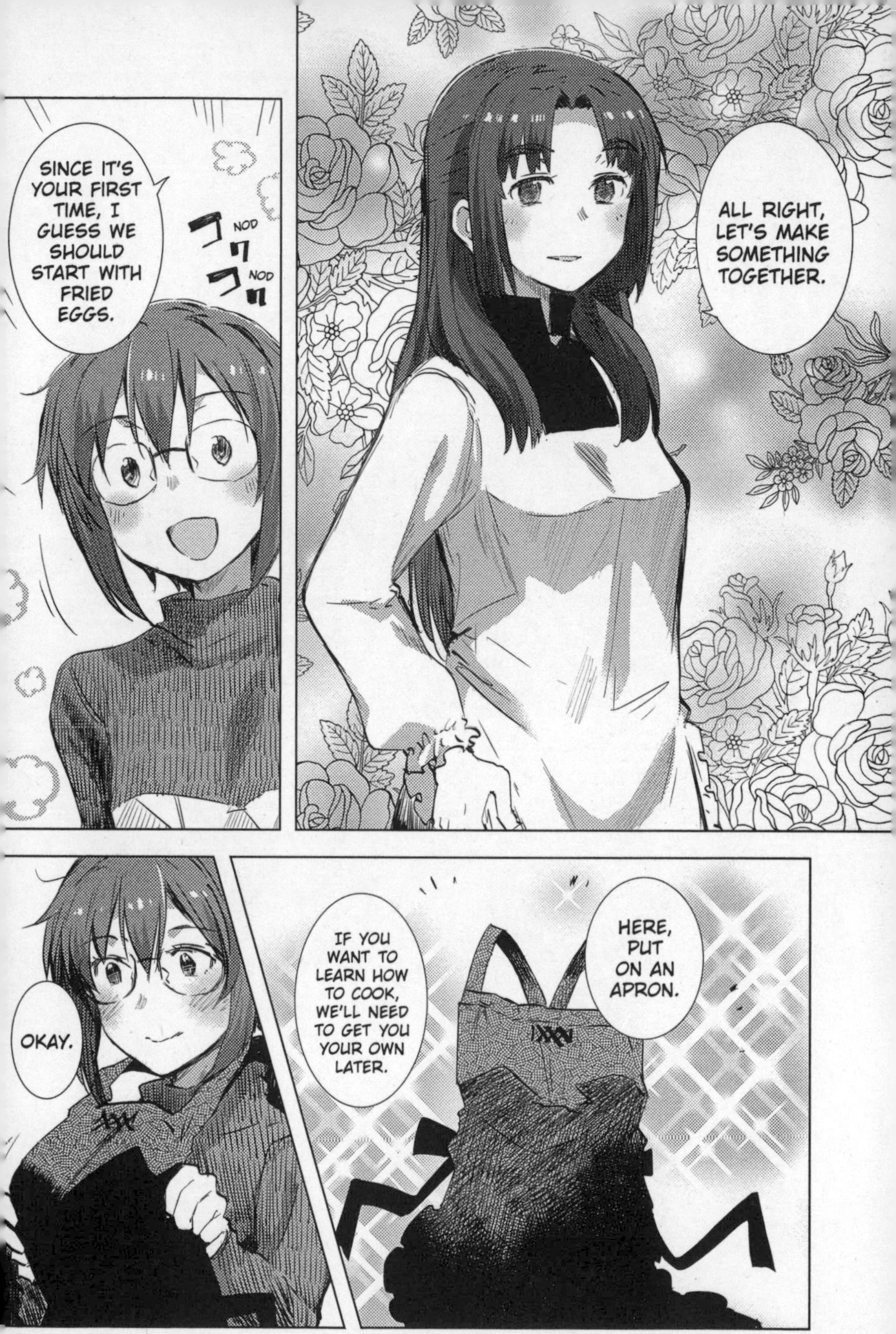
ALL RIGHT, LET'S MAKE SOMETHING TOGETHER.
SINCE IT'S YOUR FIRST TIME, I GUESS WE SHOULD START WITH FRIED EGGS.
NOD
NOD
HERE, PUT ON AN APRON.
IF YOU WANT TO LEARN HOW TO COOK, WE'LL NEED TO GET YOU YOUR OWN LATER.
OKAY.

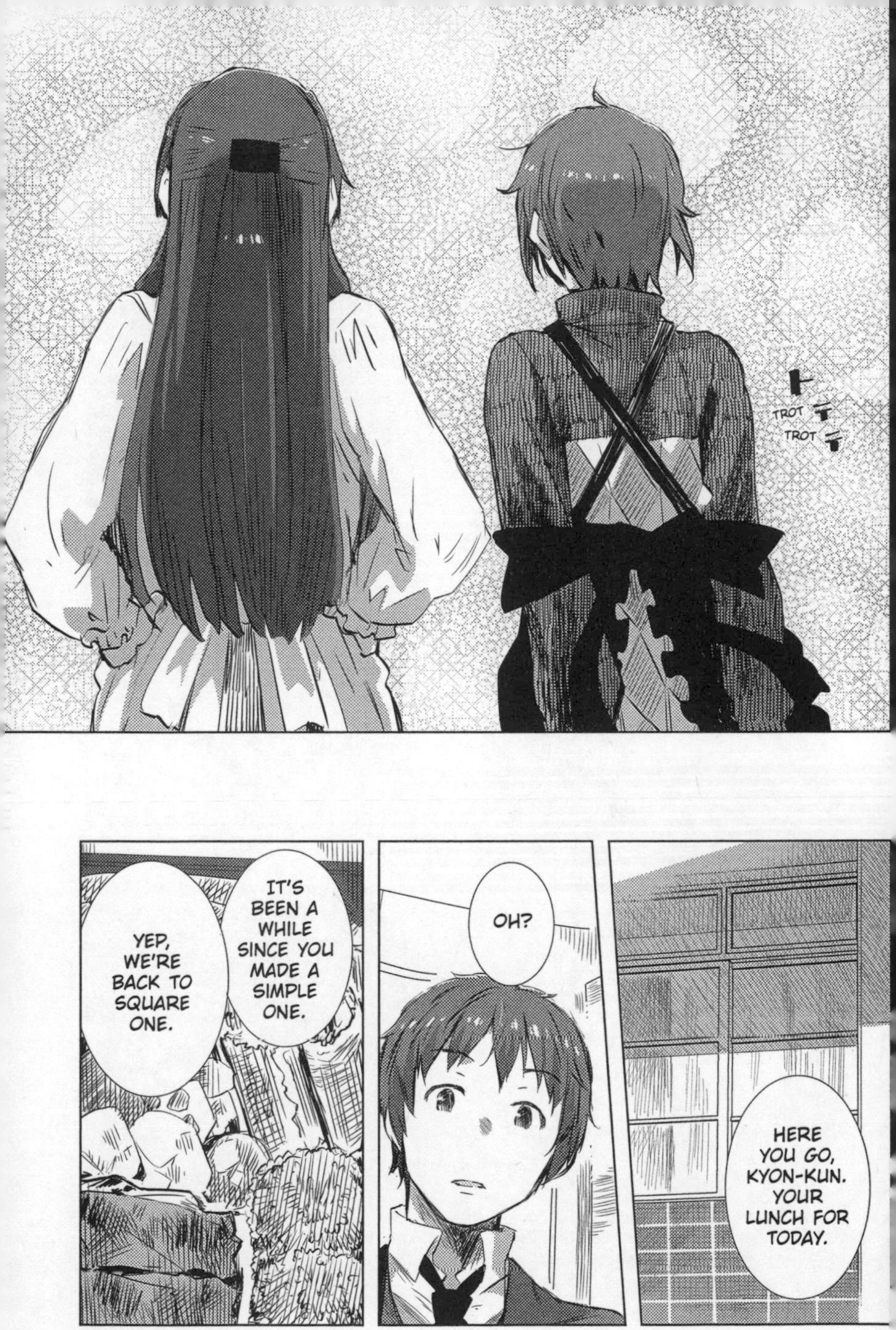
TROT
TROT
HERE YOU GO, KYON-KUN. YOUR LUNCH FOR TODAY.
OH?
IT'S BEEN A WHILE SINCE YOU MADE A SIMPLE ONE.
YEP, WE'RE BACK TO SQUARE ONE.

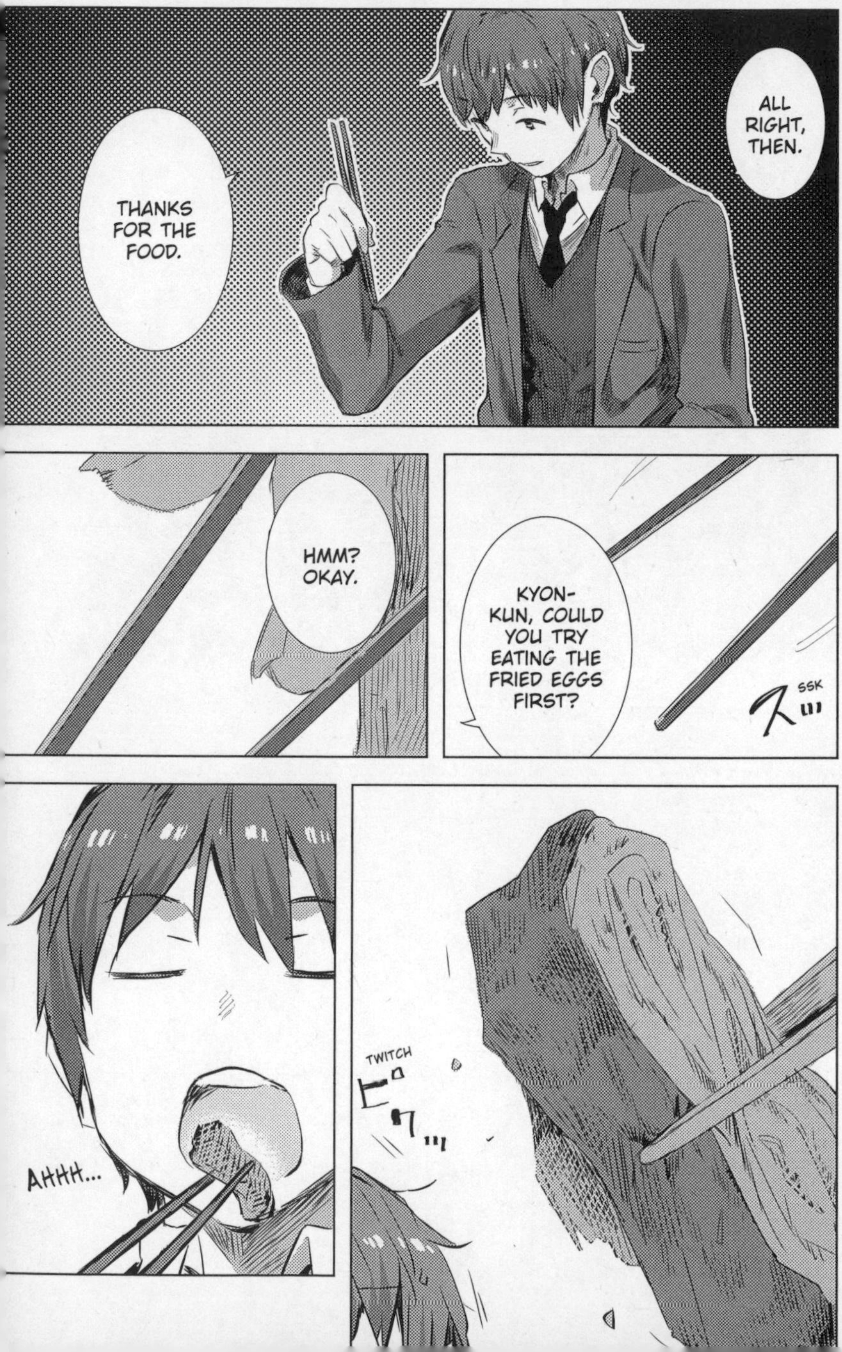
ALL RIGHT, THEN.
THANKS FOR THE FOOD.
KYON-KUN, COULD YOU TRY EATING THE FRIED EGGS FIRST?
SSK
HMM? OKAY.
TWITCH
AHHH...

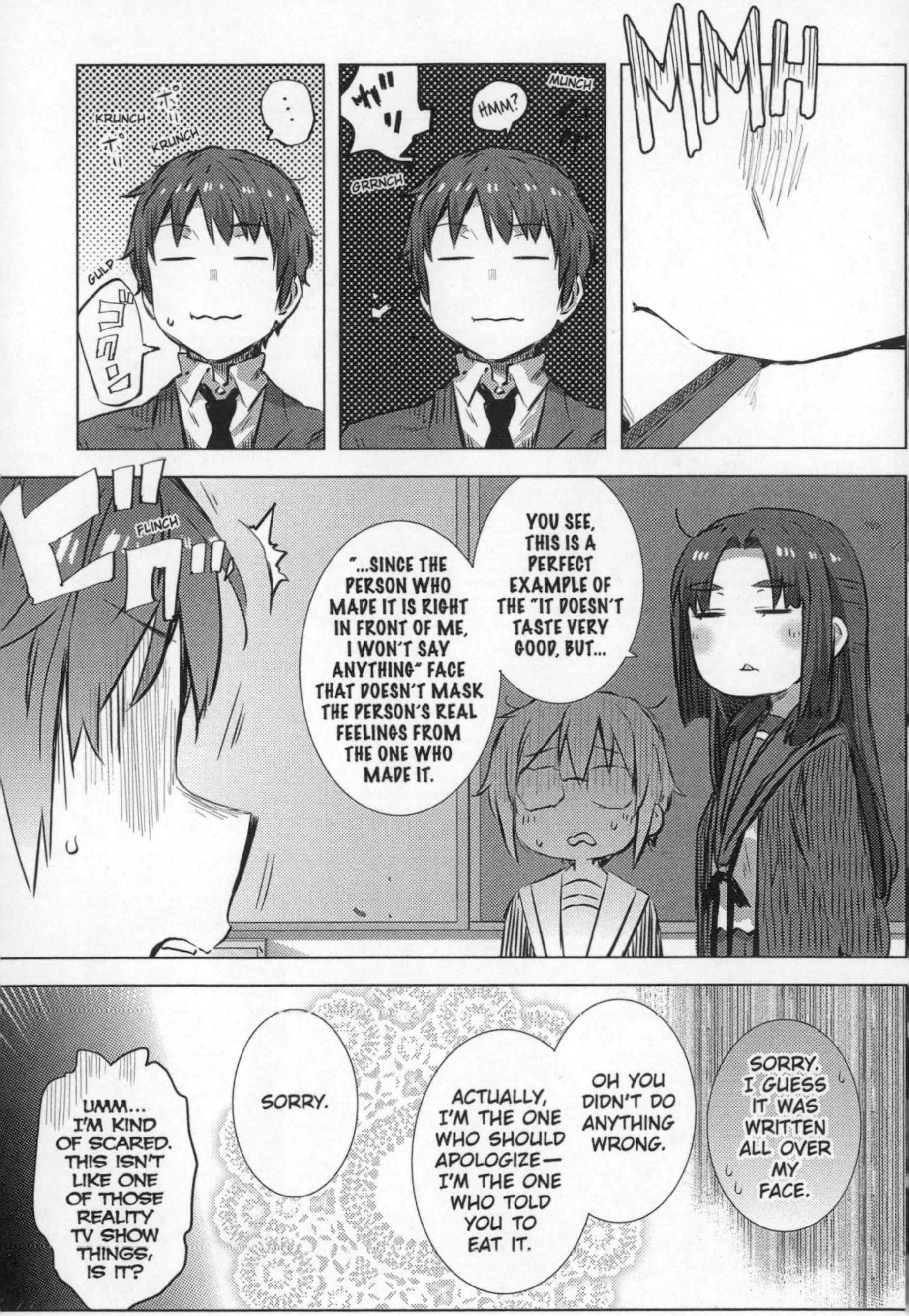
MMH
HMM?
MUNCH
GRRNCH
...
KRUNCH
KRUNCH
GULP
YOU SEE, THIS IS A PERFECT EXAMPLE OF THE "IT DOESN'T TASTE VERY GOOD, BUT...
"...SINCE THE PERSON WHO MADE IT IS RIGHT IN FRONT OF ME, I WON'T SAY ANYTHING" FACE THAT DOESN'T MASK THE PERSON'S REAL FEELINGS FROM THE ONE WHO MADE IT.
FLINCH
SORRY. I GUESS IT WAS WRITTEN ALL OVER MY FACE.
OH YOU DIDN'T DO ANYTHING WRONG.
ACTUALLY, I'M THE ONE WHO SHOULD APOLOGIZE— I'M THE ONE WHO TOLD YOU TO EAT IT.
SORRY.
UMM... I'M KIND OF SCARED. THIS ISN'T LIKE ONE OF THOSE REALITY TV SHOW THINGS, IS IT?

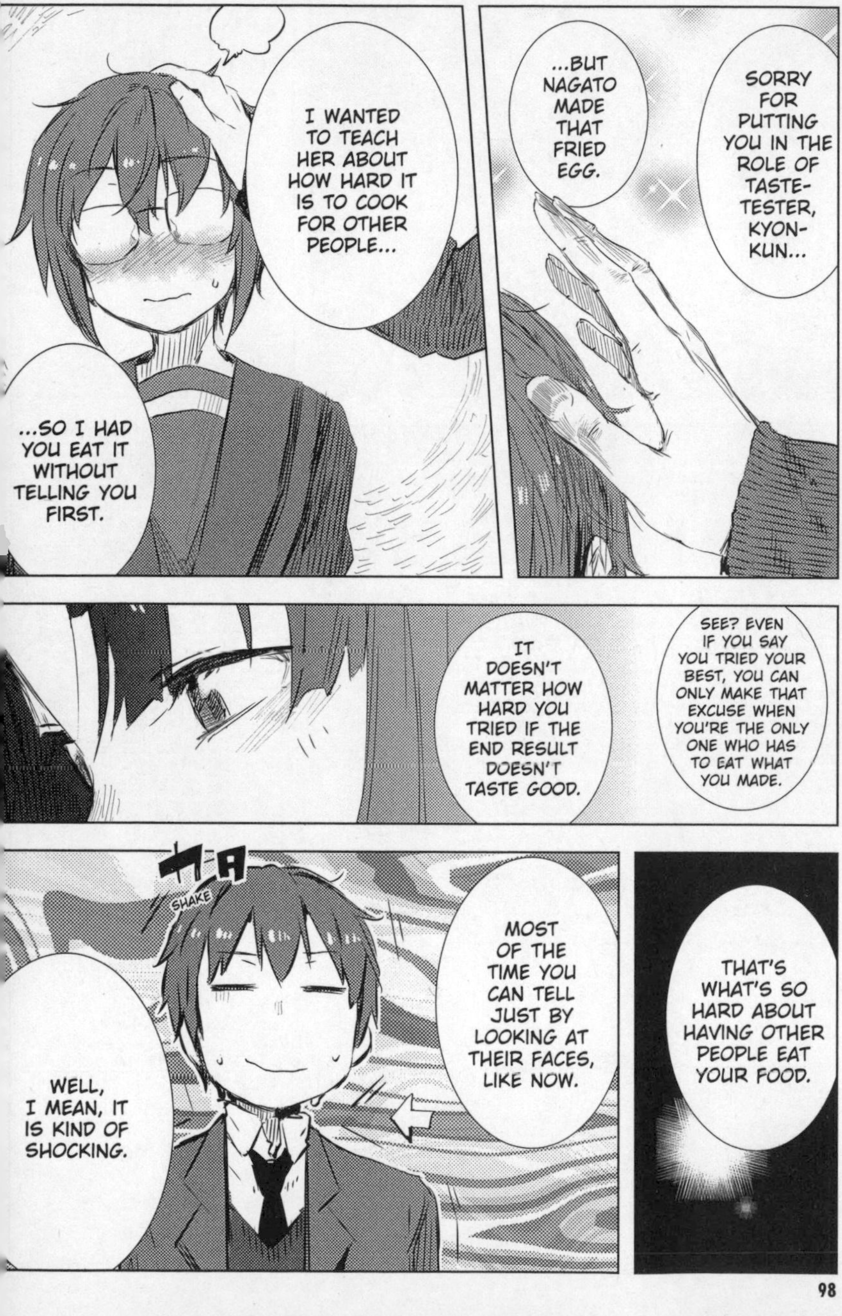
SORRY FOR PUTTING YOU IN THE ROLE OF TASTE-TESTER, KYON-KUN...
...BUT NAGATO MADE THAT FRIED EGG.
I WANTED TO TEACH HER ABOUT HOW HARD IT IS TO COOK FOR OTHER PEOPLE...
...SO I HAD YOU EAT IT WITHOUT TELLING YOU FIRST.
SEE? EVEN IF YOU SAY YOU TRIED YOUR BEST, YOU CAN ONLY MAKE THAT EXCUSE WHEN YOU'RE THE ONLY ONE WHO HAS TO EAT WHAT YOU MADE.
IT DOESN'T MATTER HOW HARD YOU TRIED IF THE END RESULT DOESN'T TASTE GOOD.
THAT'S WHAT'S SO HARD ABOUT HAVING OTHER PEOPLE EAT YOUR FOOD.
MOST OF THE TIME YOU CAN TELL JUST BY LOOKING AT THEIR FACES, LIKE NOW.
SHAKE
WELL, I MEAN, IT IS KIND OF SHOCKING.

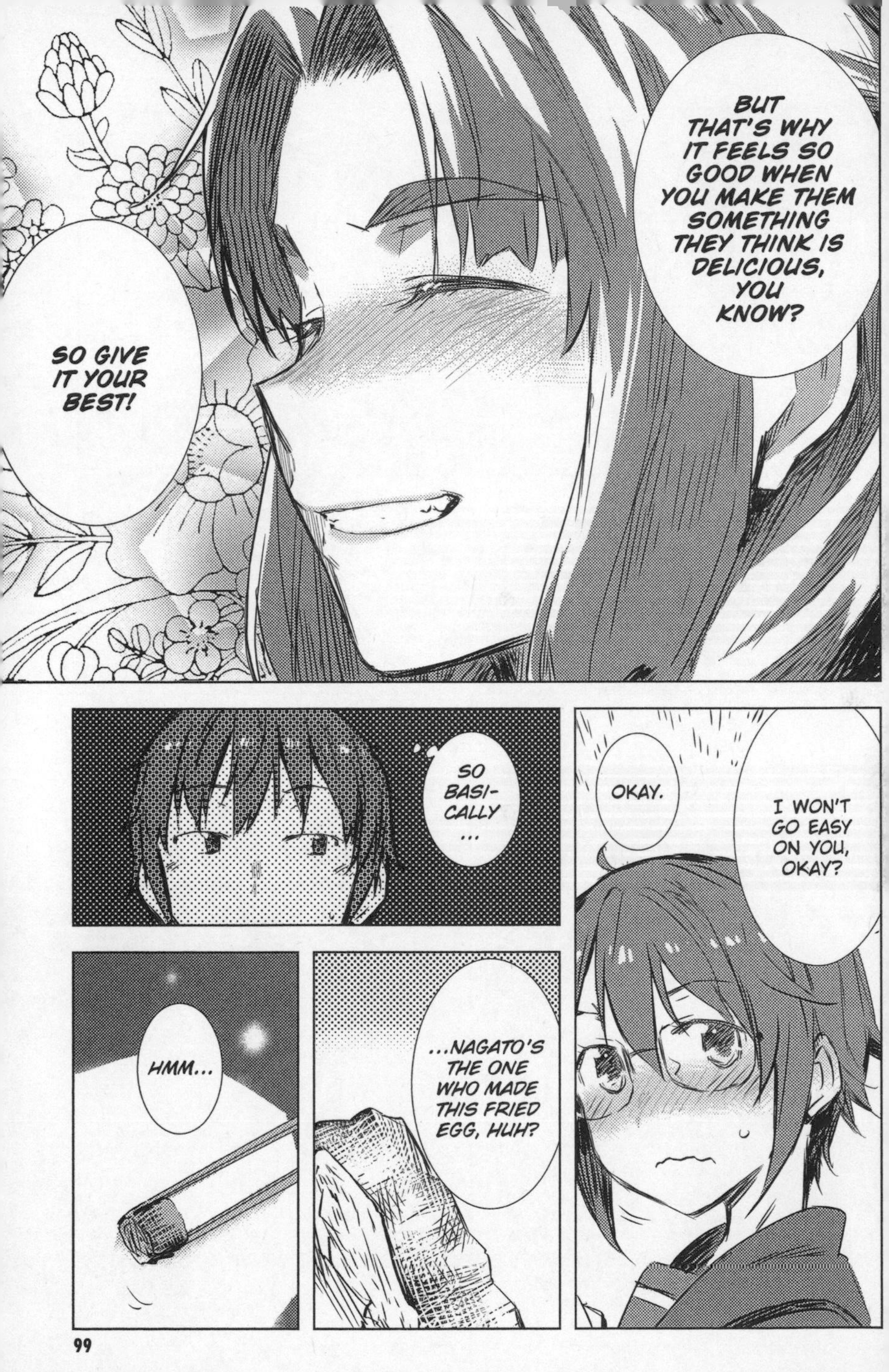
BUT THAT'S WHY IT FEELS SO GOOD WHEN YOU MAKE THEM SOMETHING THEY THINK IS DELICIOUS, YOU KNOW?
SO GIVE IT YOUR BEST!
I WON'T GO EASY ON YOU, OKAY?
OKAY.
SO BASI-CALLY ...
...NAGATO'S THE ONE WHO MADE THIS FRIED EGG, HUH?
HMM...

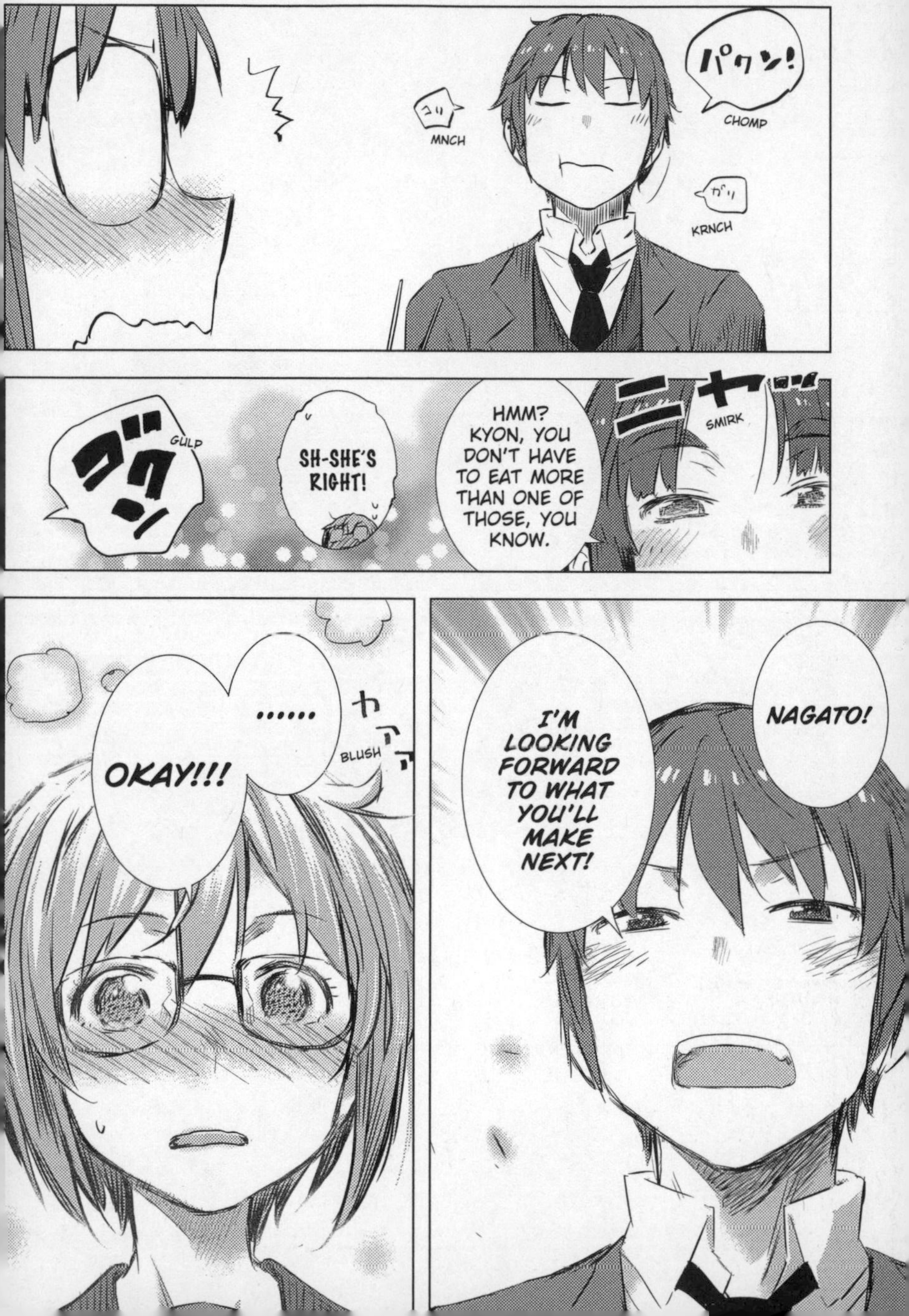
パクン!
CHOMP
コリ
MNCH
ガリ
KRNCH
ニヤッ
SMIRK
HMM? KYON, YOU DON'T HAVE TO EAT MORE THAN ONE OF THOSE, YOU KNOW.
SH-SHE'S RIGHT!
ゴクン
GULP
NAGATO!
I'M LOOKING FORWARD TO WHAT YOU'LL MAKE NEXT!
カァァ
BLUSH
......
OKAY!!!

Epilogue 62>> Club Activities

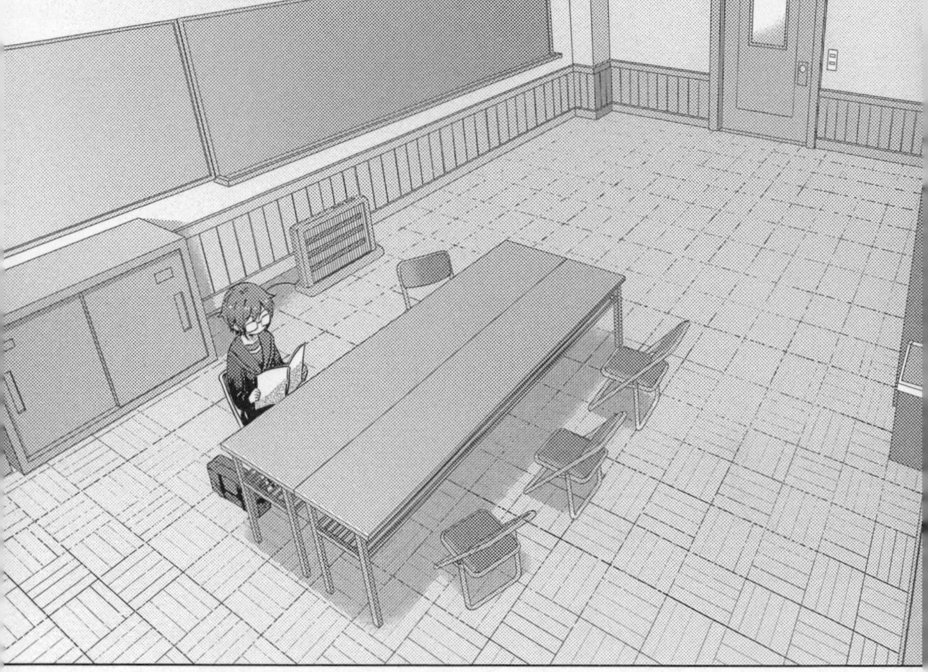

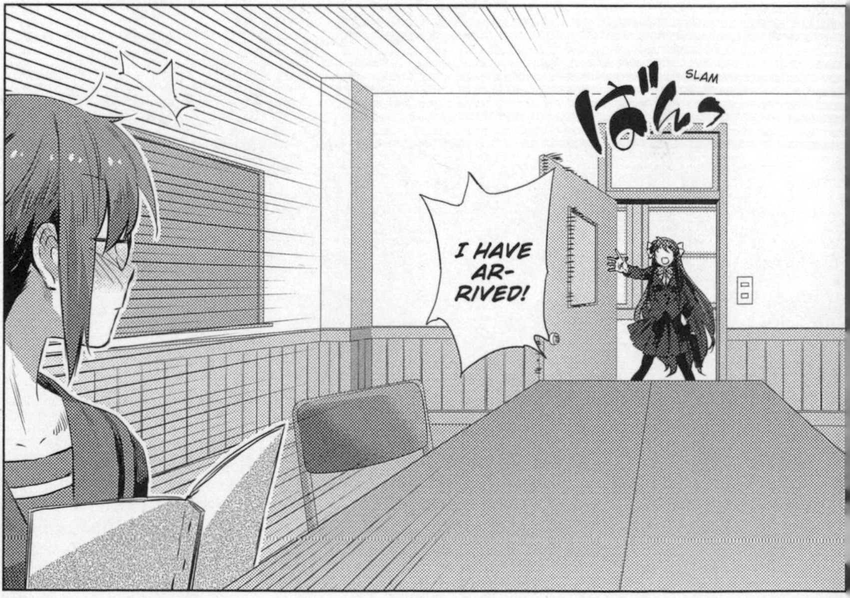
ばんっ
SLAM
I HAVE AR-RIVED!

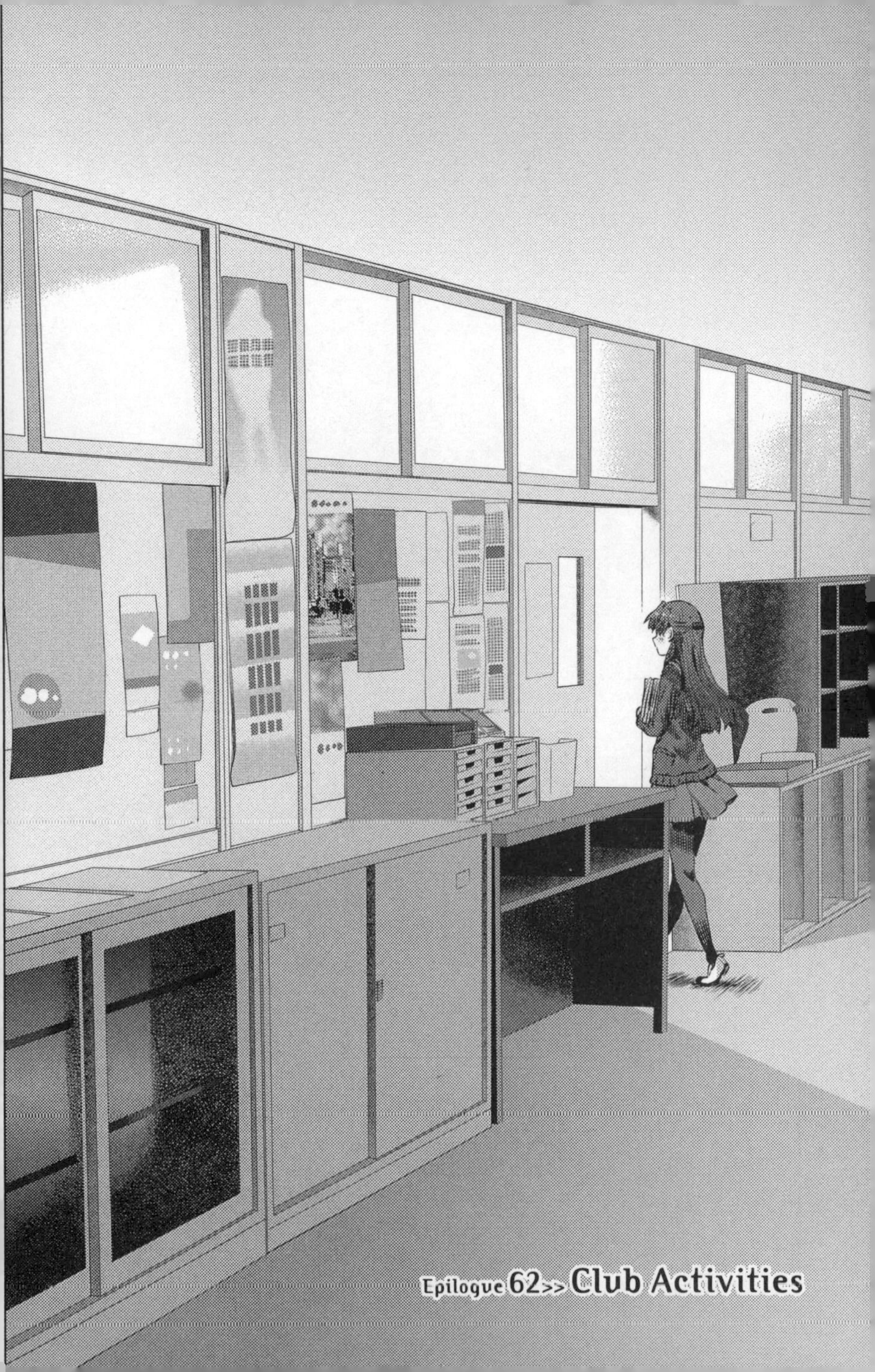
Epilogue 62>> Club Activities

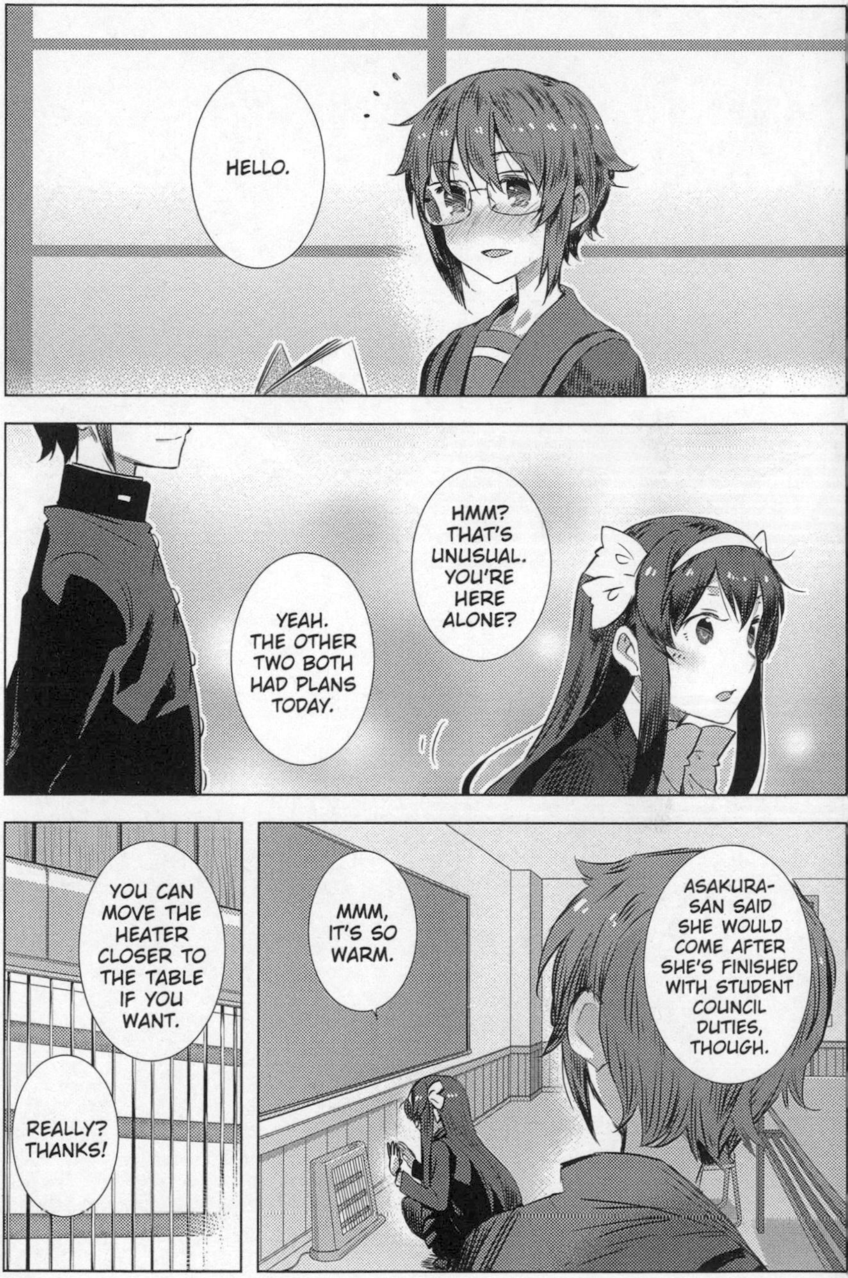
HELLO.
HMM? THAT'S UNUSUAL. YOU'RE HERE ALONE?
YEAH. THE OTHER TWO BOTH HAD PLANS TODAY.
ASAKURA-SAN SAID SHE WOULD COME AFTER SHE'S FINISHED WITH STUDENT COUNCIL DUTIES, THOUGH.
MMM, IT'S SO WARM.
YOU CAN MOVE THE HEATER CLOSER TO THE TABLE IF YOU WANT.
REALLY? THANKS!

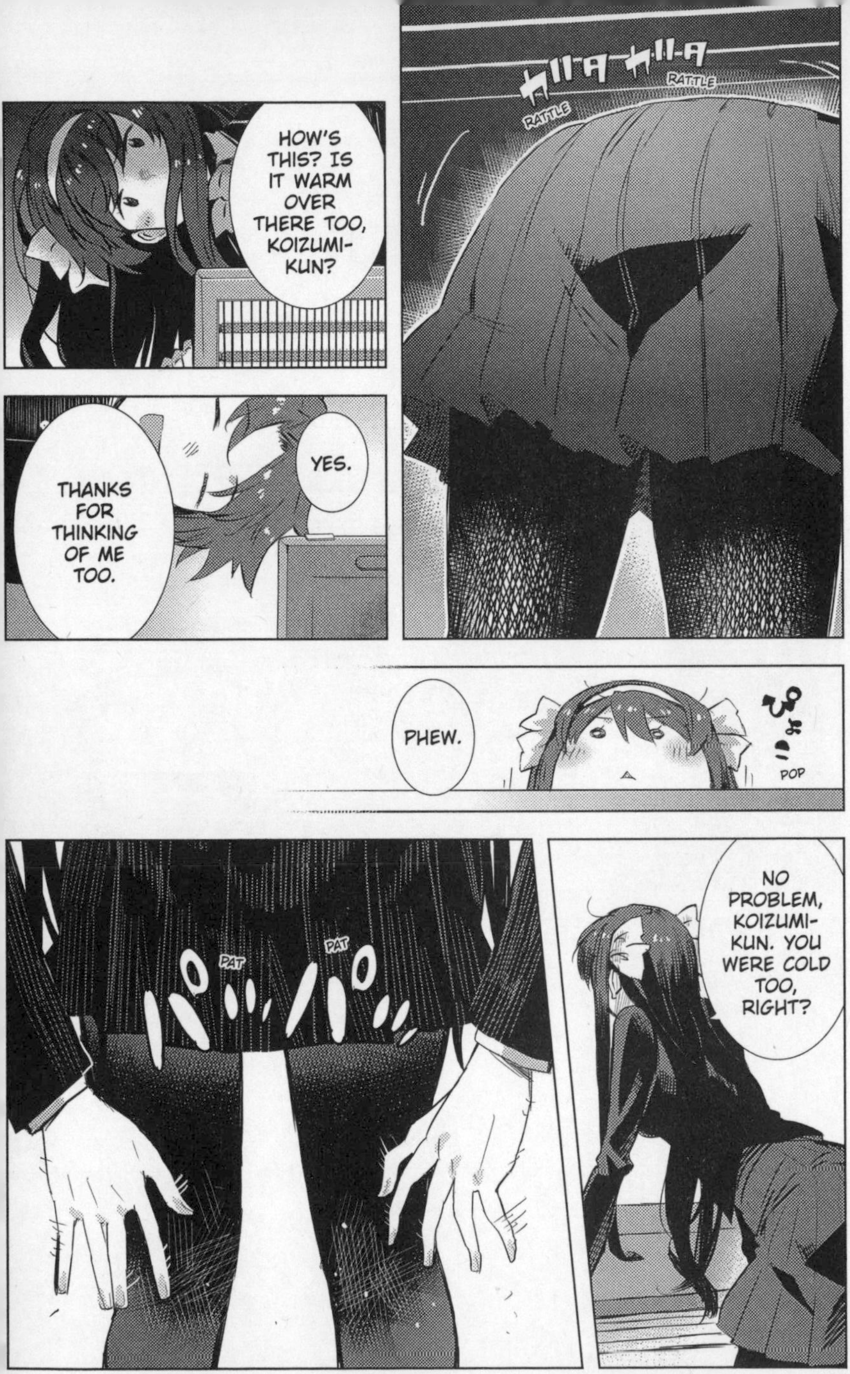
RATTLE
RATTLE
HOW'S THIS? IS IT WARM OVER THERE TOO, KOIZUMI-KUN?
YES.
THANKS FOR THINKING OF ME TOO.
POP
PHEW.
NO PROBLEM, KOIZUMI-KUN. YOU WERE COLD TOO, RIGHT?
PAT
PAT

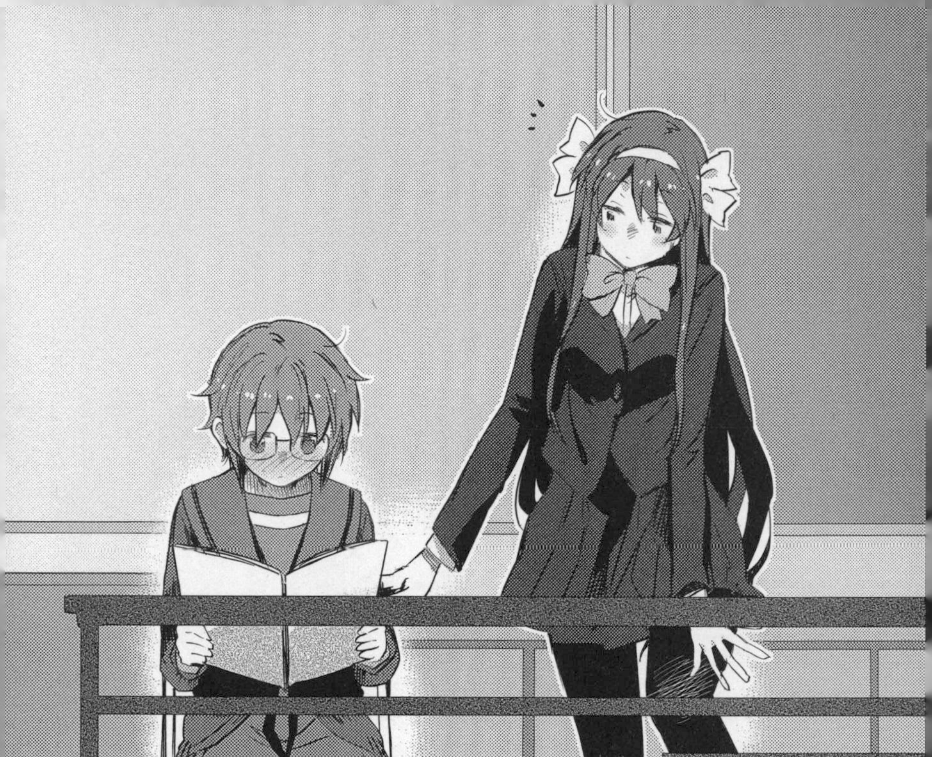

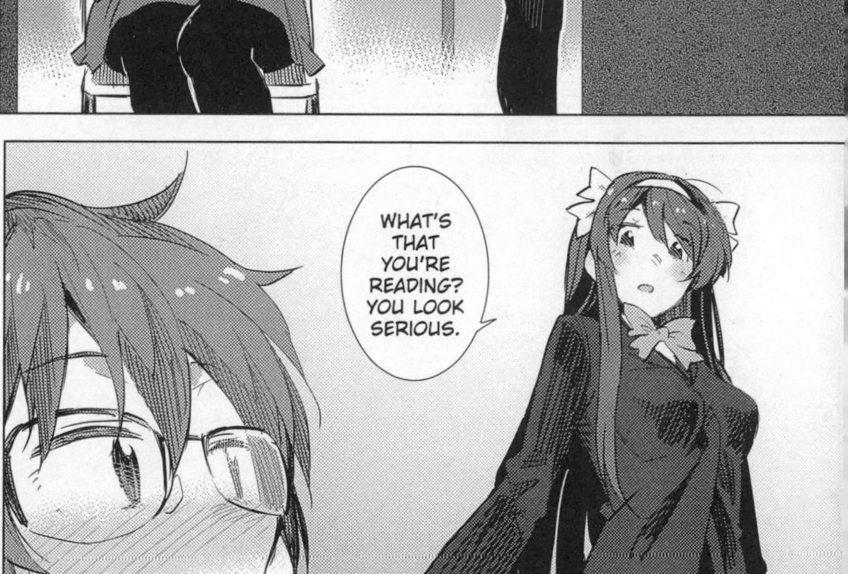
WHAT'S THAT YOU'RE READING? YOU LOOK SERIOUS.

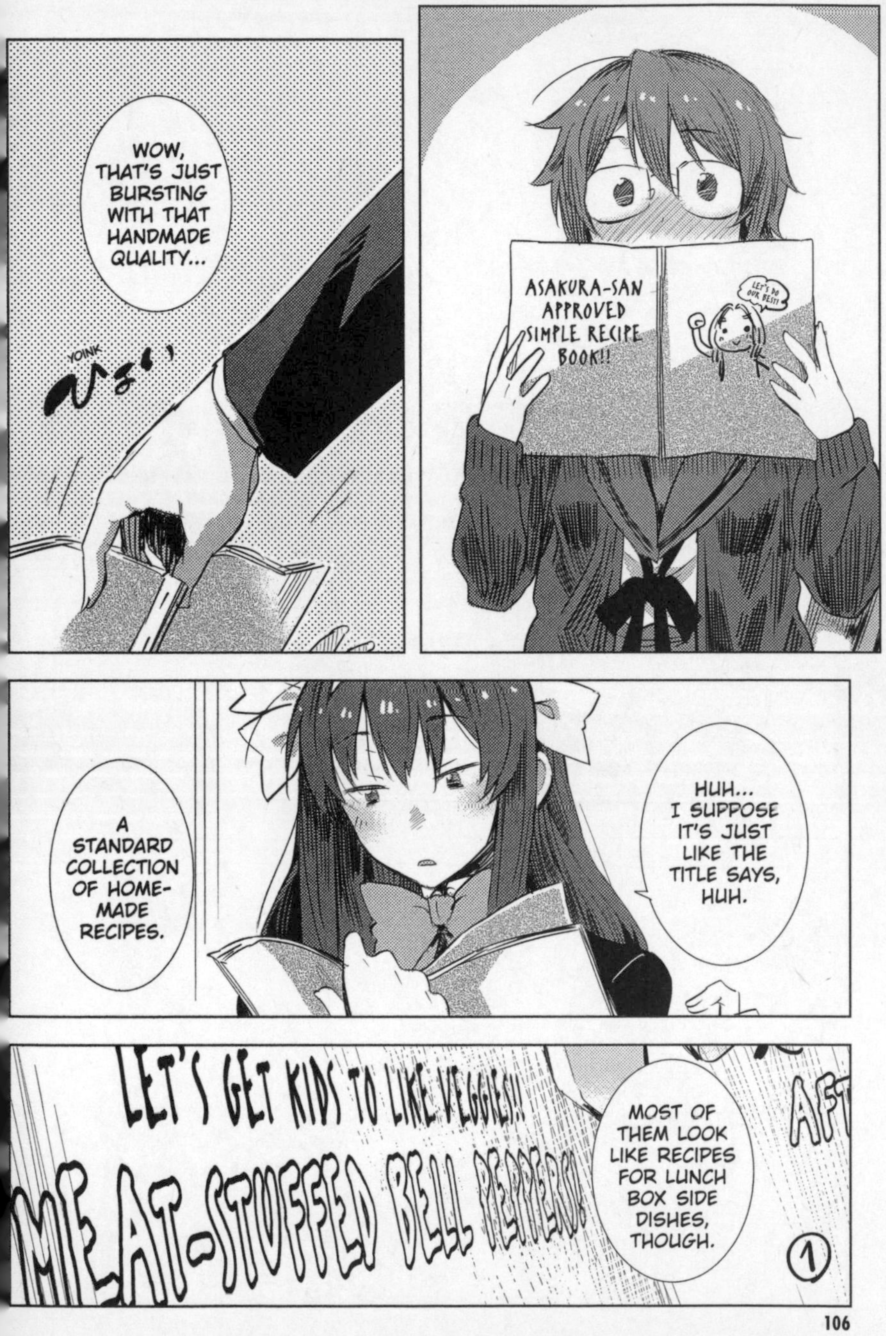
ASAKURA-SAN APPROVED SIMPLE RECIPE BOOK!!
LET'S DO OUR BEST!
WOW, THAT'S JUST BURSTING WITH THAT HANDMADE QUALITY...
YOINK
HUH... I SUPPOSE IT'S JUST LIKE THE TITLE SAYS, HUH.
A STANDARD COLLECTION OF HOME-MADE RECIPES.
MOST OF THEM LOOK LIKE RECIPES FOR LUNCH BOX SIDE DISHES, THOUGH.
LET'S GET KIDS TO LIKE VEGGIES!!
MEAT-STUFFED BELL PEPPERS!
1

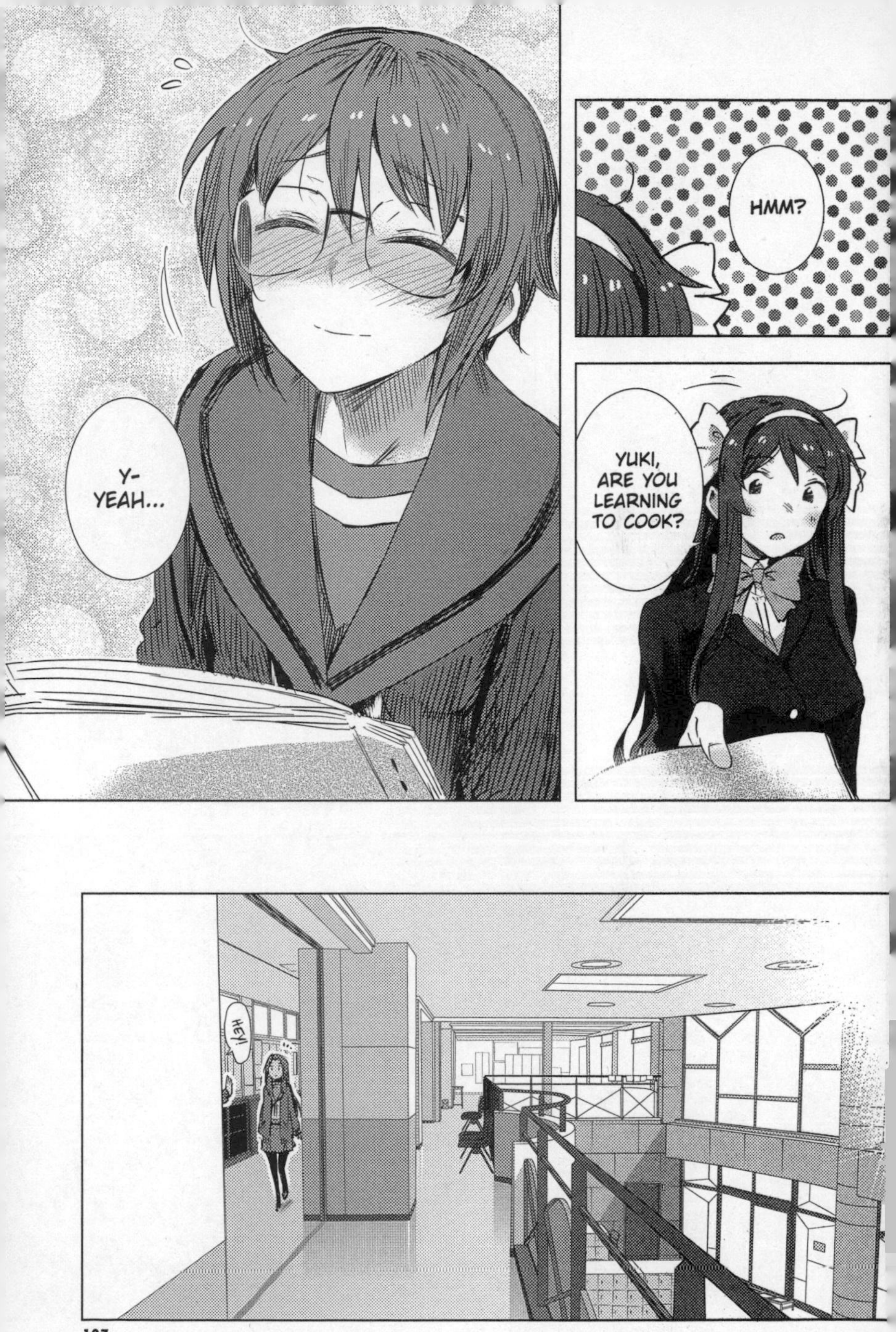
HMM?
YUKI, ARE YOU LEARNING TO COOK?
Y-YEAH...
HEY!

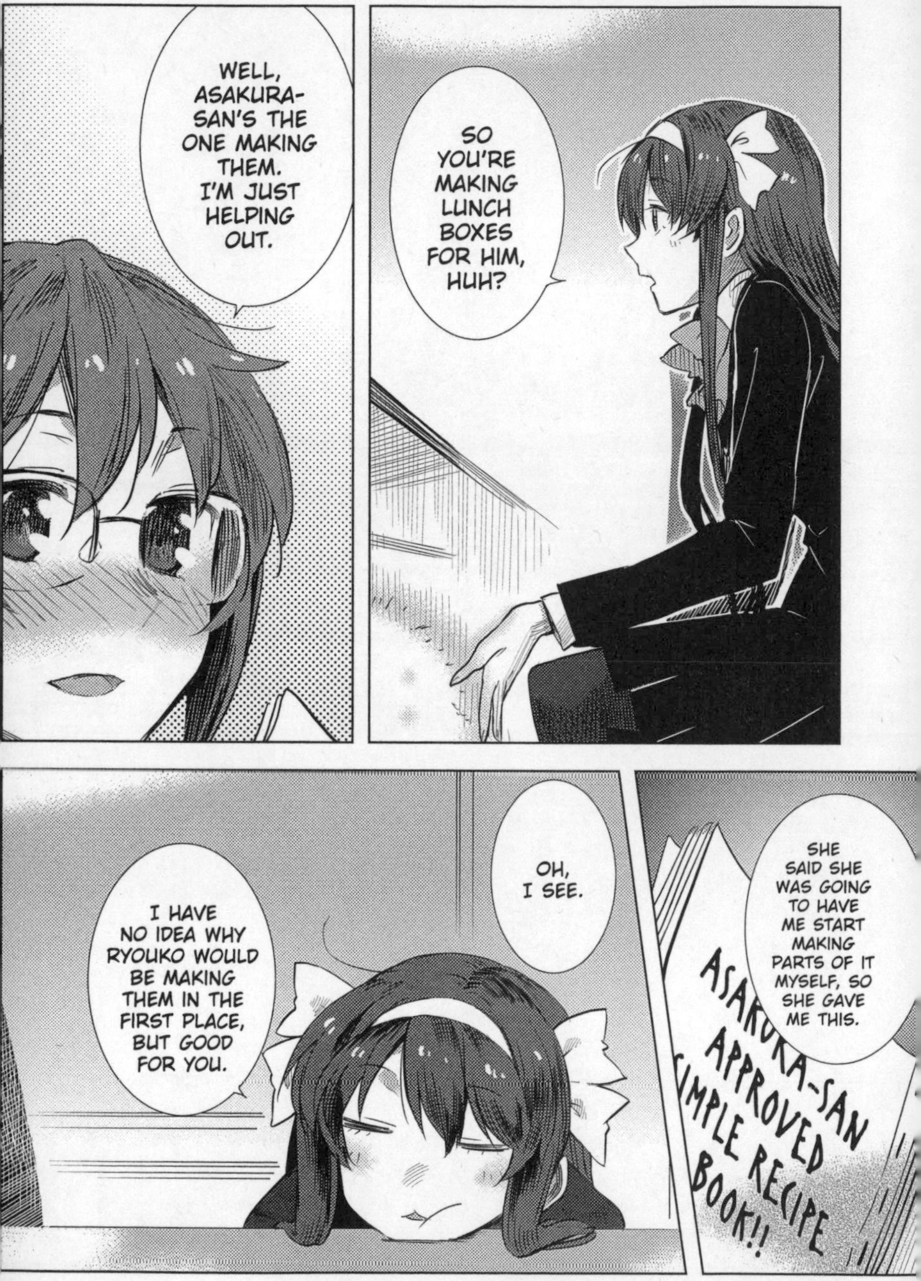
SO YOU'RE MAKING LUNCH BOXES FOR HIM, HUH?
WELL, ASAKURA-SAN'S THE ONE MAKING THEM. I'M JUST HELPING OUT.
SHE SAID SHE WAS GOING TO HAVE ME START MAKING PARTS OF IT MYSELF, SO SHE GAVE ME THIS.
ASAKURA-SAN APPROVED SIMPLE RECIPE BOOK!!
OH, I SEE.
I HAVE NO IDEA WHY RYOUKO WOULD BE MAKING THEM IN THE FIRST PLACE, BUT GOOD FOR YOU.

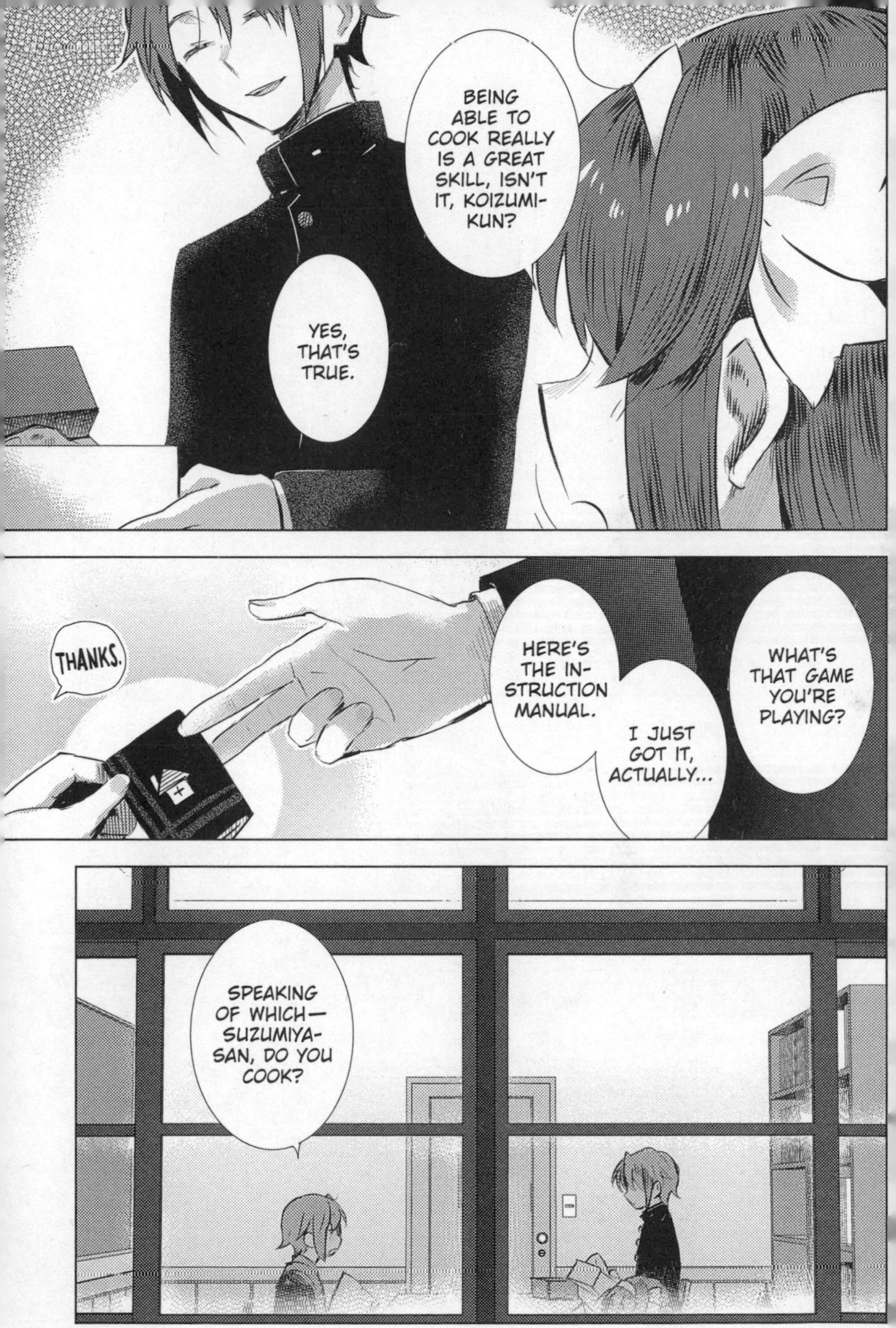
BEING ABLE TO COOK REALLY IS A GREAT SKILL, ISN'T IT, KOIZUMI-KUN?
YES, THAT'S TRUE.
WHAT'S THAT GAME YOU'RE PLAYING?
I JUST GOT IT, ACTUALLY...
HERE'S THE IN-STRUCTION MANUAL.
THANKS.
SPEAKING OF WHICH— SUZUMIYA-SAN, DO YOU COOK?

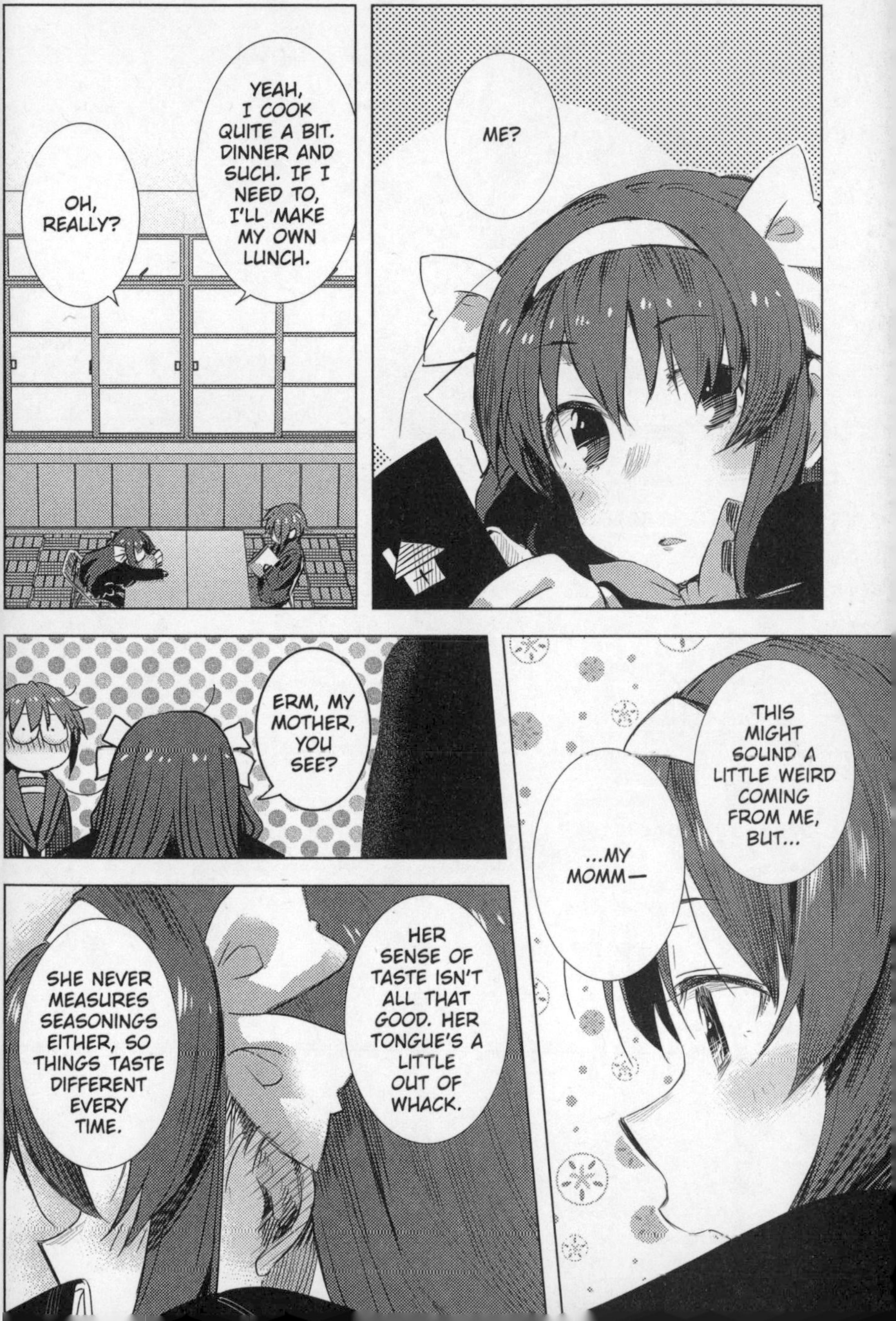
ME?
YEAH, I COOK QUITE A BIT. DINNER AND SUCH. IF I NEED TO, I'LL MAKE MY OWN LUNCH.
OH, REALLY?
THIS MIGHT SOUND A LITTLE WEIRD COMING FROM ME, BUT...
...MY MOMM—
ERM, MY MOTHER, YOU SEE?
HER SENSE OF TASTE ISN'T ALL THAT GOOD. HER TONGUE'S A LITTLE OUT OF WHACK.
SHE NEVER MEASURES SEASONINGS EITHER, SO THINGS TASTE DIFFERENT EVERY TIME.

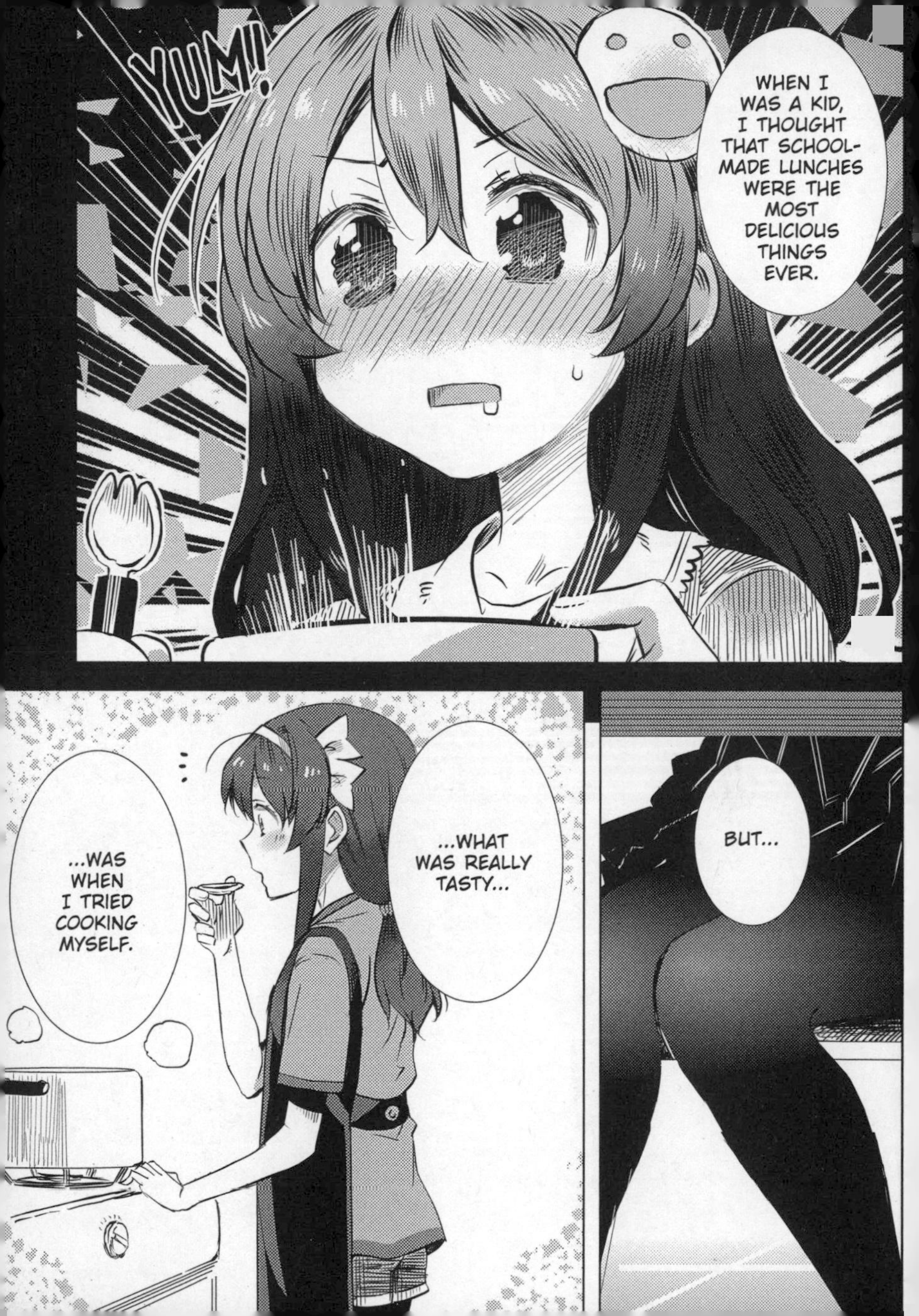
WHEN I WAS A KID, I THOUGHT THAT SCHOOL-MADE LUNCHES WERE THE MOST DELICIOUS THINGS EVER.
YUM!
BUT...
...WHAT WAS REALLY TASTY...
...WAS WHEN I TRIED COOKING MYSELF.

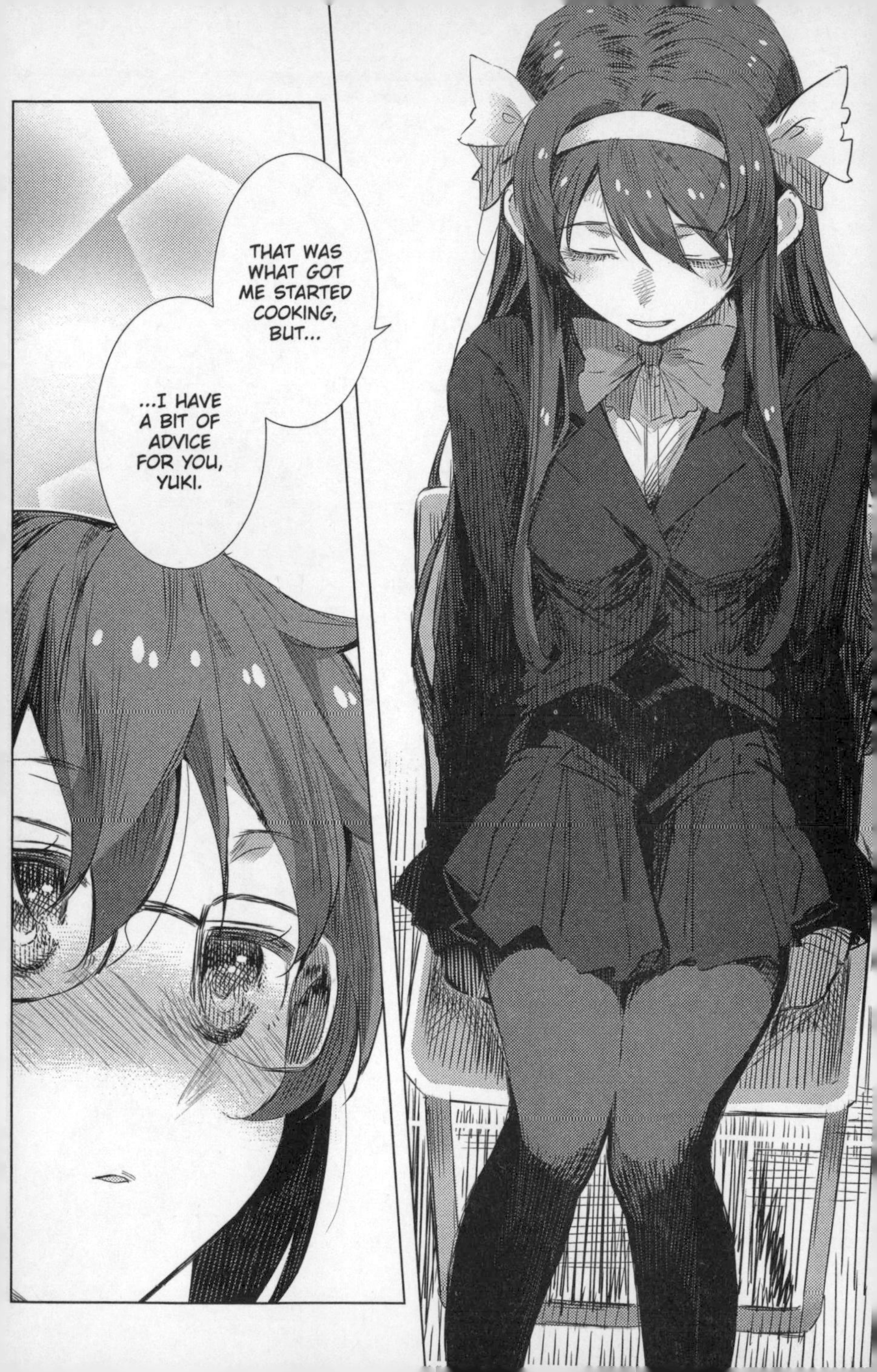
THAT WAS WHAT GOT ME STARTED COOKING, BUT...
...I HAVE A BIT OF ADVICE FOR YOU, YUKI.

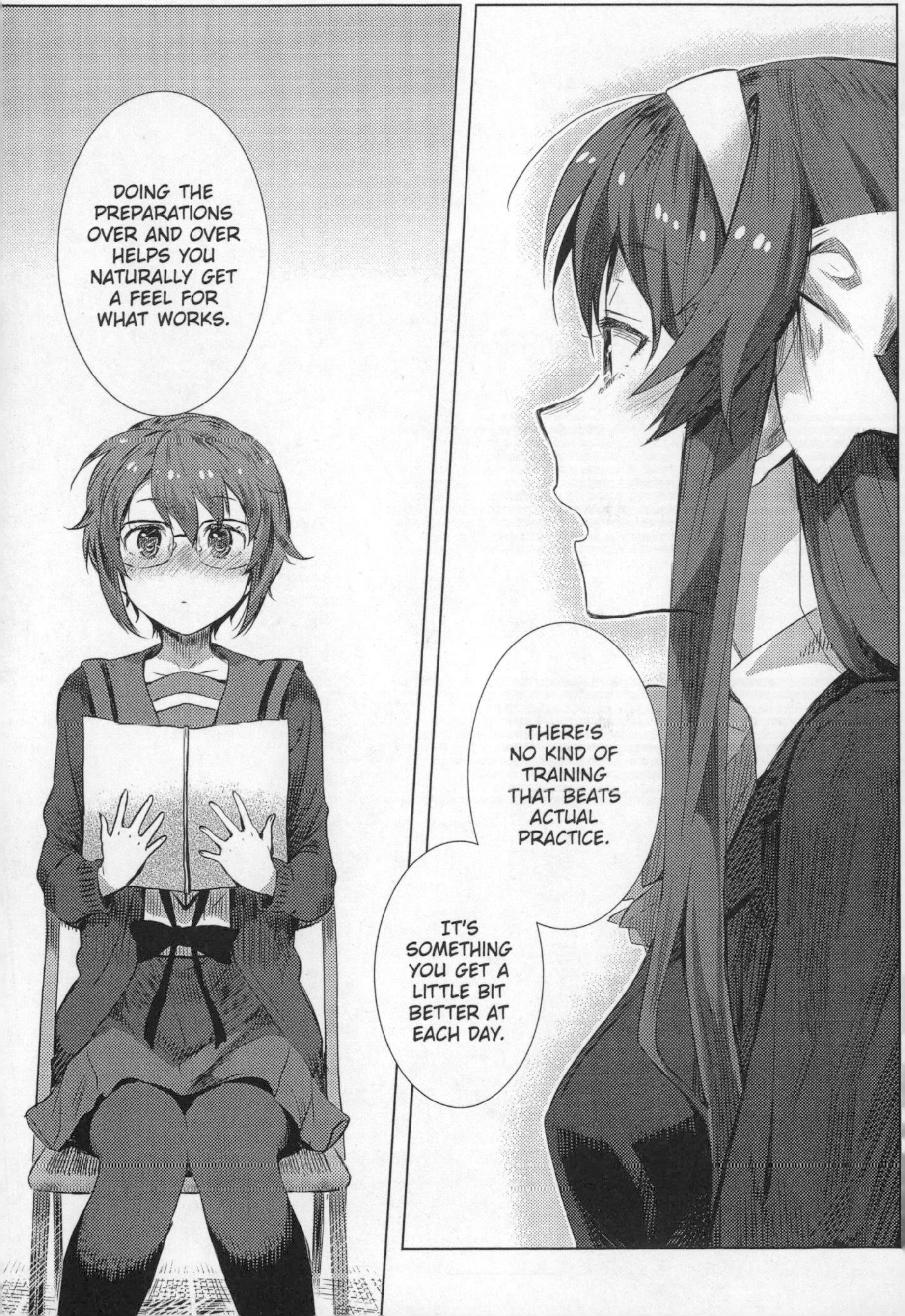
THERE'S NO KIND OF TRAINING THAT BEATS ACTUAL PRACTICE.
IT'S SOMETHING YOU GET A LITTLE BIT BETTER AT EACH DAY.
DOING THE PREPARATIONS OVER AND OVER HELPS YOU NATURALLY GET A FEEL FOR WHAT WORKS.

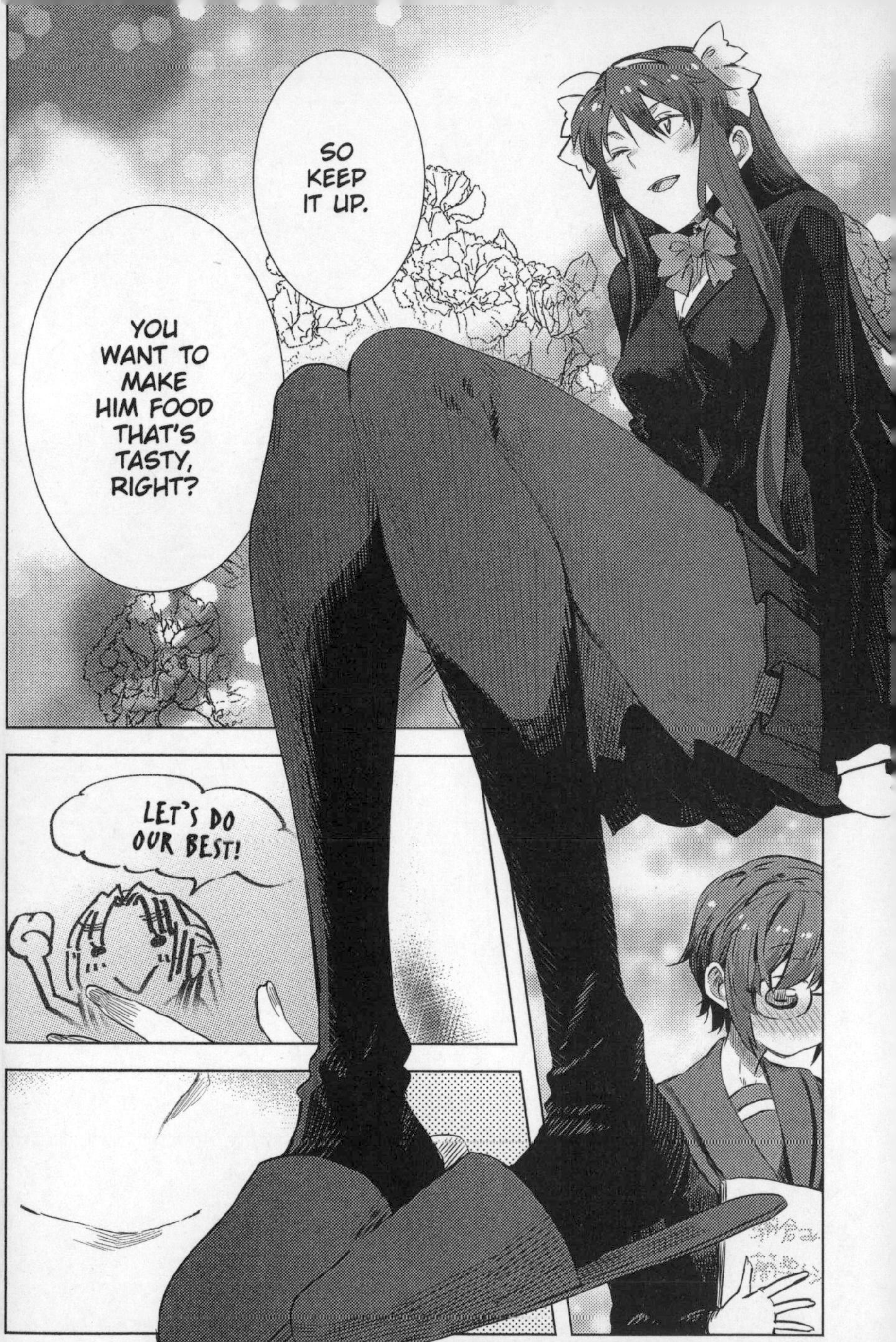
SO KEEP IT UP.
YOU WANT TO MAKE HIM FOOD THAT'S TASTY, RIGHT?
LET'S DO OUR BEST!

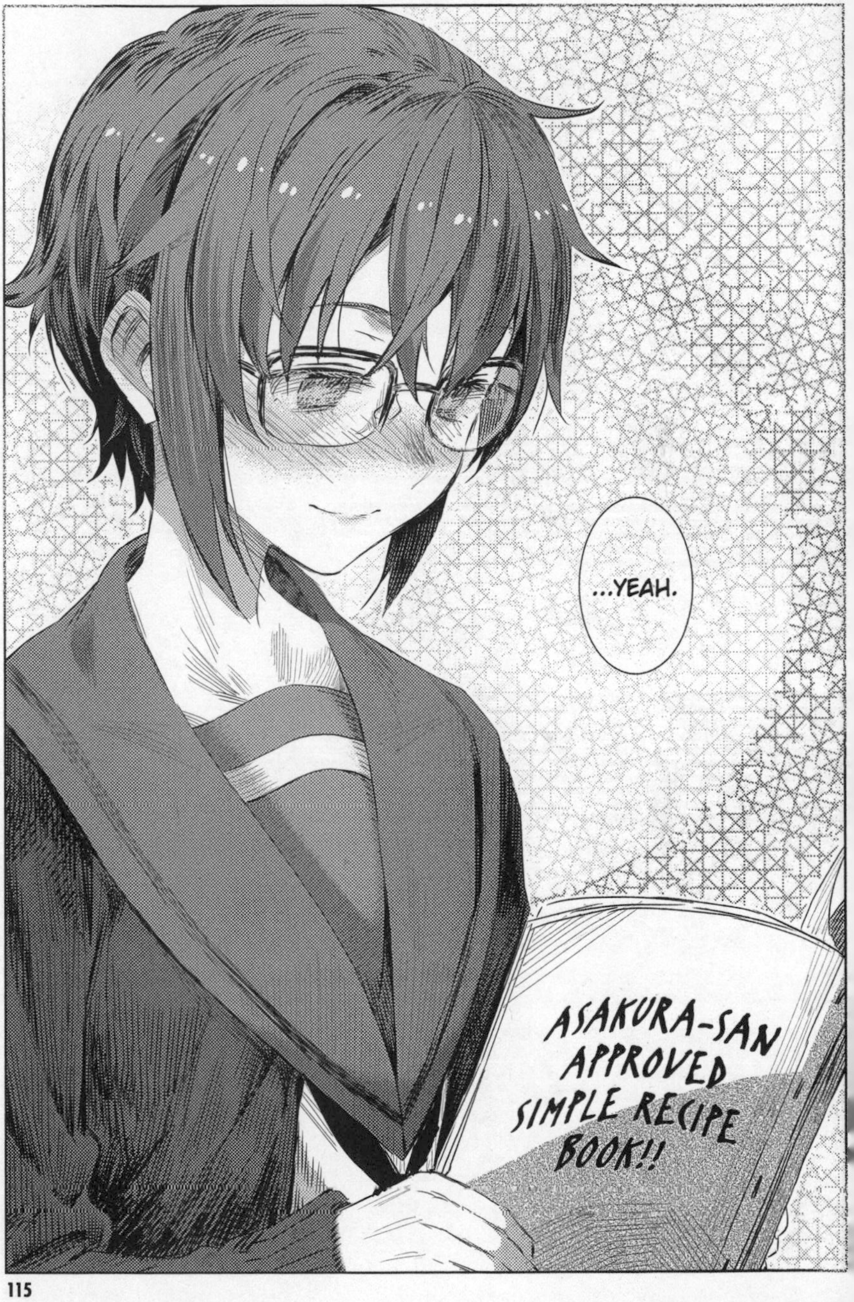
...YEAH.
ASAKURA-SAN APPROVED SIMPLE RECIPE BOOK!!

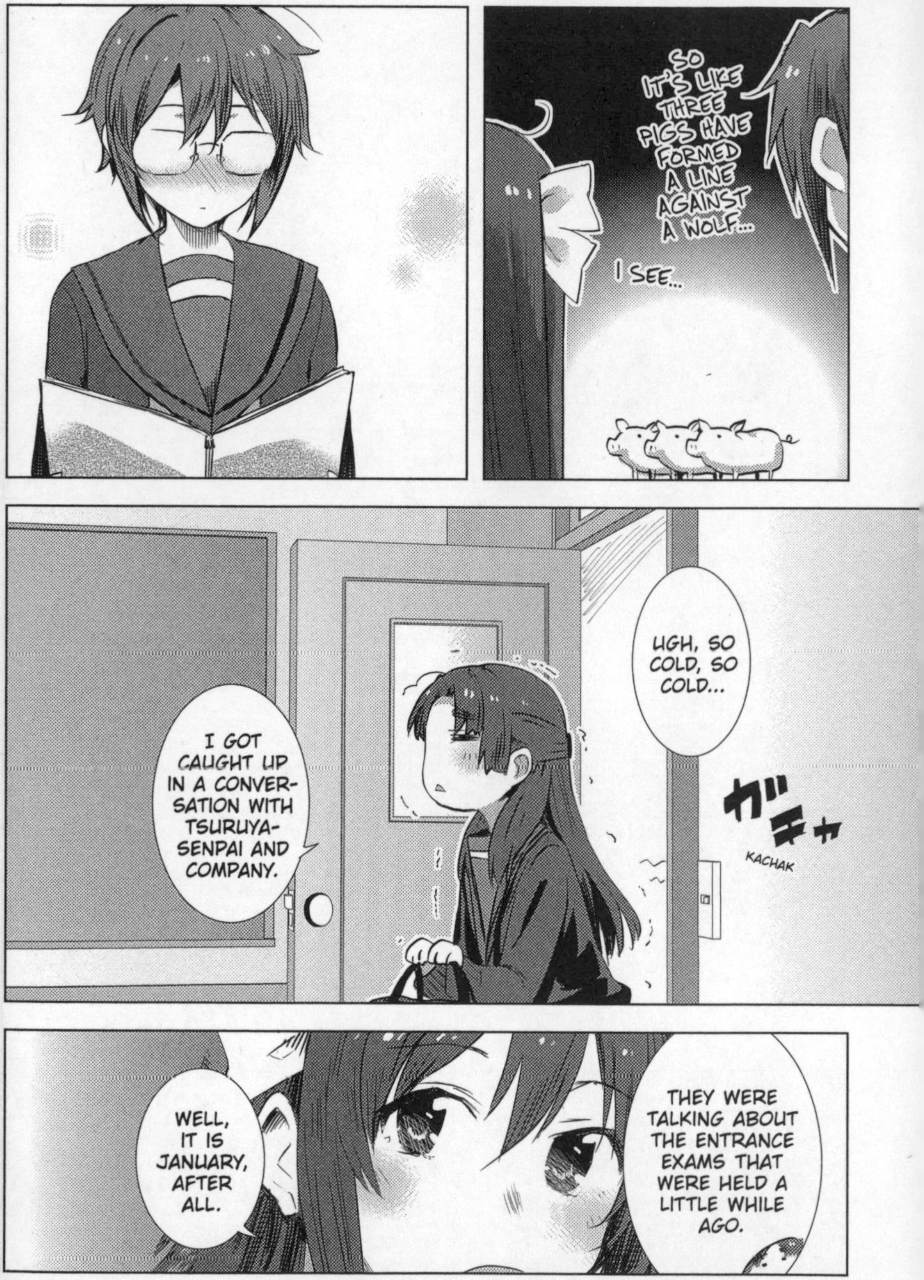
SO IT'S LIKE THREE PIGS HAVE FORMED A LINE AGAINST A WOLF...
I SEE...
UGH, SO COLD, SO COLD...
ガチャ
KACHAK
I GOT CAUGHT UP IN A CONVERSATION WITH TSURUYA-SENPAI AND COMPANY.
THEY WERE TALKING ABOUT THE ENTRANCE EXAMS THAT WERE HELD A LITTLE WHILE AGO.
WELL, IT IS JANUARY, AFTER ALL.

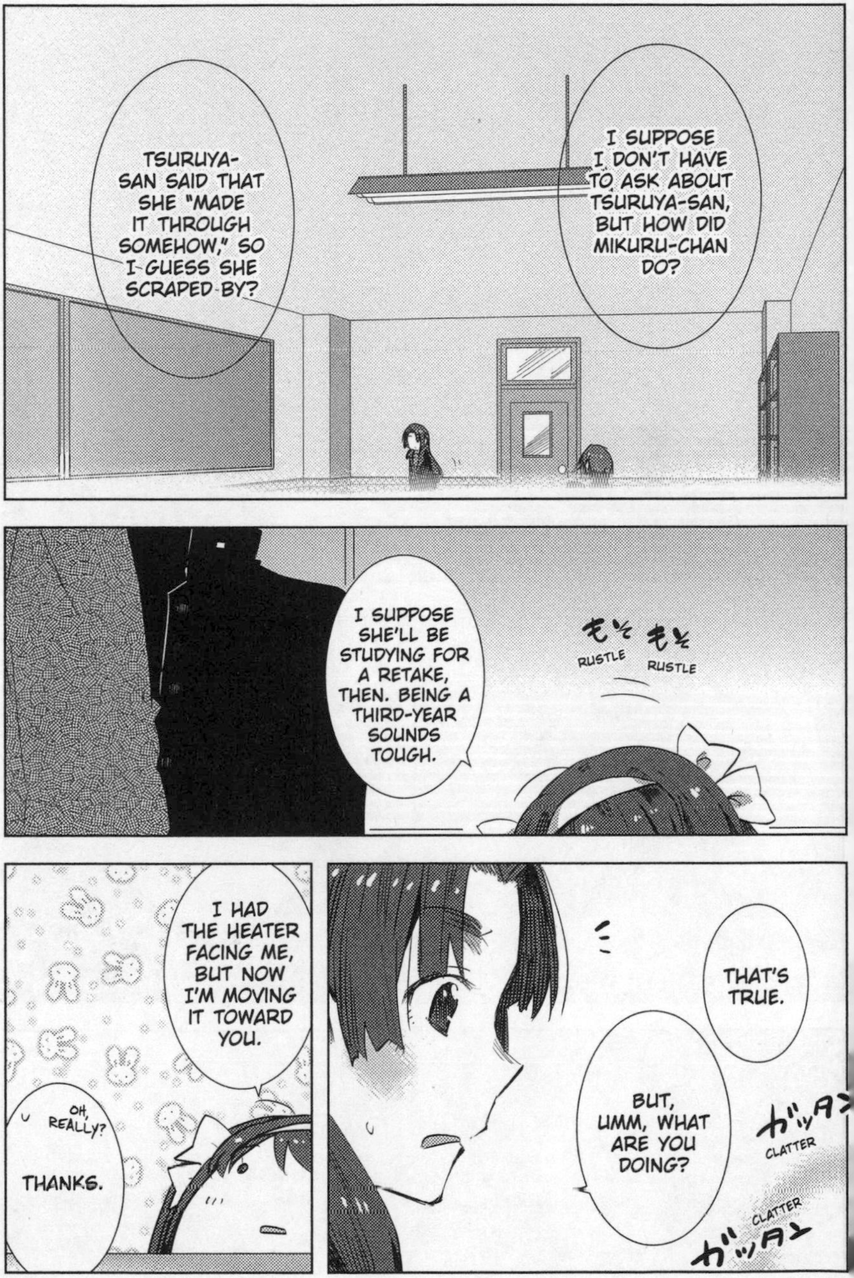
I SUPPOSE I DON'T HAVE TO ASK ABOUT TSURUYA-SAN, BUT HOW DID MIKURU-CHAN DO?
TSURUYA-SAN SAID THAT SHE "MADE IT THROUGH SOMEHOW," SO I GUESS SHE SCRAPED BY?
RUSTLE
RUSTLE
I SUPPOSE SHE'LL BE STUDYING FOR A RETAKE, THEN. BEING A THIRD-YEAR SOUNDS TOUGH.
THAT'S TRUE.
BUT, UMM, WHAT ARE YOU DOING?
CLATTER
CLATTER
I HAD THE HEATER FACING ME, BUT NOW I'M MOVING IT TOWARD YOU.
OH, REALLY?
THANKS.

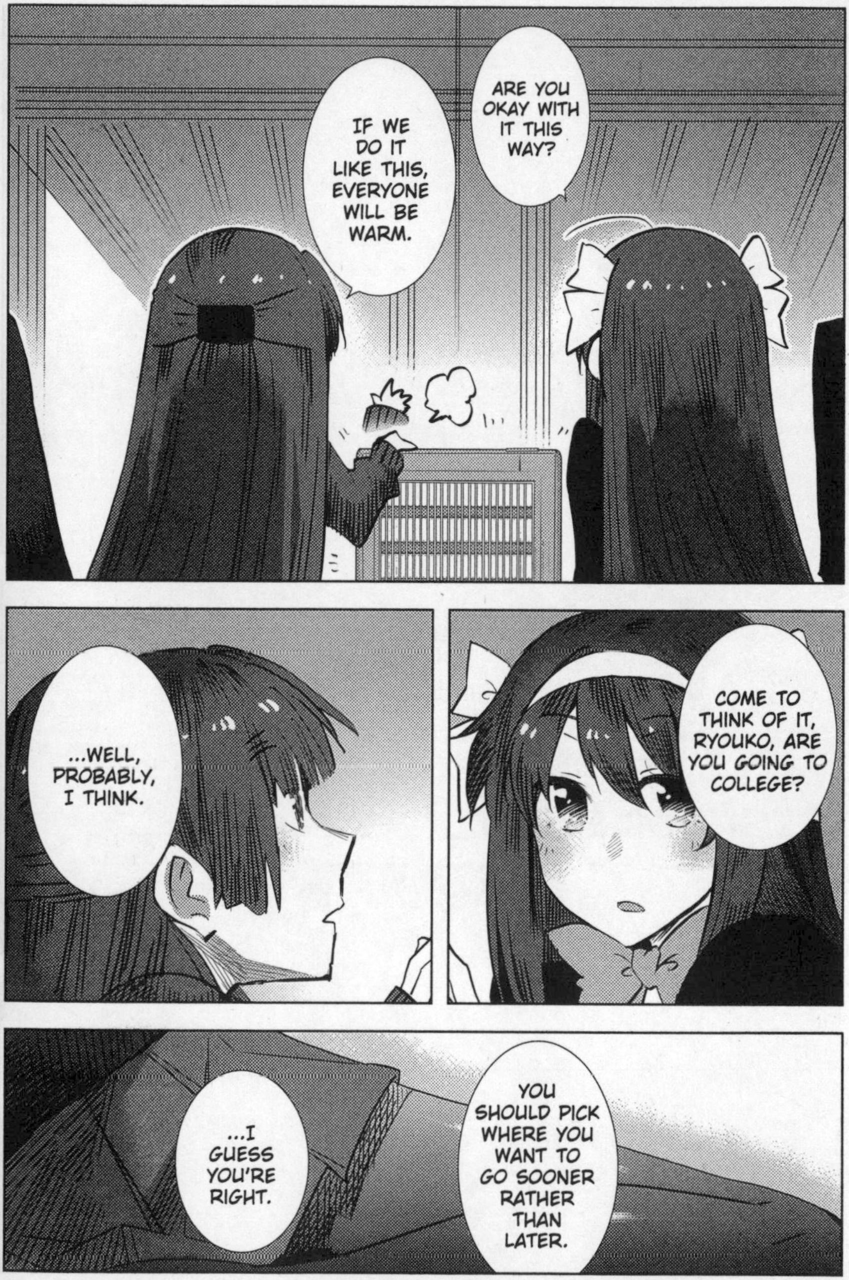
ARE YOU OKAY WITH IT THIS WAY?
IF WE DO IT LIKE THIS, EVERYONE WILL BE WARM.
COME TO THINK OF IT, RYOUKO, ARE YOU GOING TO COLLEGE?
...WELL, PROBABLY, I THINK.
YOU SHOULD PICK WHERE YOU WANT TO GO SOONER RATHER THAN LATER.
...I GUESS YOU'RE RIGHT.

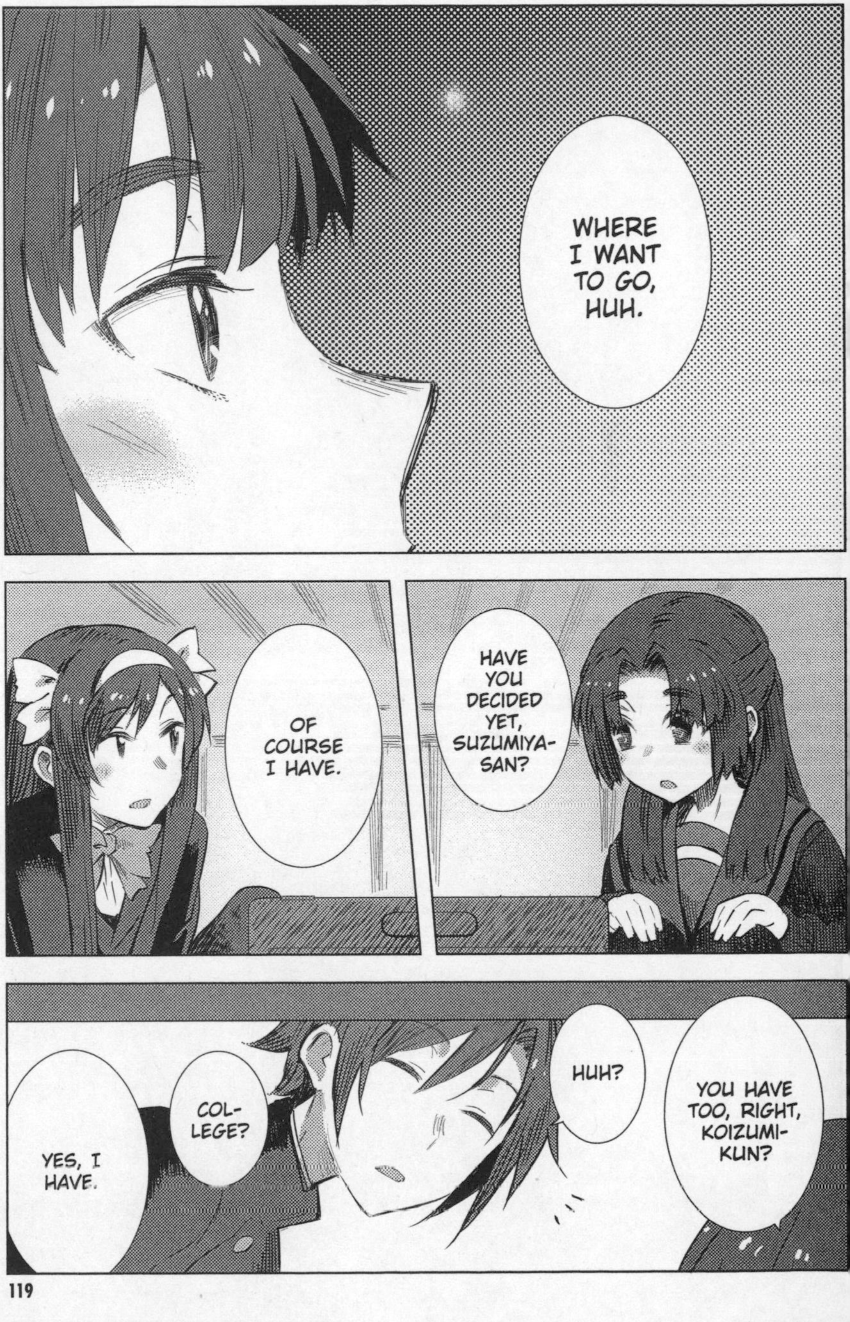
WHERE I WANT TO GO, HUH.
HAVE YOU DECIDED YET, SUZUMIYA-SAN?
OF COURSE I HAVE.
YOU HAVE TOO, RIGHT, KOIZUMI-KUN?
HUH?
COL-LEGE?
YES, I HAVE.

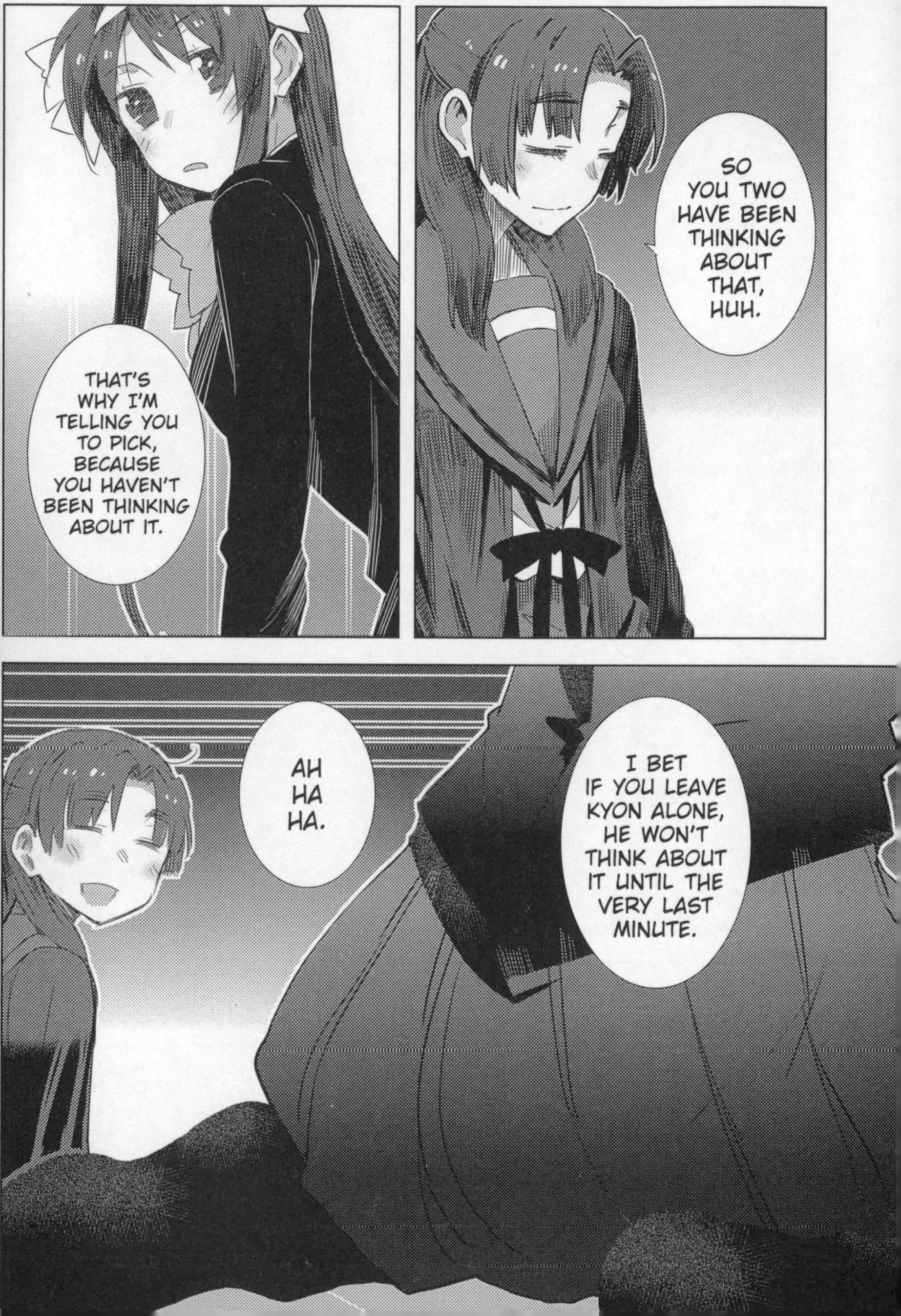
SO YOU TWO HAVE BEEN THINKING ABOUT THAT, HUH.
THAT'S WHY I'M TELLING YOU TO PICK, BECAUSE YOU HAVEN'T BEEN THINKING ABOUT IT.
I BET IF YOU LEAVE KYON ALONE, HE WON'T THINK ABOUT IT UNTIL THE VERY LAST MINUTE.
AH HA HA.

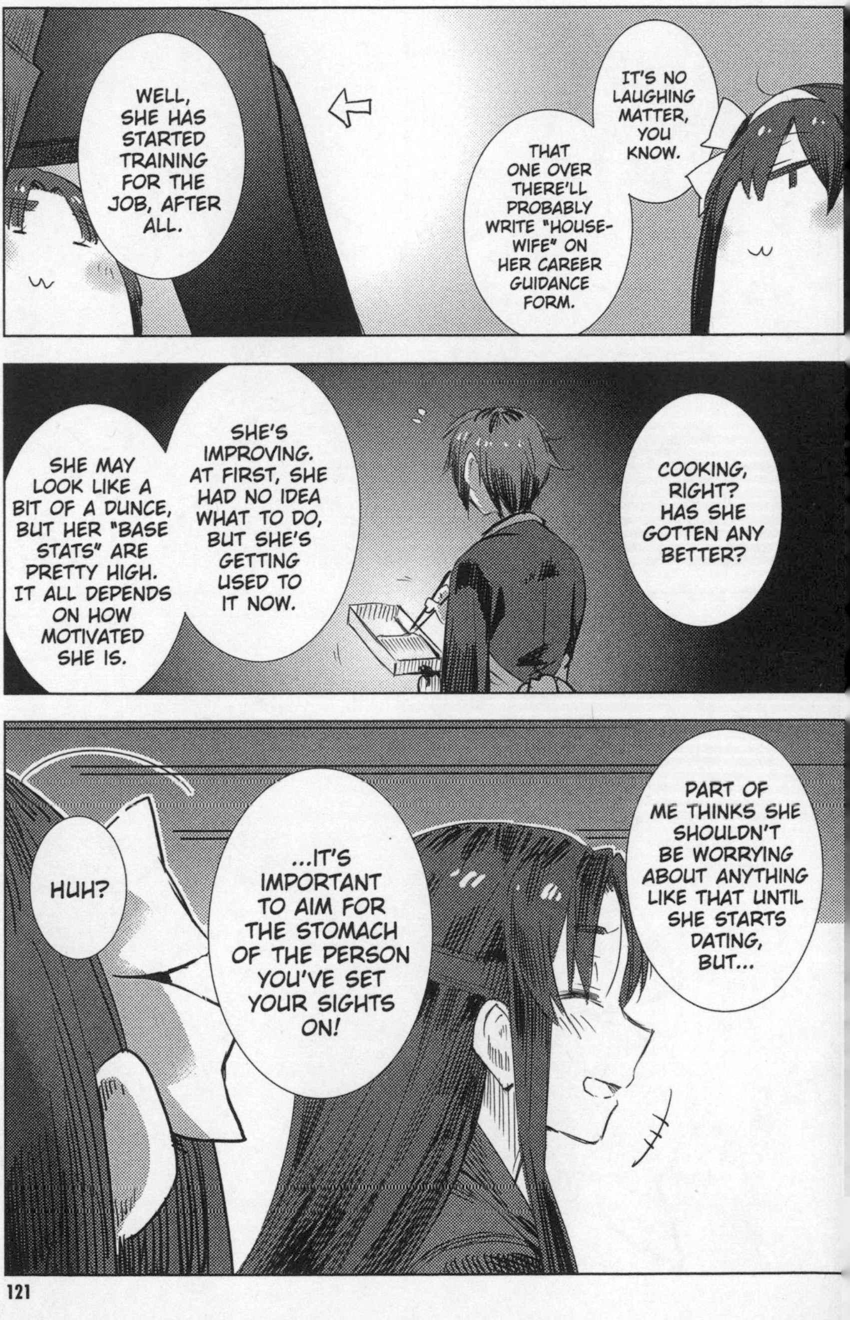
IT'S NO LAUGHING MATTER, YOU KNOW.
THAT ONE OVER THERE'LL PROBABLY WRITE "HOUSE-WIFE" ON HER CAREER GUIDANCE FORM.
WELL, SHE HAS STARTED TRAINING FOR THE JOB, AFTER ALL.
COOKING, RIGHT? HAS SHE GOTTEN ANY BETTER?
SHE'S IMPROVING. AT FIRST, SHE HAD NO IDEA WHAT TO DO, BUT SHE'S GETTING USED TO IT NOW.
SHE MAY LOOK LIKE A BIT OF A DUNCE, BUT HER "BASE STATS" ARE PRETTY HIGH. IT ALL DEPENDS ON HOW MOTIVATED SHE IS.
PART OF ME THINKS SHE SHOULDN'T BE WORRYING ABOUT ANYTHING LIKE THAT UNTIL SHE STARTS DATING, BUT...
...IT'S IMPORTANT TO AIM FOR THE STOMACH OF THE PERSON YOU'VE SET YOUR SIGHTS ON!
HUH?

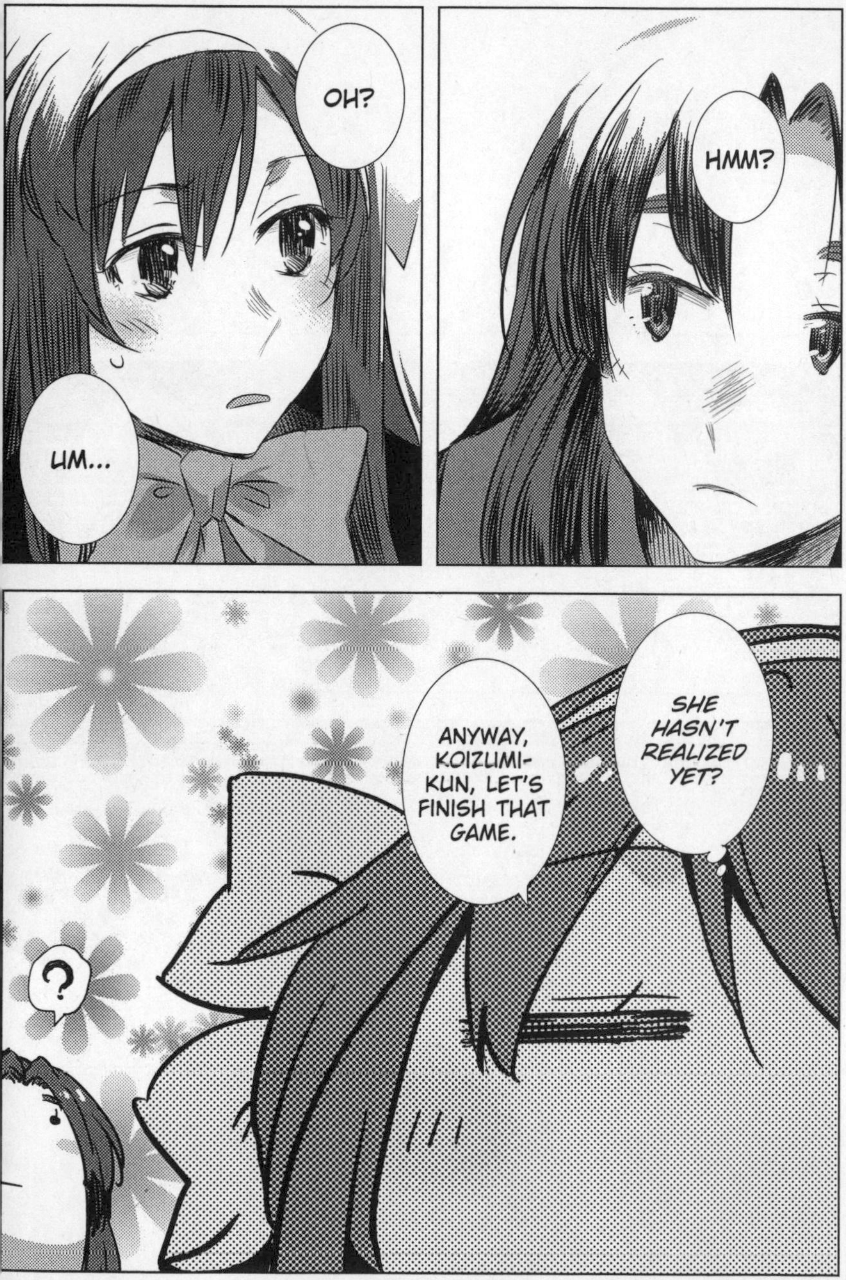
HMM?
OH?
UM...
SHE HASN'T REALIZED YET?
ANYWAY, KOIZUMI-KUN, LET'S FINISH THAT GAME.
?

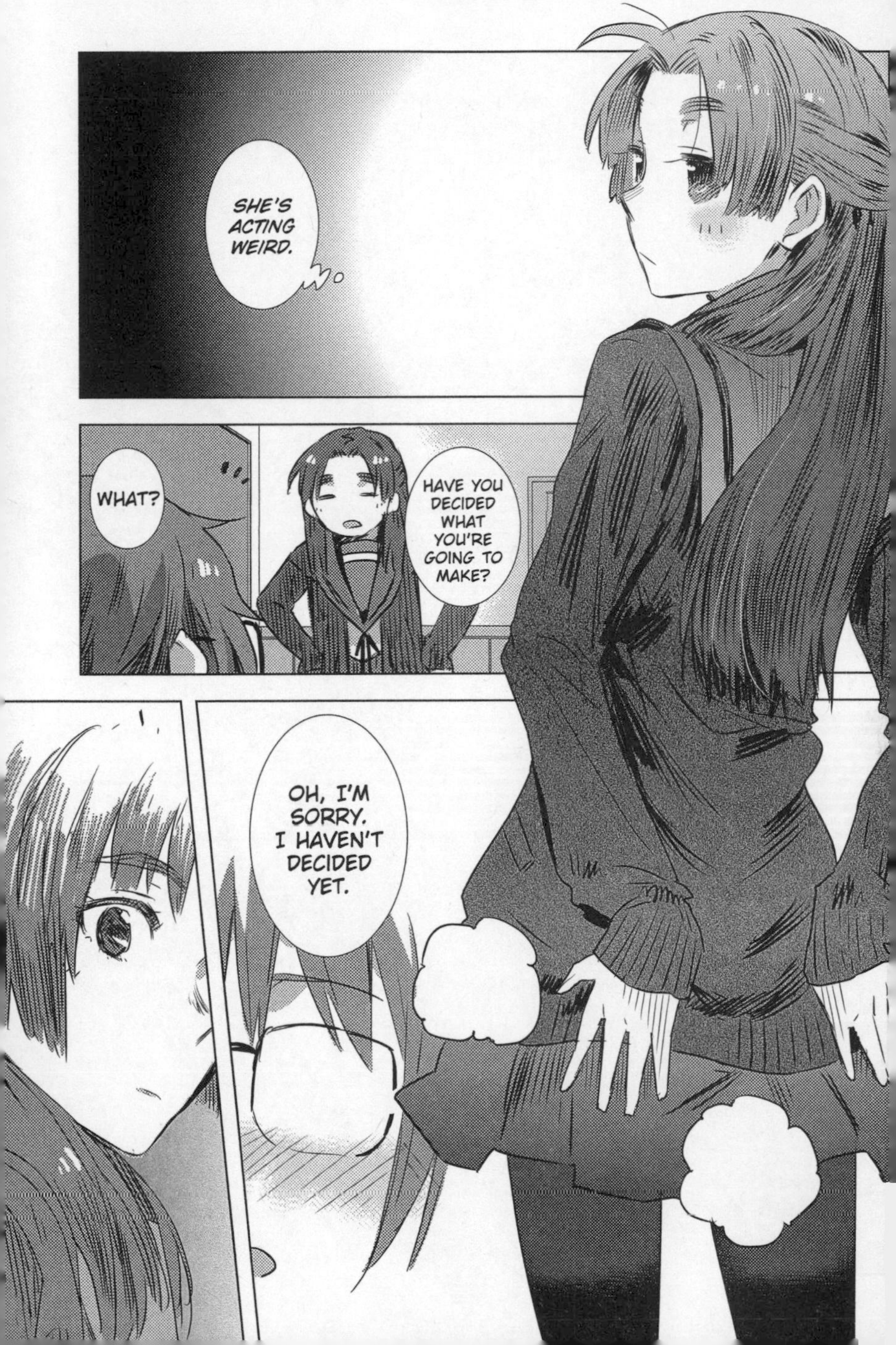
SHE'S ACTING WEIRD.
HAVE YOU DECIDED WHAT YOU'RE GOING TO MAKE?
WHAT?
OH, I'M SORRY. I HAVEN'T DECIDED YET.

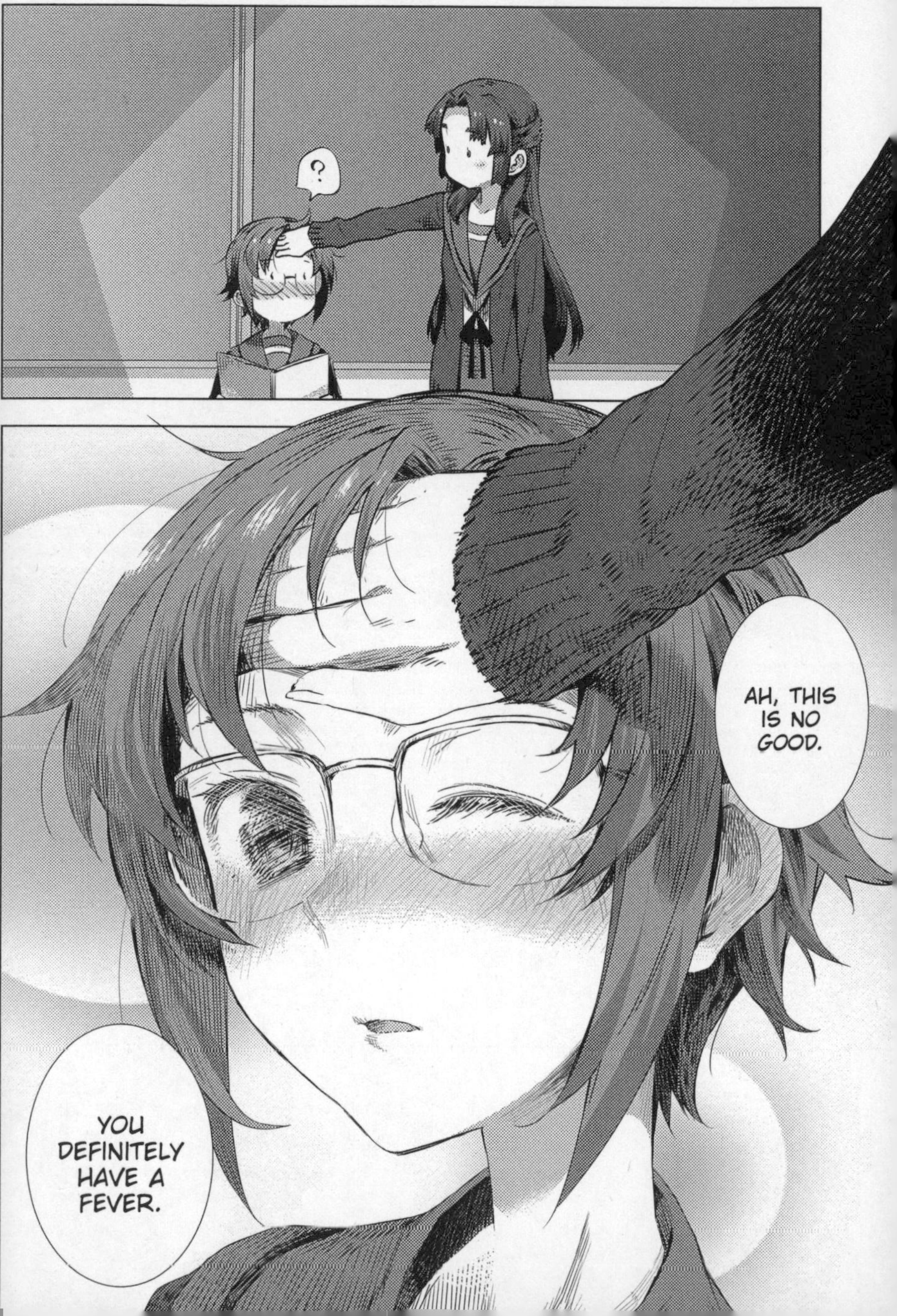
?
AH, THIS IS NO GOOD.
YOU DEFINITELY HAVE A FEVER.

GOING STRAIGHT HOME.

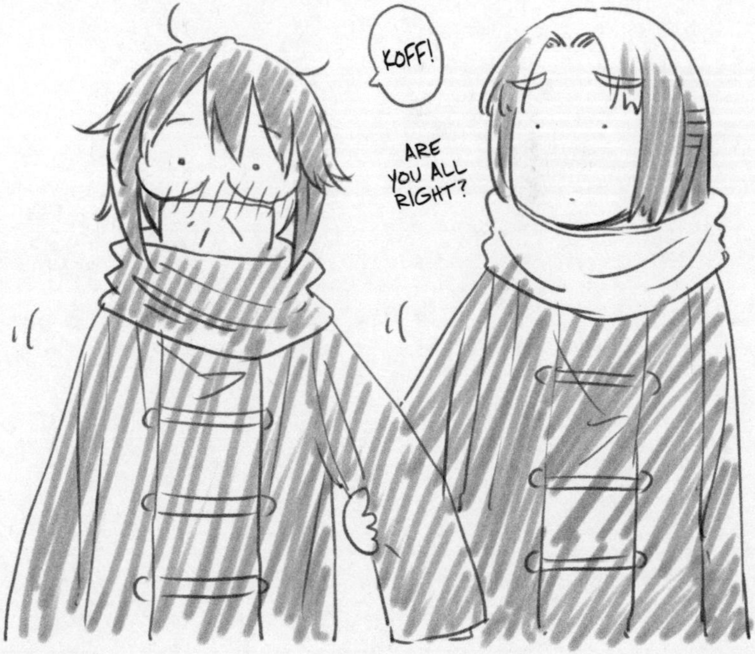
KOFF!
ARE YOU ALL RIGHT?

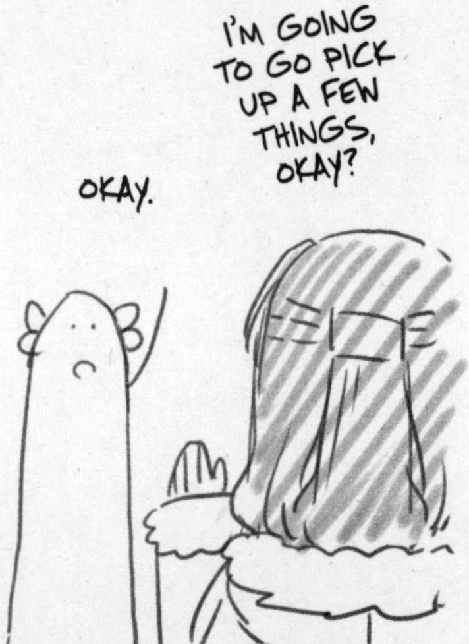
I'M GOING TO GO PICK UP A FEW THINGS, OKAY?
OKAY.

Epilogue 63>> Cold

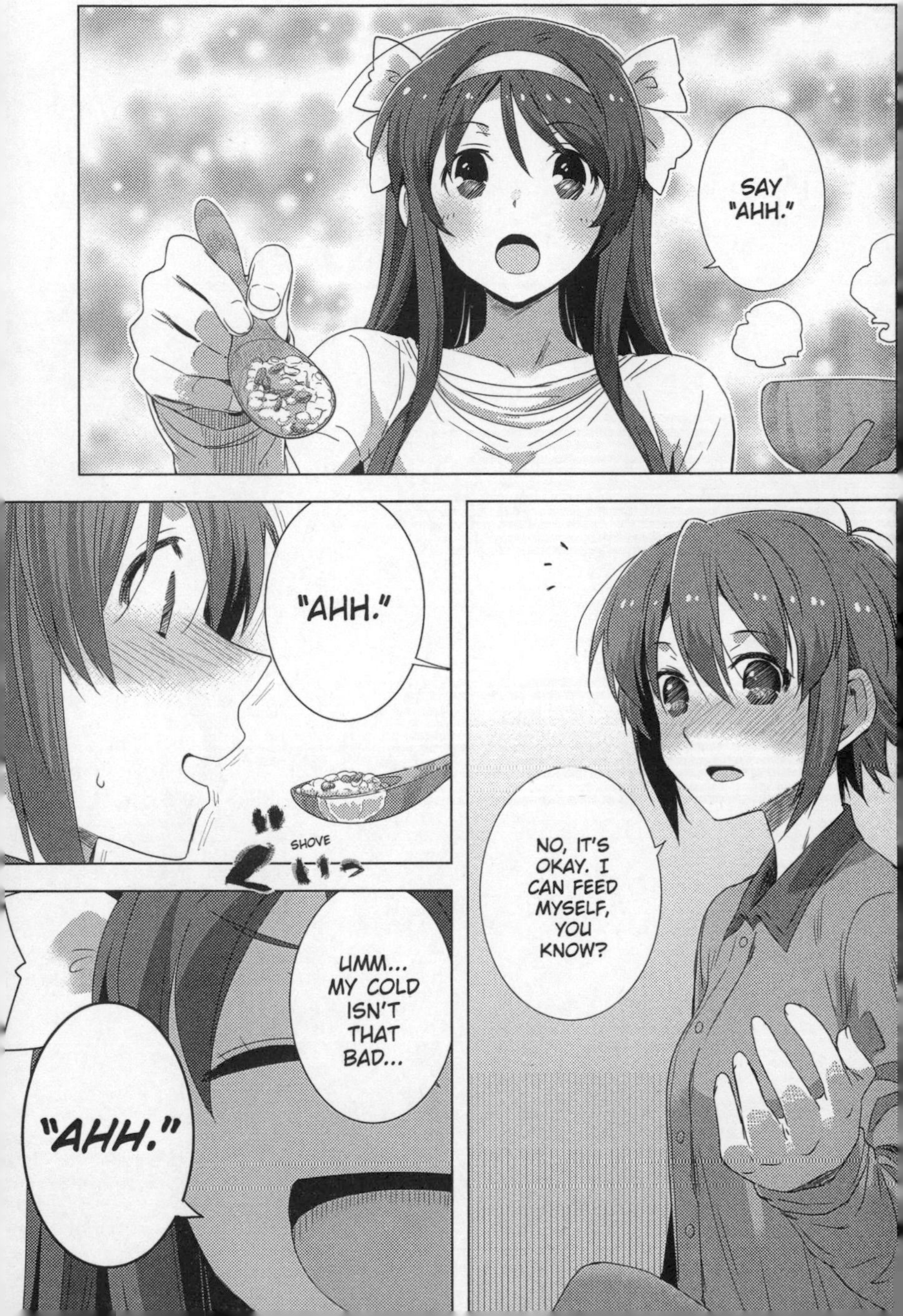

SAY "AHH."
NO, IT'S OKAY. I CAN FEED MYSELF, YOU KNOW?
"AHH."
SHOVE
UMM... MY COLD ISN'T THAT BAD...
"AHH."

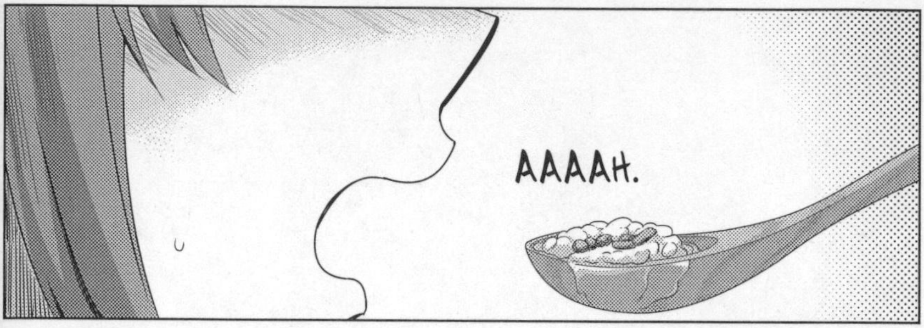
AAAAH.

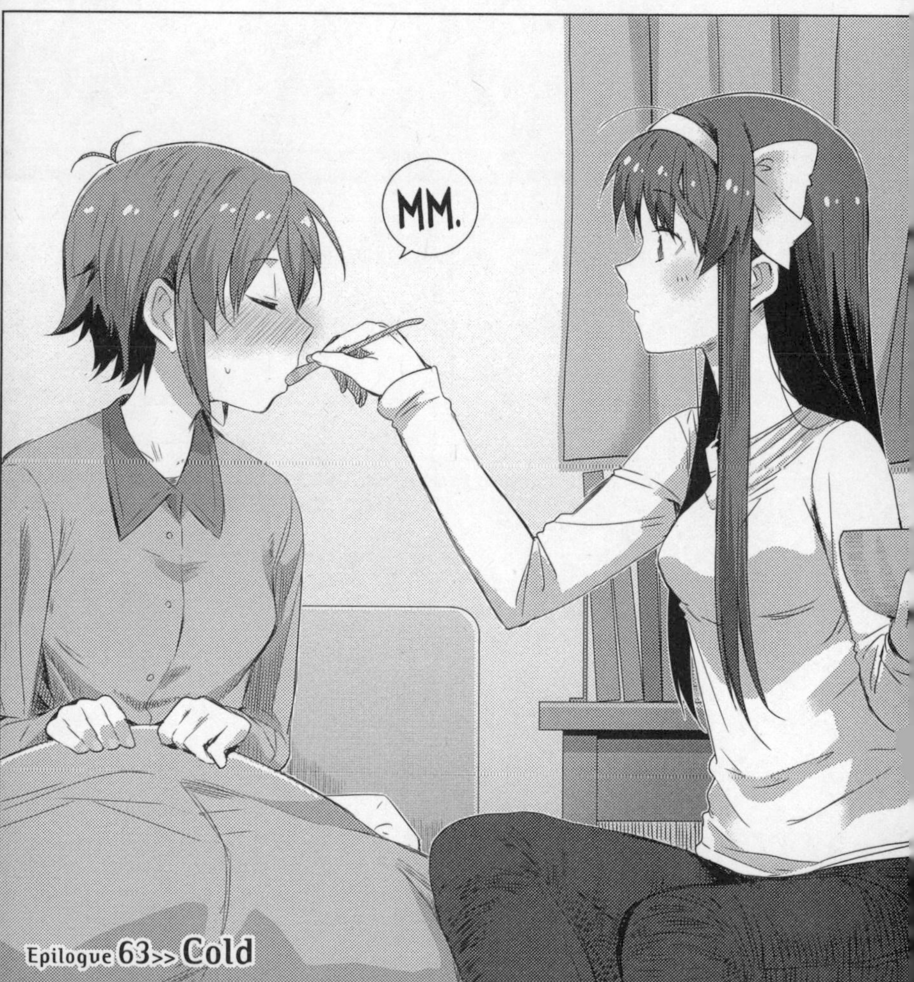
MM.
Epilogue 63>> Cold

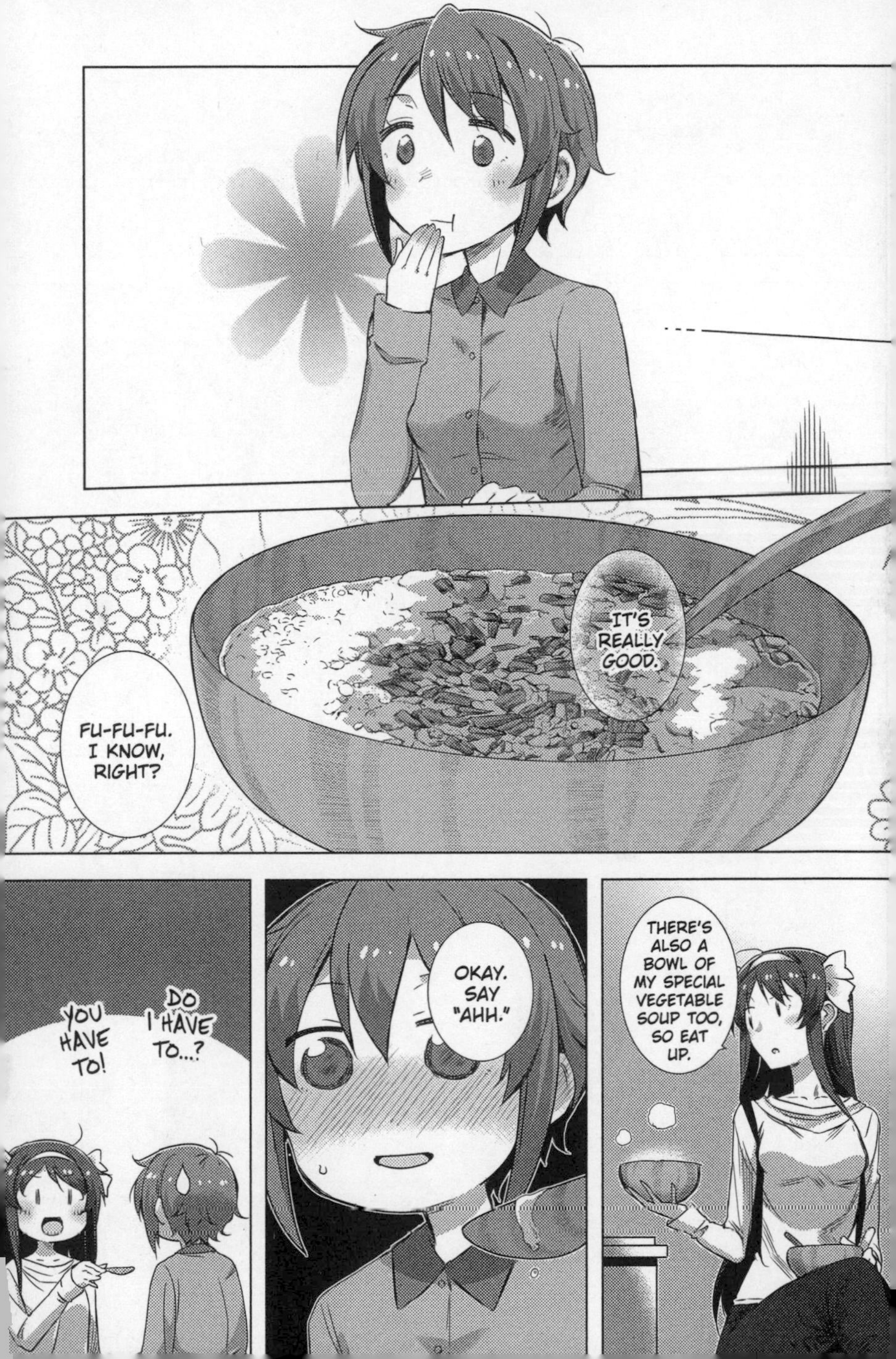
IT'S REALLY GOOD.
FU-FU-FU. I KNOW, RIGHT?
THERE'S ALSO A BOWL OF MY SPECIAL VEGETABLE SOUP TOO, SO EAT UP.
OKAY. SAY "AHH."
DO I HAVE TO...?
YOU HAVE TO!

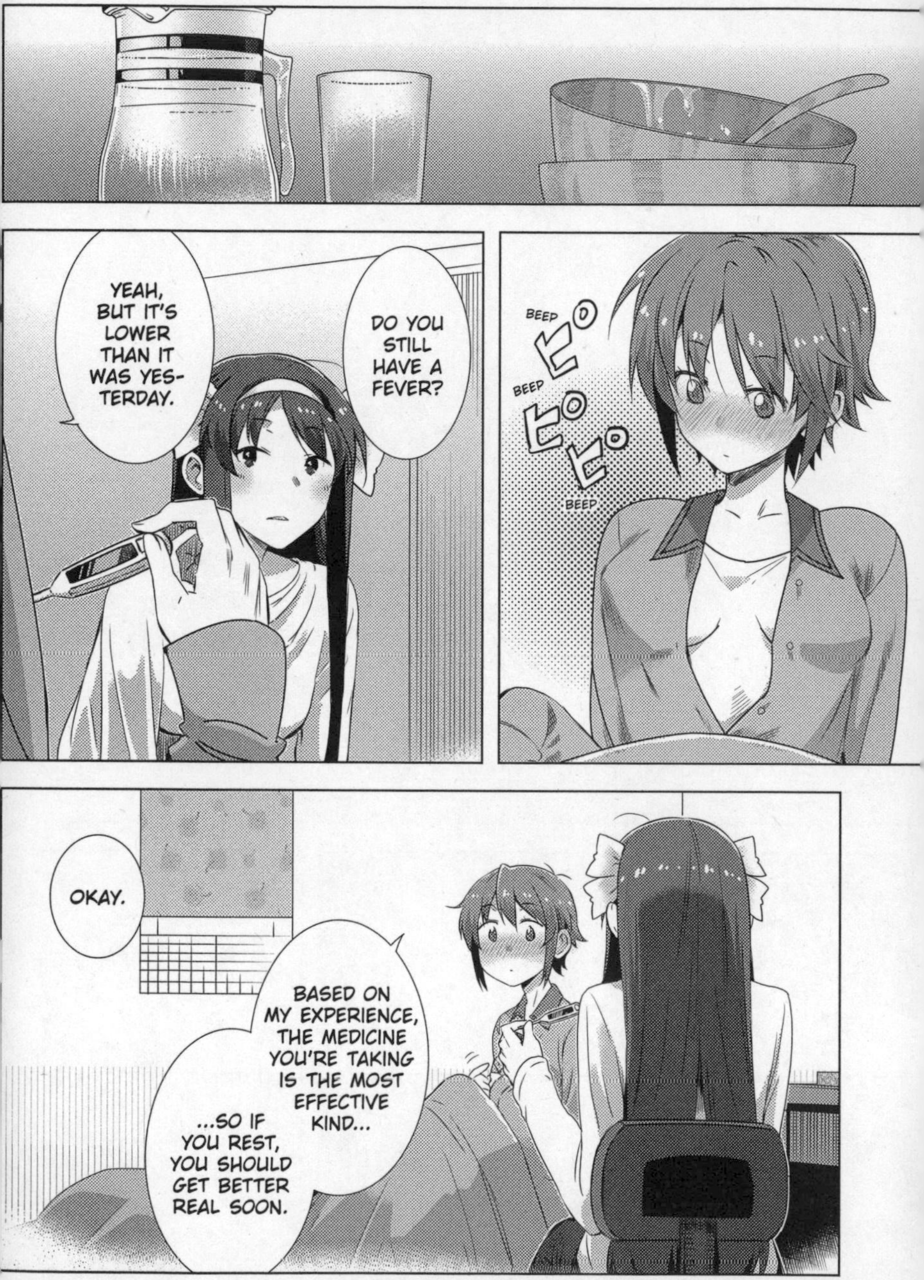
BEEP
ピ
BEEP
ピ
ピ
BEEP
DO YOU STILL HAVE A FEVER?
YEAH, BUT IT'S LOWER THAN IT WAS YES-TERDAY.
BASED ON MY EXPERIENCE, THE MEDICINE YOU'RE TAKING IS THE MOST EFFECTIVE KIND...
...SO IF YOU REST, YOU SHOULD GET BETTER REAL SOON.
OKAY.

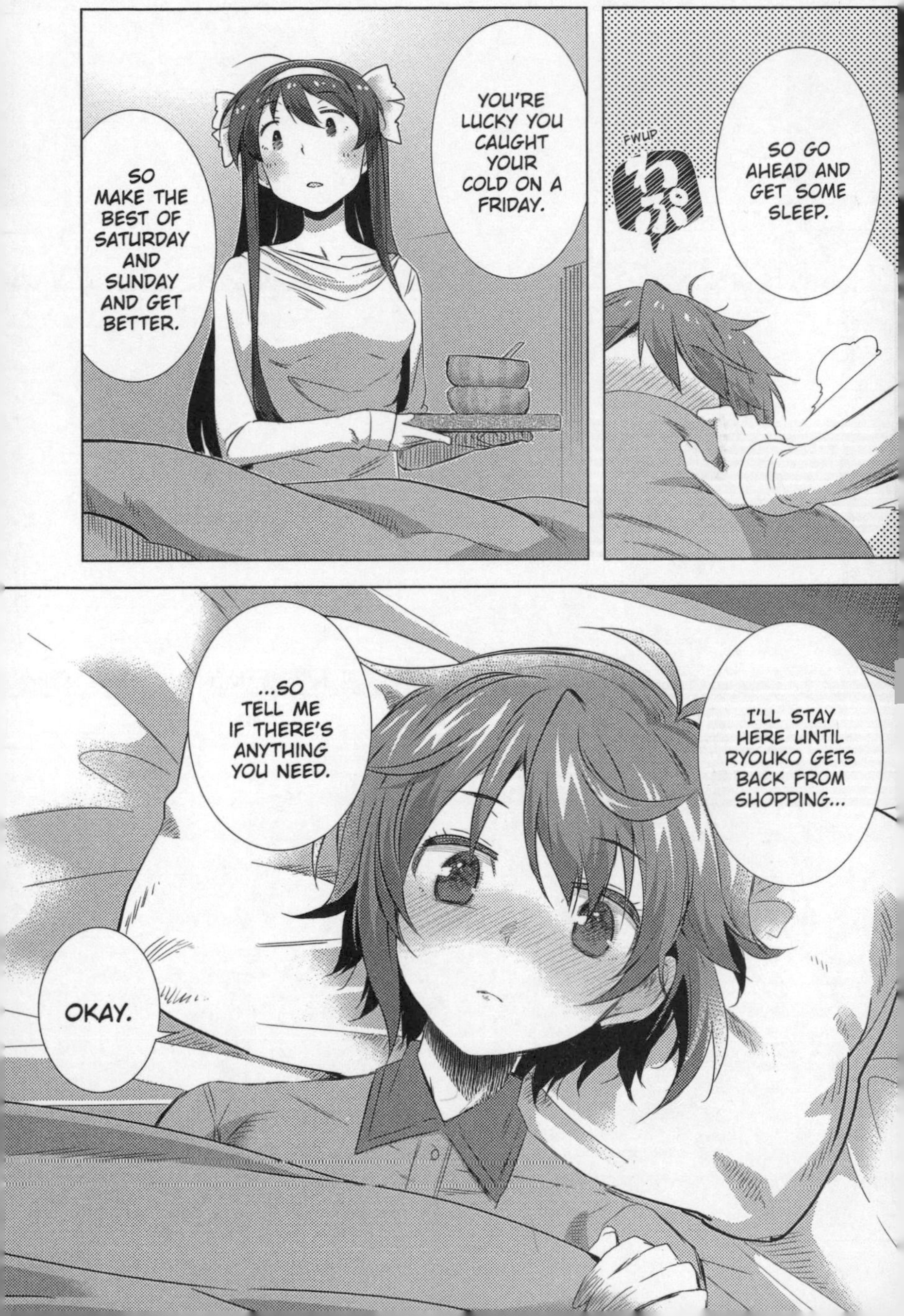
SO GO AHEAD AND GET SOME SLEEP.
わぷ
FWUP
YOU'RE LUCKY YOU CAUGHT YOUR COLD ON A FRIDAY.
SO MAKE THE BEST OF SATURDAY AND SUNDAY AND GET BETTER.
I'LL STAY HERE UNTIL RYOUKO GETS BACK FROM SHOPPING...
...SO TELL ME IF THERE'S ANYTHING YOU NEED.
OKAY.

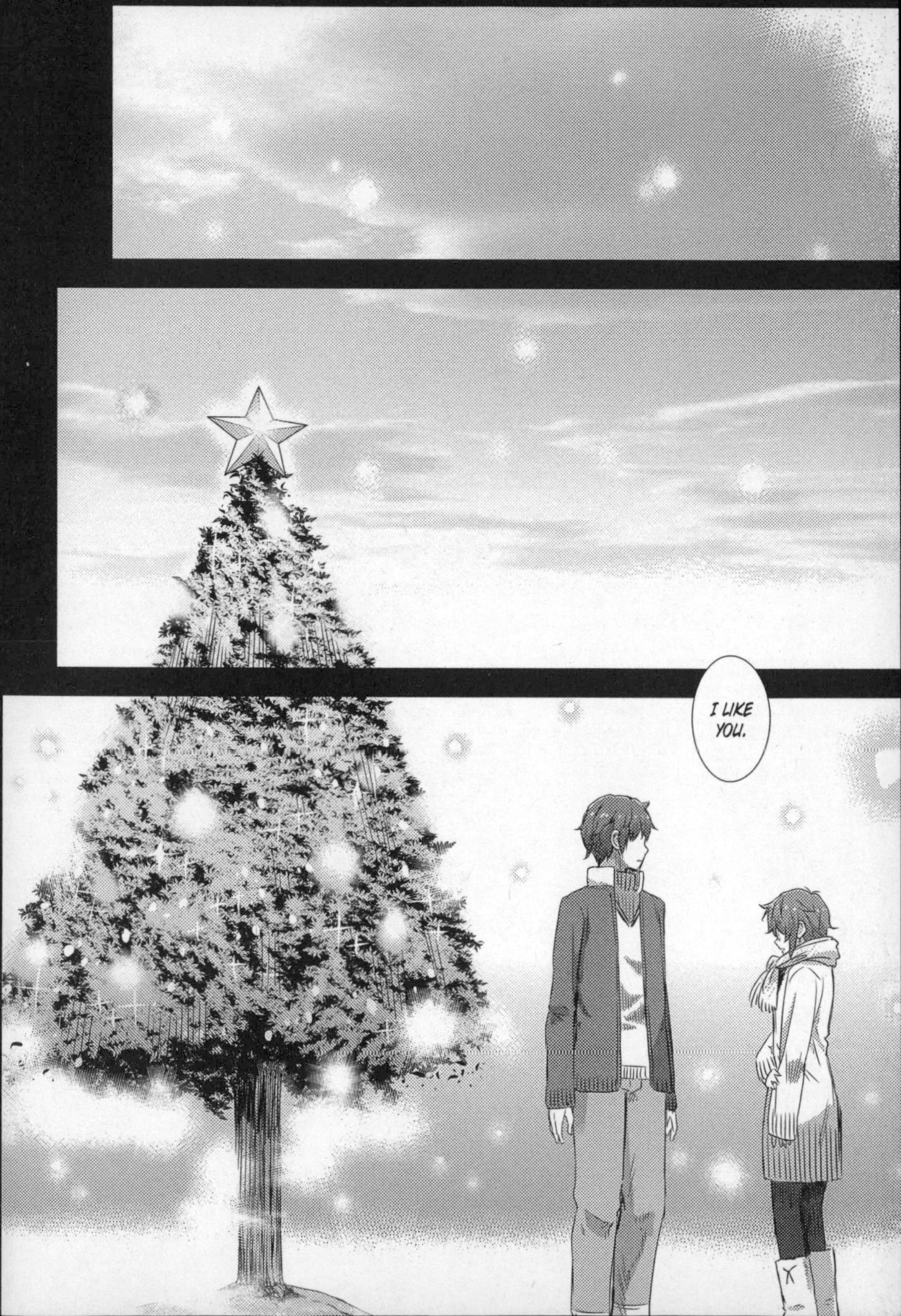
I LIKE YOU.

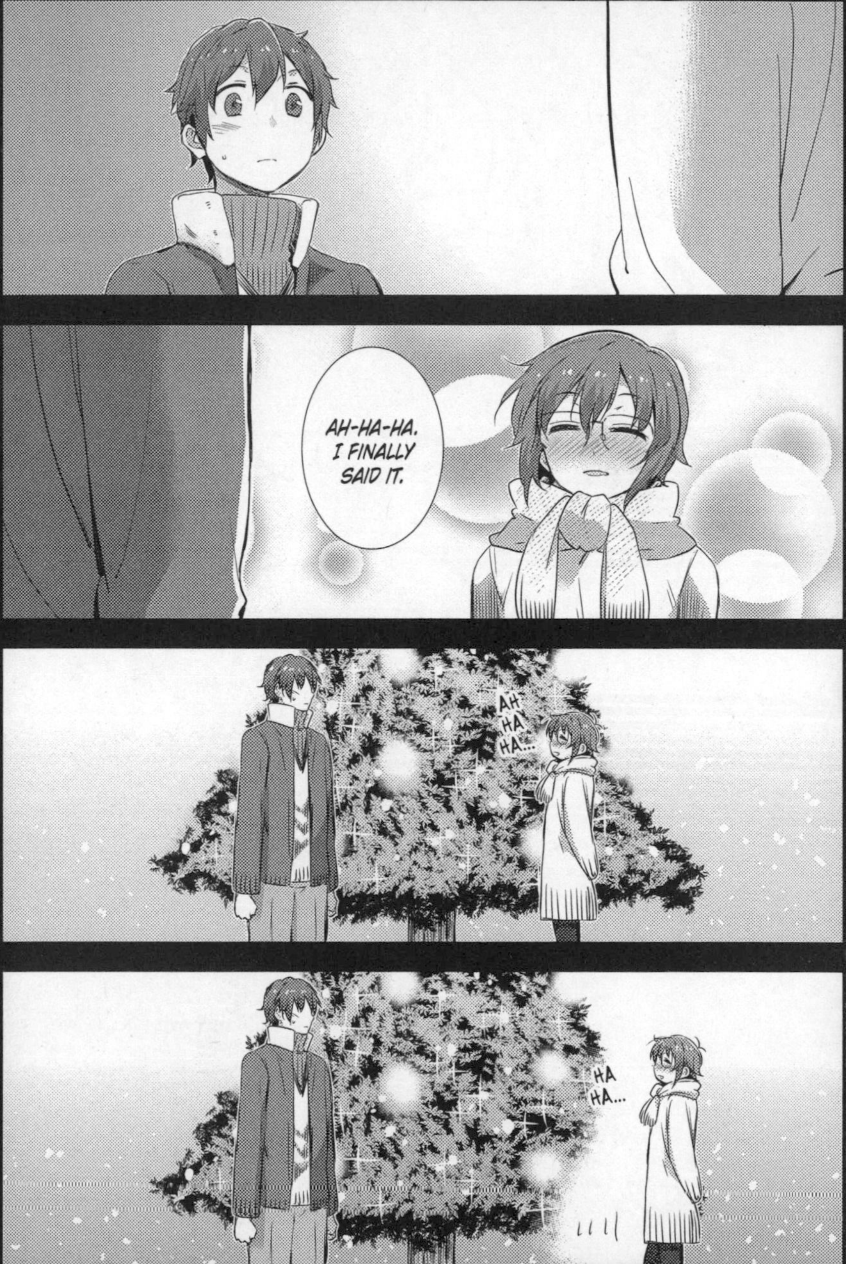
AH-HA-HA. I FINALLY SAID IT.
AH HA HA...
HA HA...

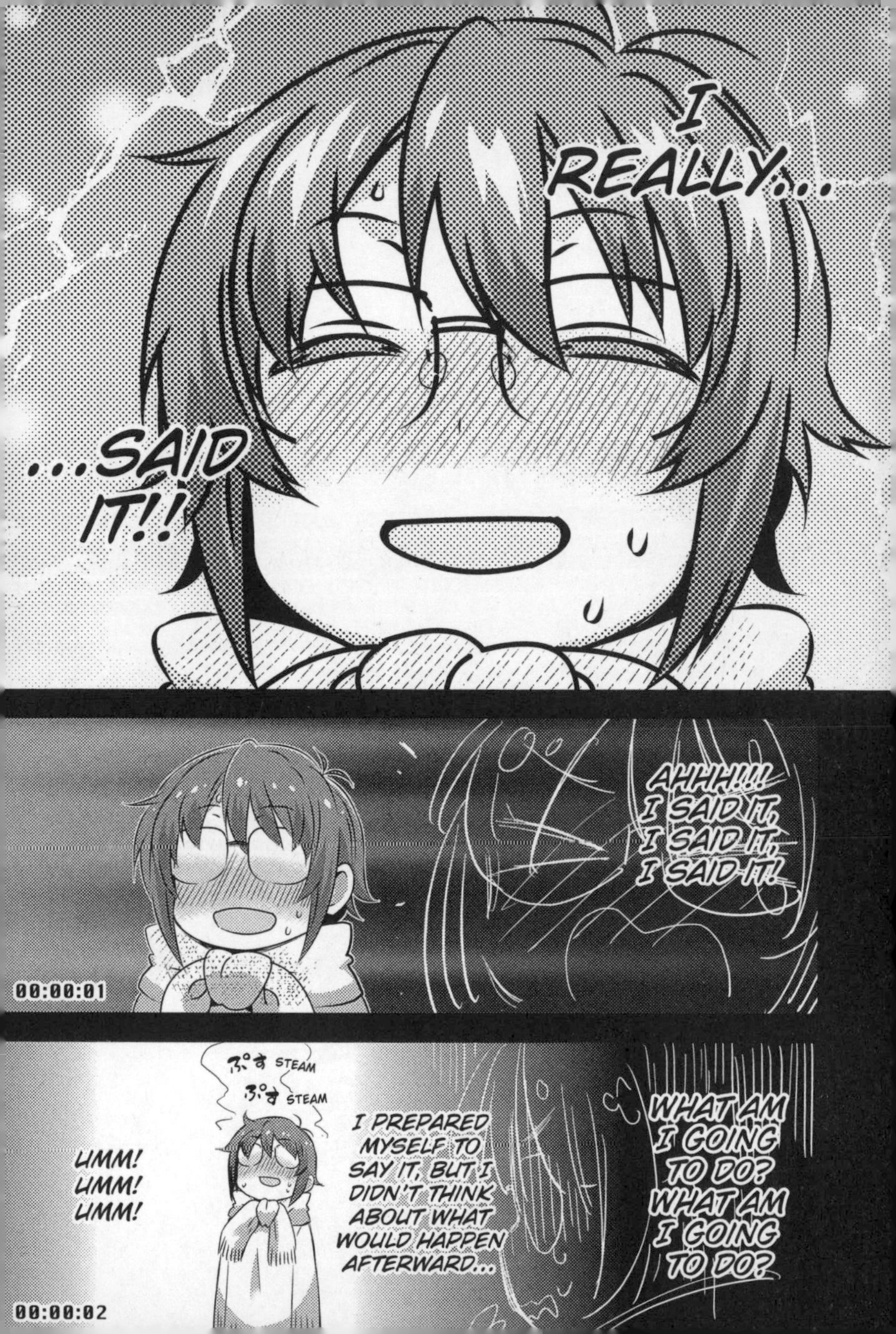
I REALLY...
...SAID IT!!
AHHH!!! I SAID IT, I SAID IT, I SAID IT!
00:00:01
WHAT AM I GOING TO DO? WHAT AM I GOING TO DO?
I PREPARED MYSELF TO SAY IT, BUT I DIDN'T THINK ABOUT WHAT WOULD HAPPEN AFTERWARD...
ぷす STEAM
ぷす STEAM
UMM! UMM! UMM!
00:00:02

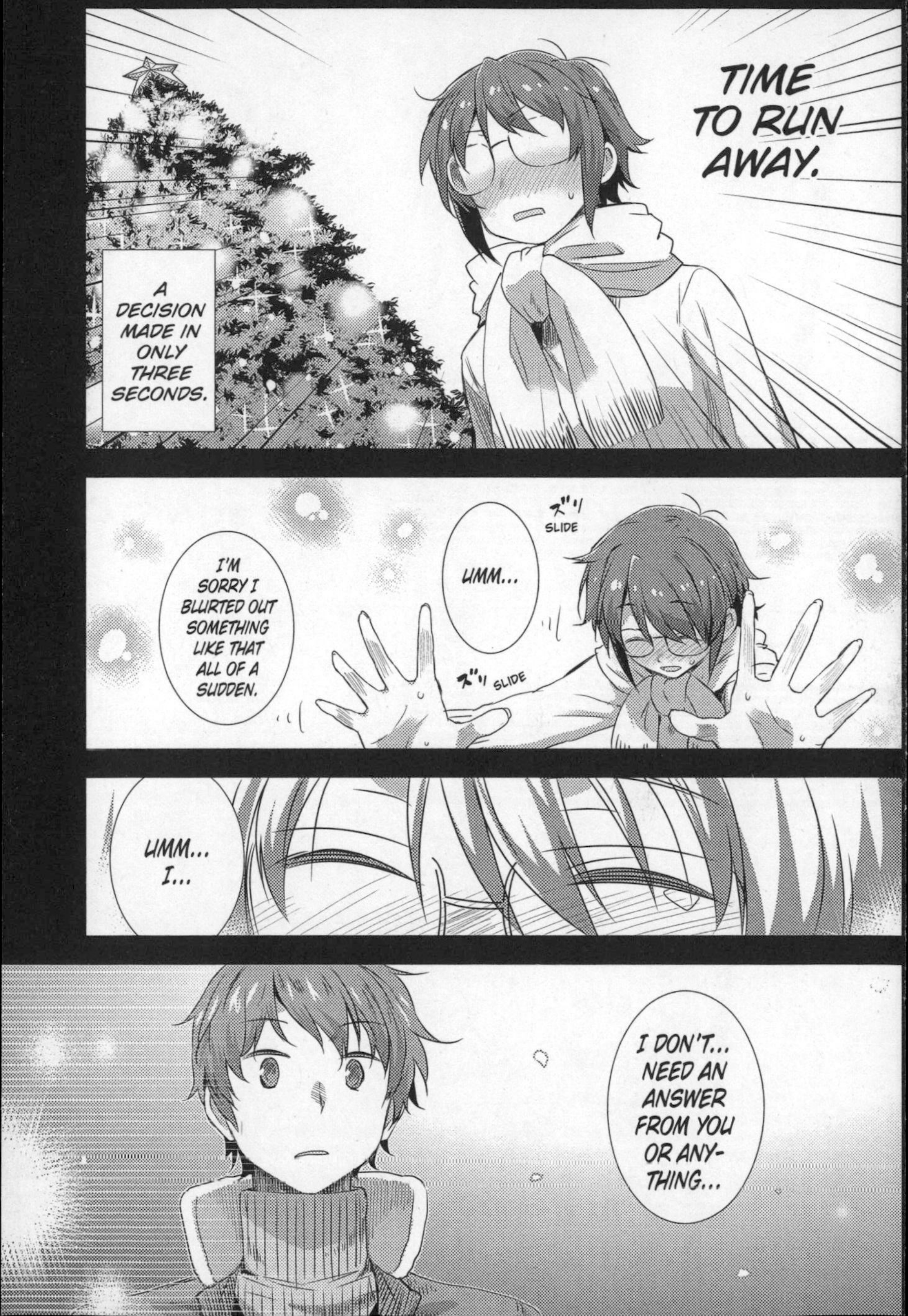
TIME TO RUN AWAY.
A DECISION MADE IN ONLY THREE SECONDS.
ズリ SLIDE
UMM...
I'M SORRY I BLURTED OUT SOMETHING LIKE THAT ALL OF A SUDDEN.
ズリ SLIDE
UMM... I...
I DON'T... NEED AN ANSWER FROM YOU OR ANY-THING...

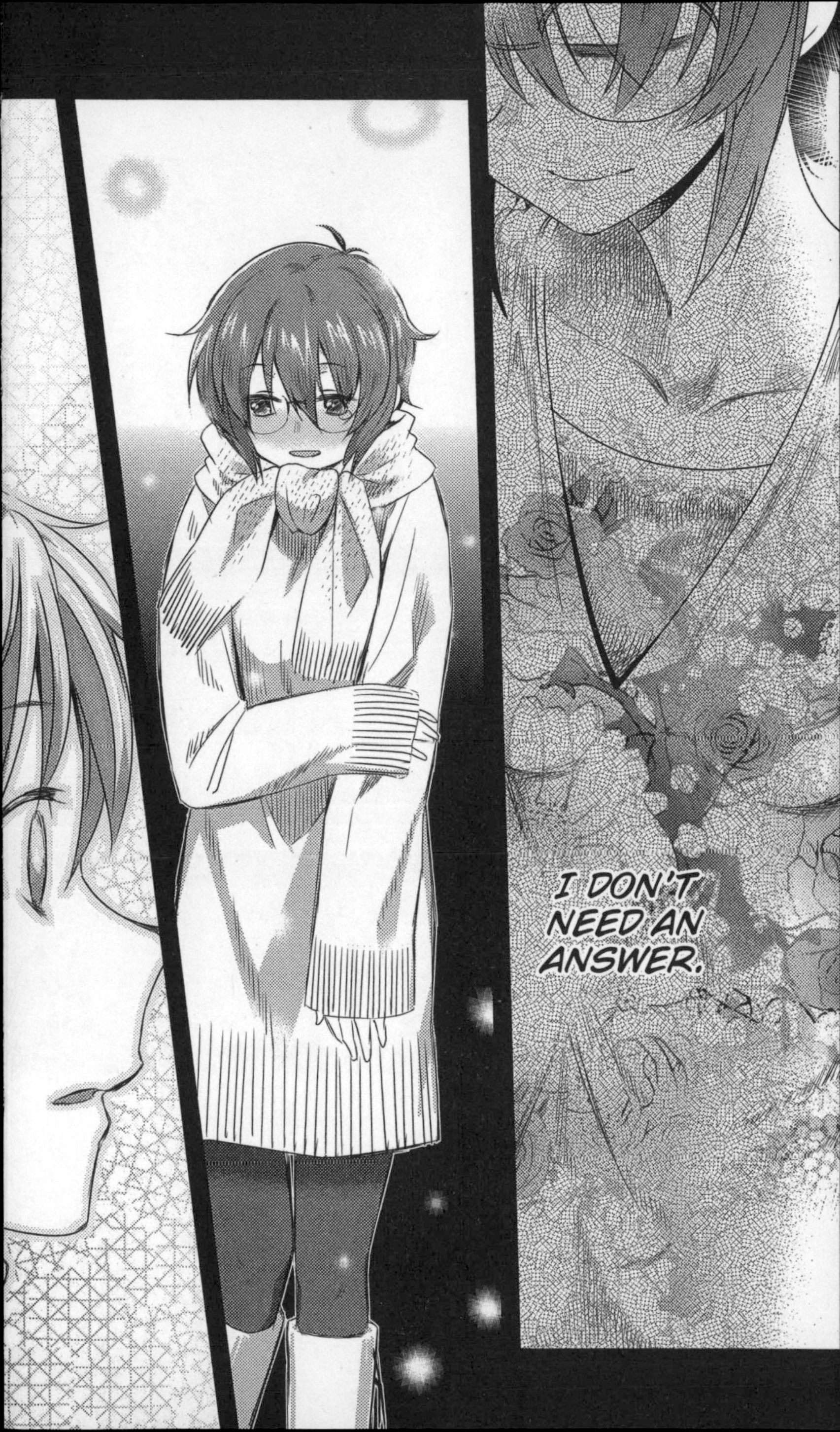
I DON'T NEED AN ANSWER.

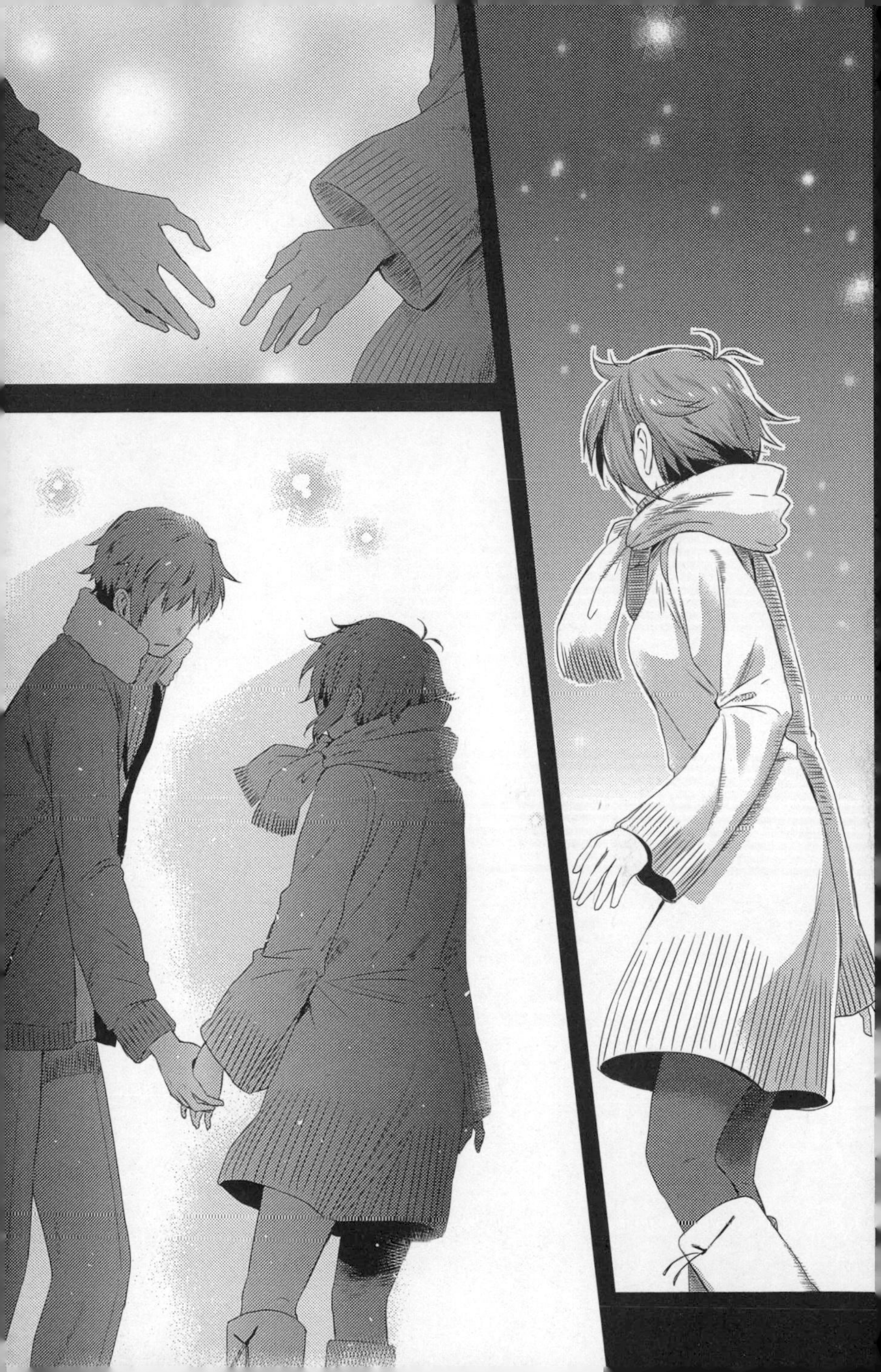

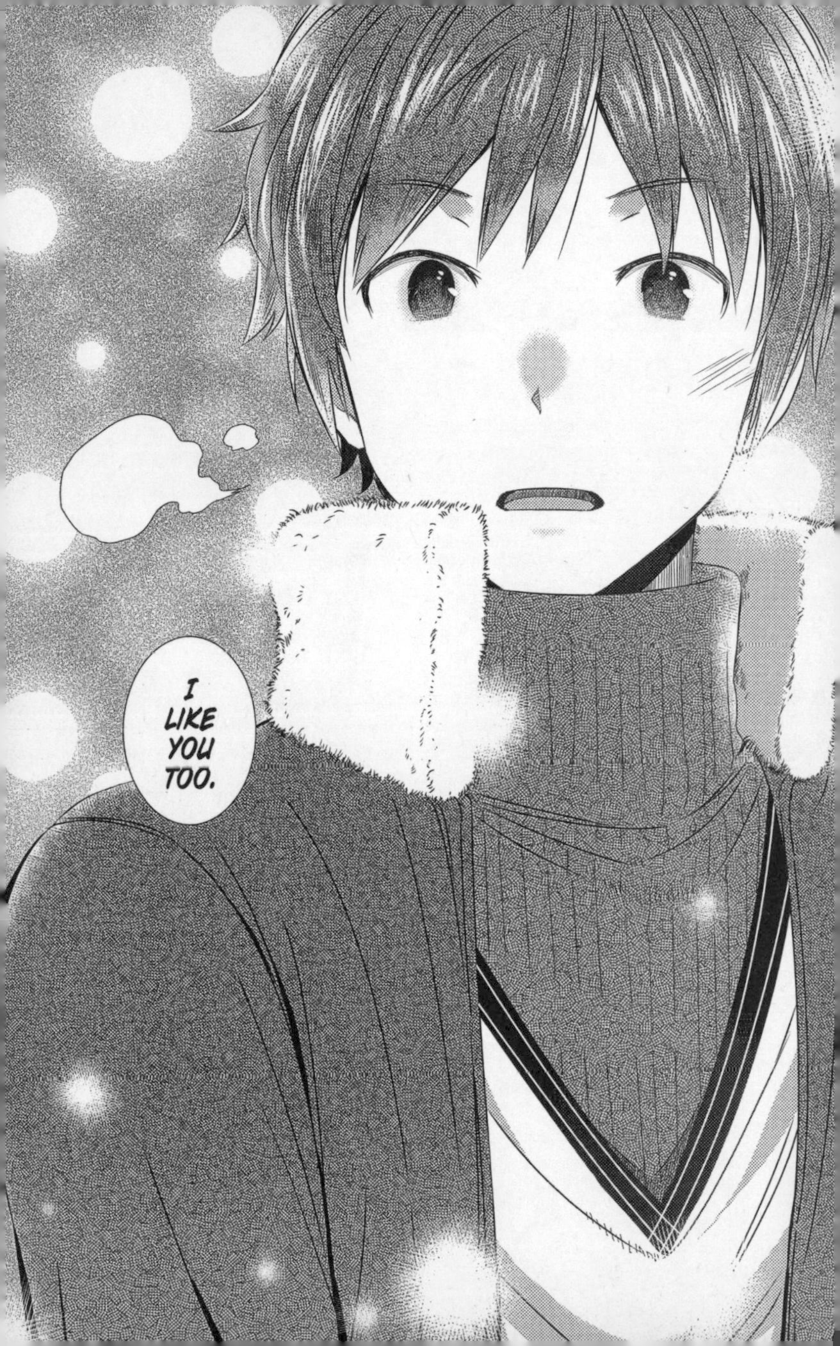
I LIKE YOU TOO.

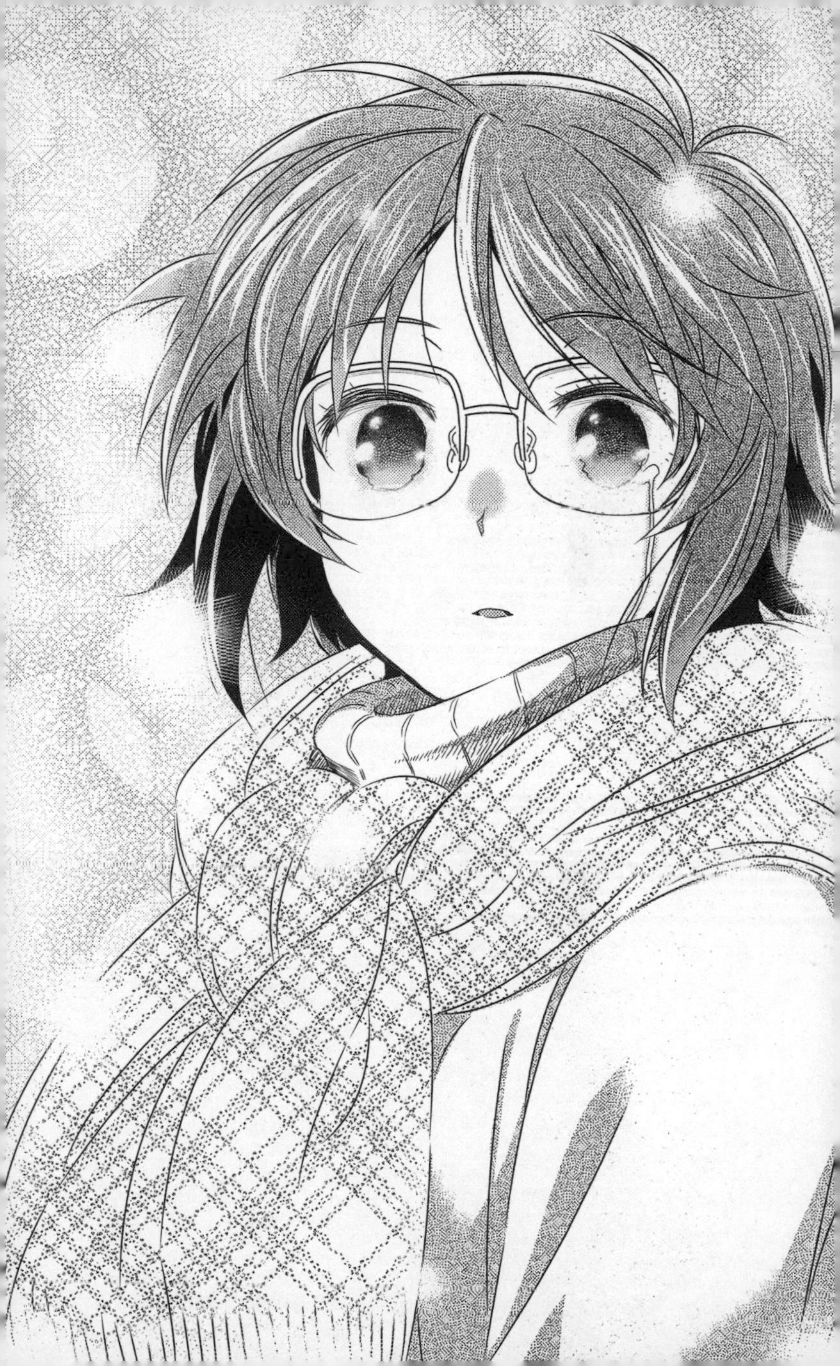

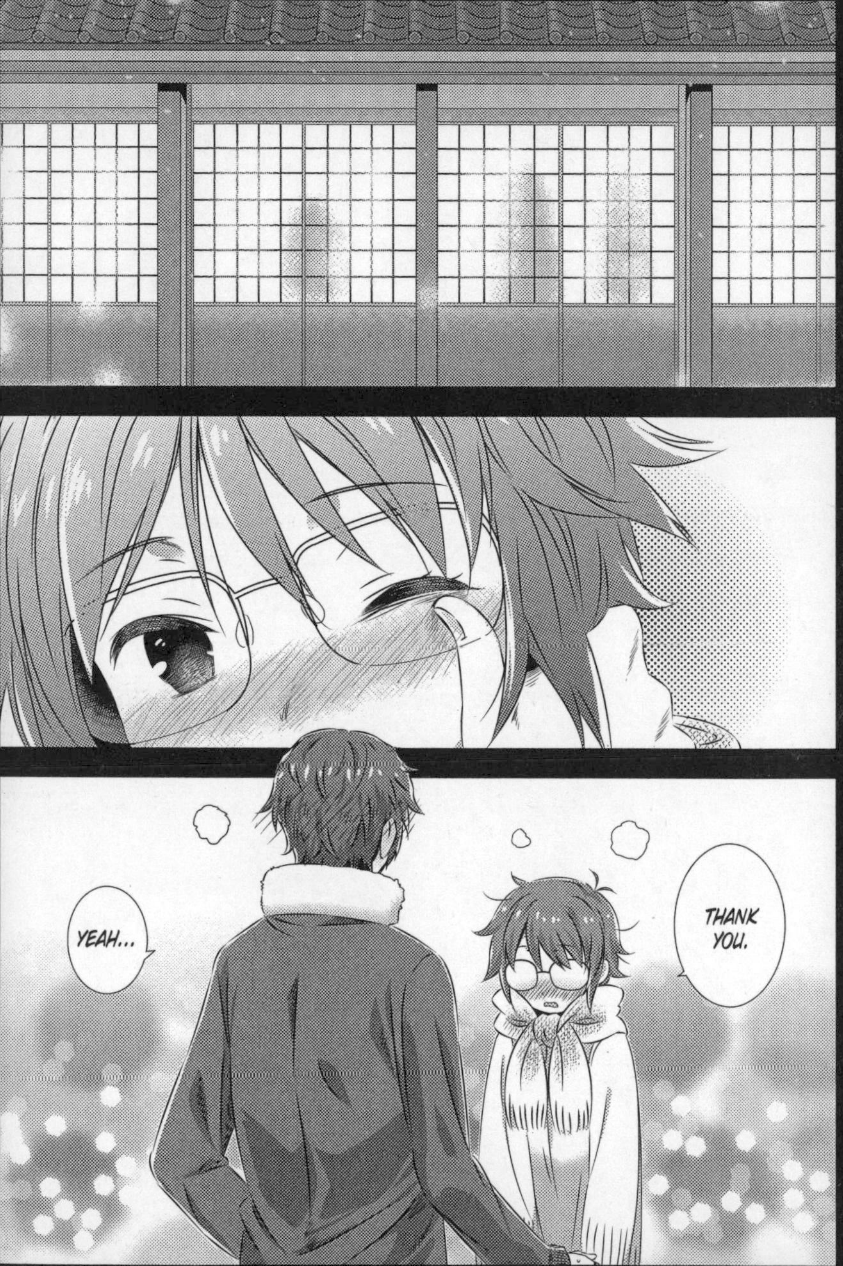
THANK YOU.
YEAH...

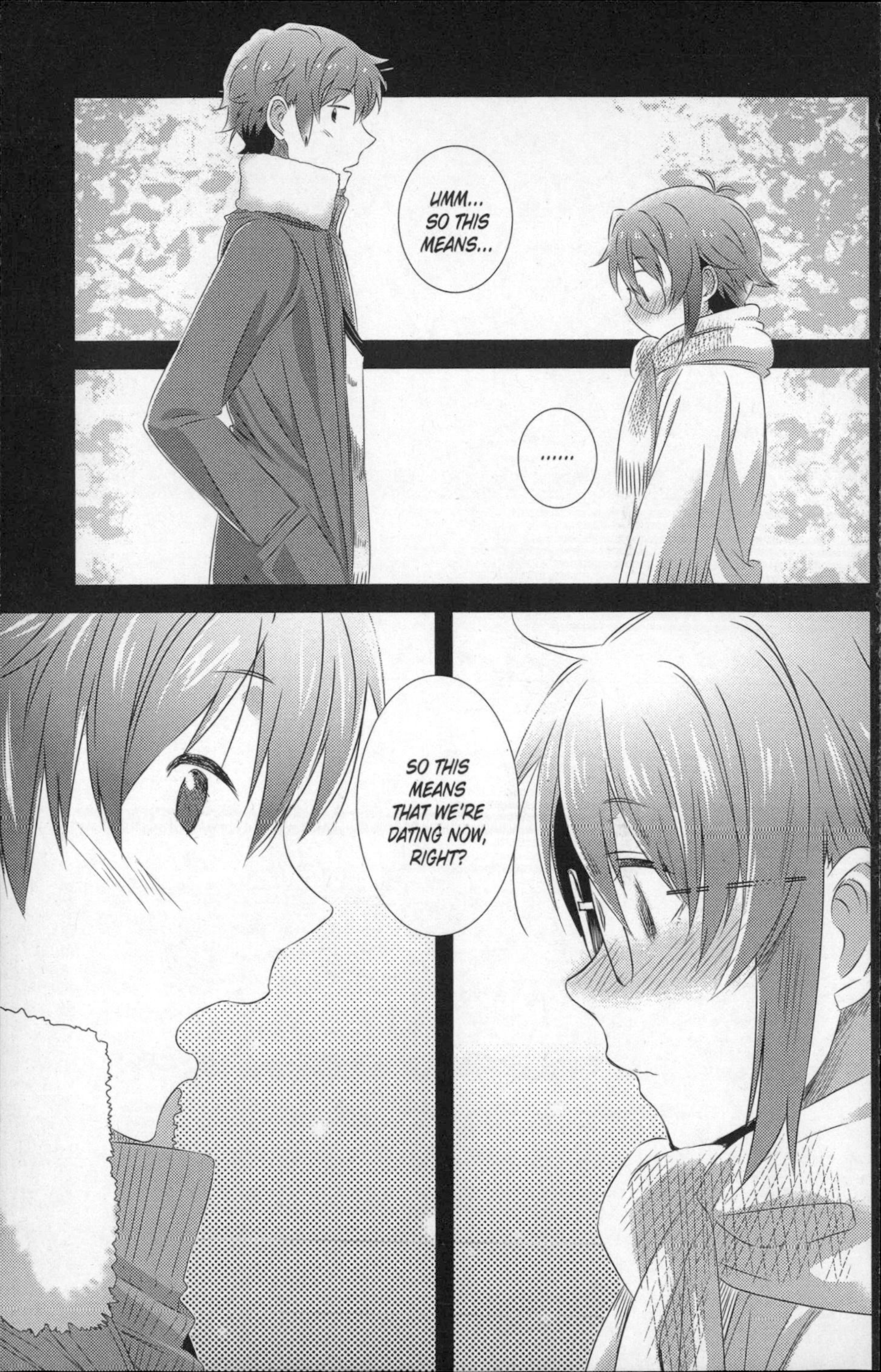
UMM... SO THIS MEANS...
......
SO THIS MEANS THAT WE'RE DATING NOW, RIGHT?

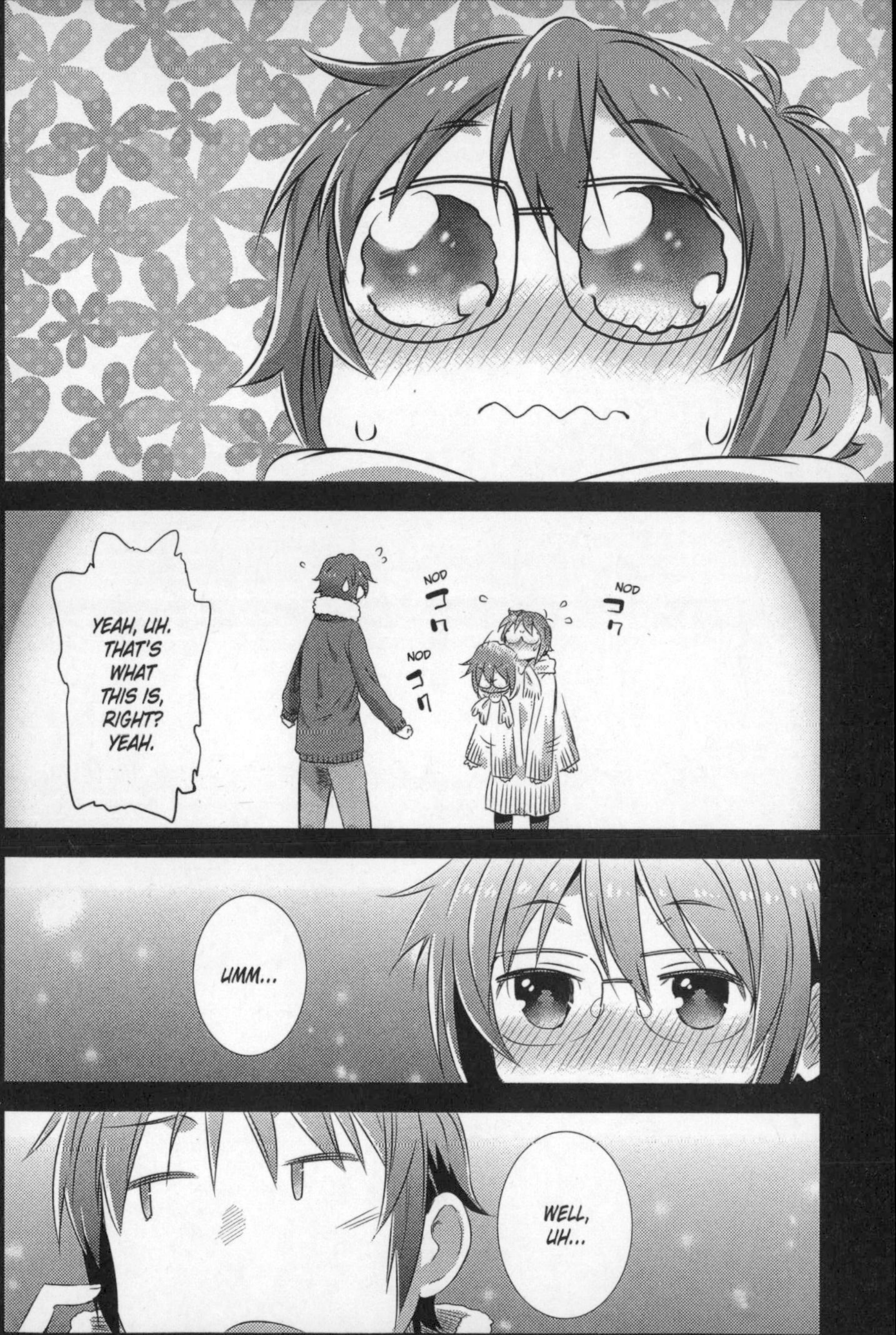
NOD
コク
NOD
コク
NOD
コク
YEAH, UH. THAT'S WHAT THIS IS, RIGHT? YEAH.
UMM...
WELL, UH...

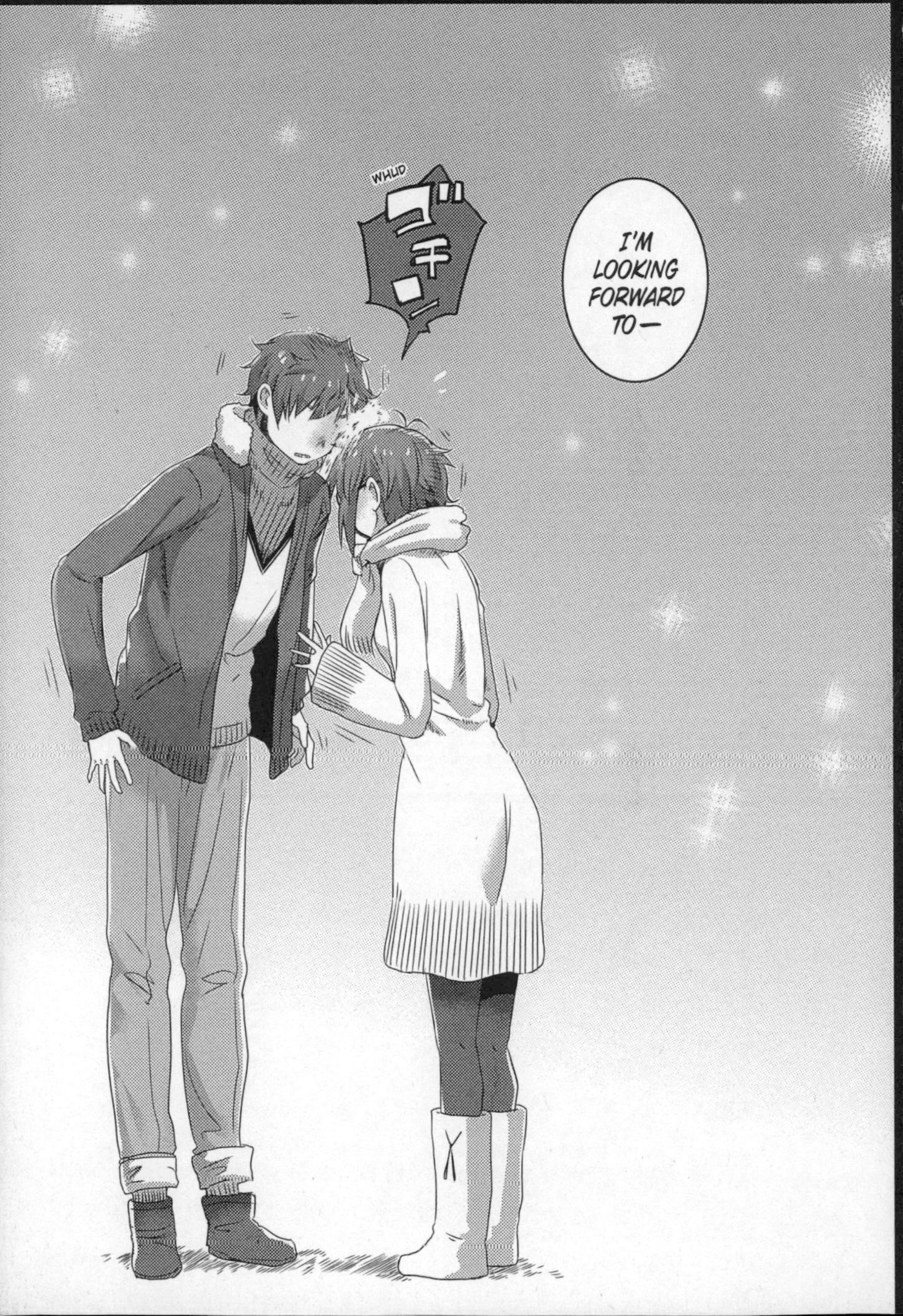
WHUD
ゴチーン
I'M LOOKING FORWARD TO—

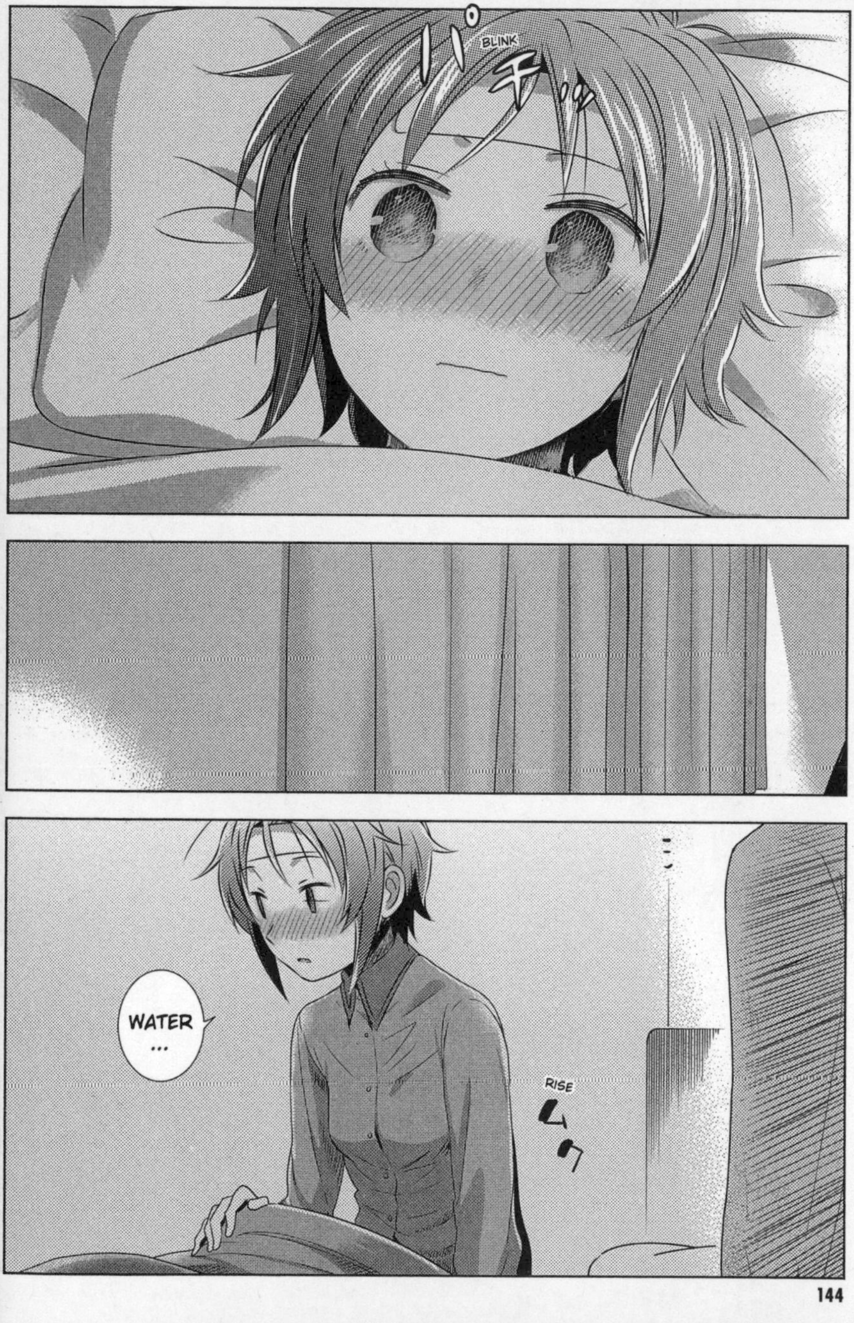
BLINK
RISE
WATER
...

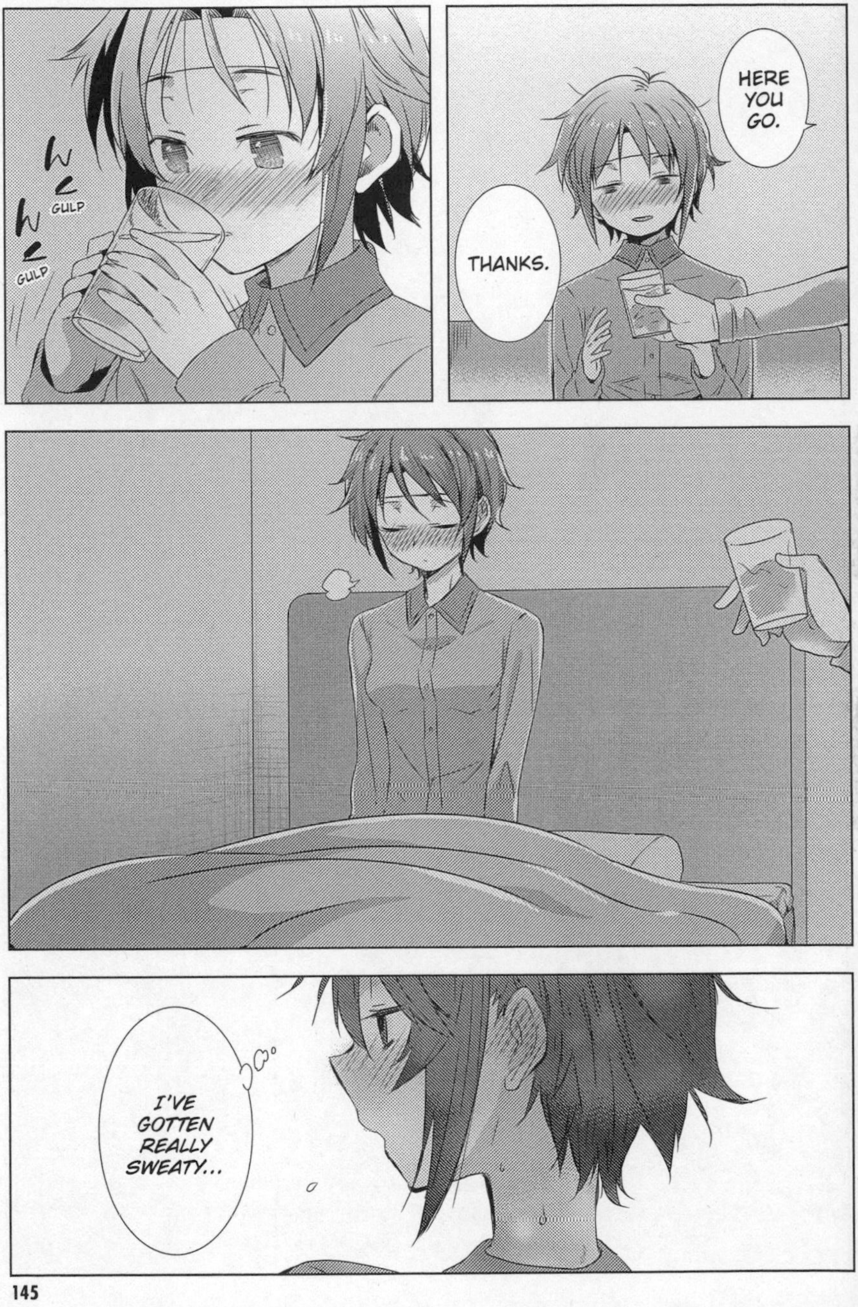
HERE YOU GO.
THANKS.
GULP
GULP
I'VE GOTTEN REALLY SWEATY...

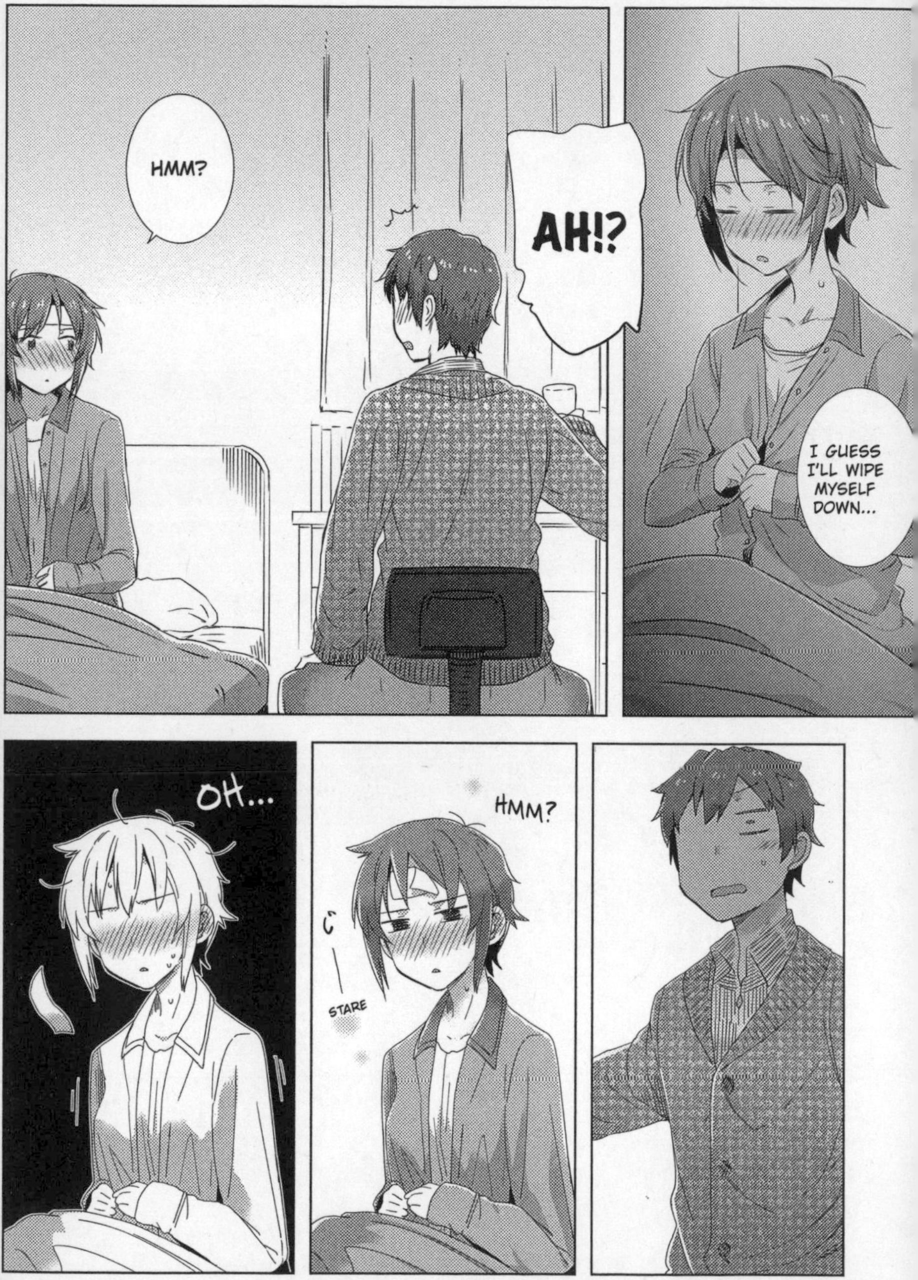
I GUESS I'LL WIPE MYSELF DOWN...
AH!?
HMM?
HMM?
じ
STARE
OH...

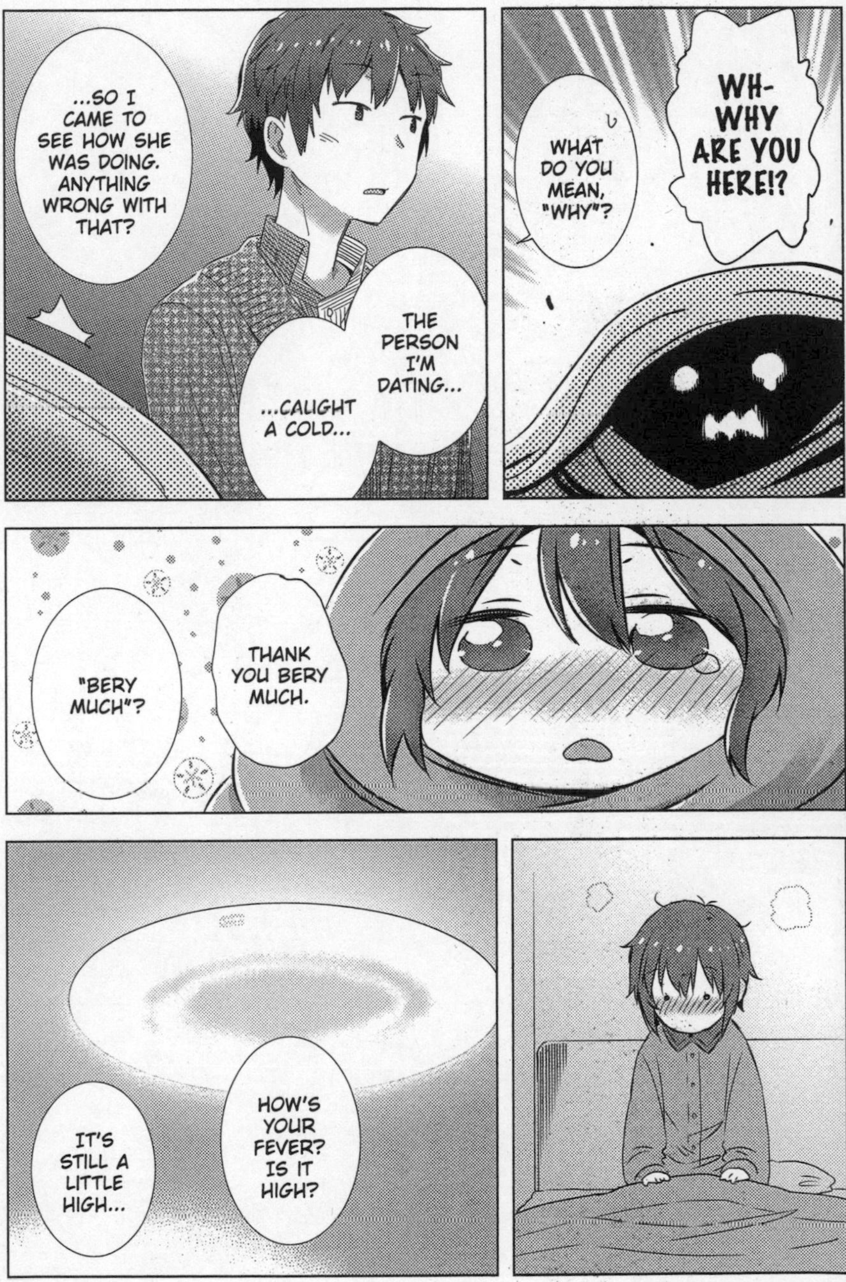
WH- WHY ARE YOU HERE!?
WHAT DO YOU MEAN, "WHY"?
THE PERSON I'M DATING...
...CAUGHT A COLD...
...SO I CAME TO SEE HOW SHE WAS DOING. ANYTHING WRONG WITH THAT?
THANK YOU BERY MUCH.
"BERY MUCH"?
HOW'S YOUR FEVER? IS IT HIGH?
IT'S STILL A LITTLE HIGH...

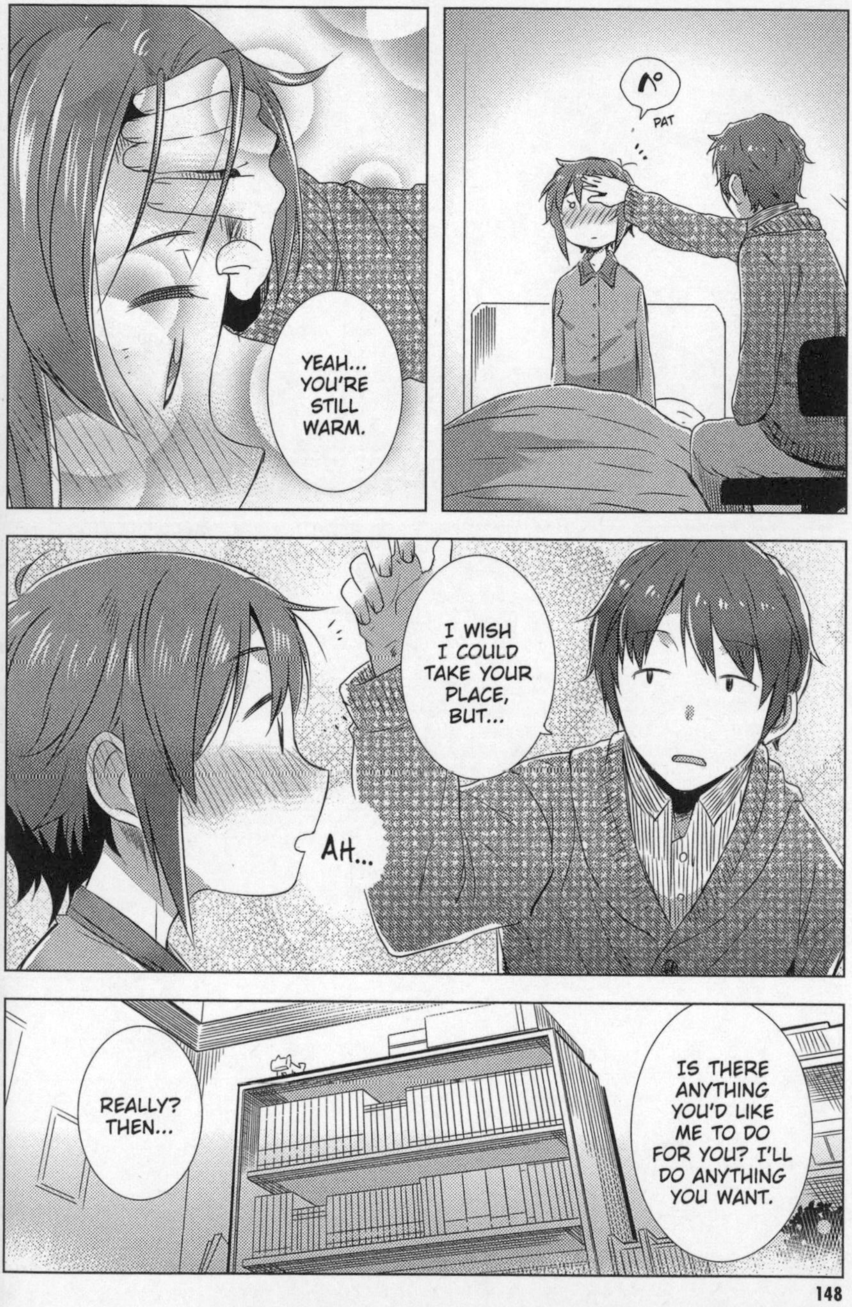
PAT
YEAH... YOU'RE STILL WARM.
I WISH I COULD TAKE YOUR PLACE, BUT...
AH...
IS THERE ANYTHING YOU'D LIKE ME TO DO FOR YOU? I'LL DO ANYTHING YOU WANT.
REALLY? THEN...

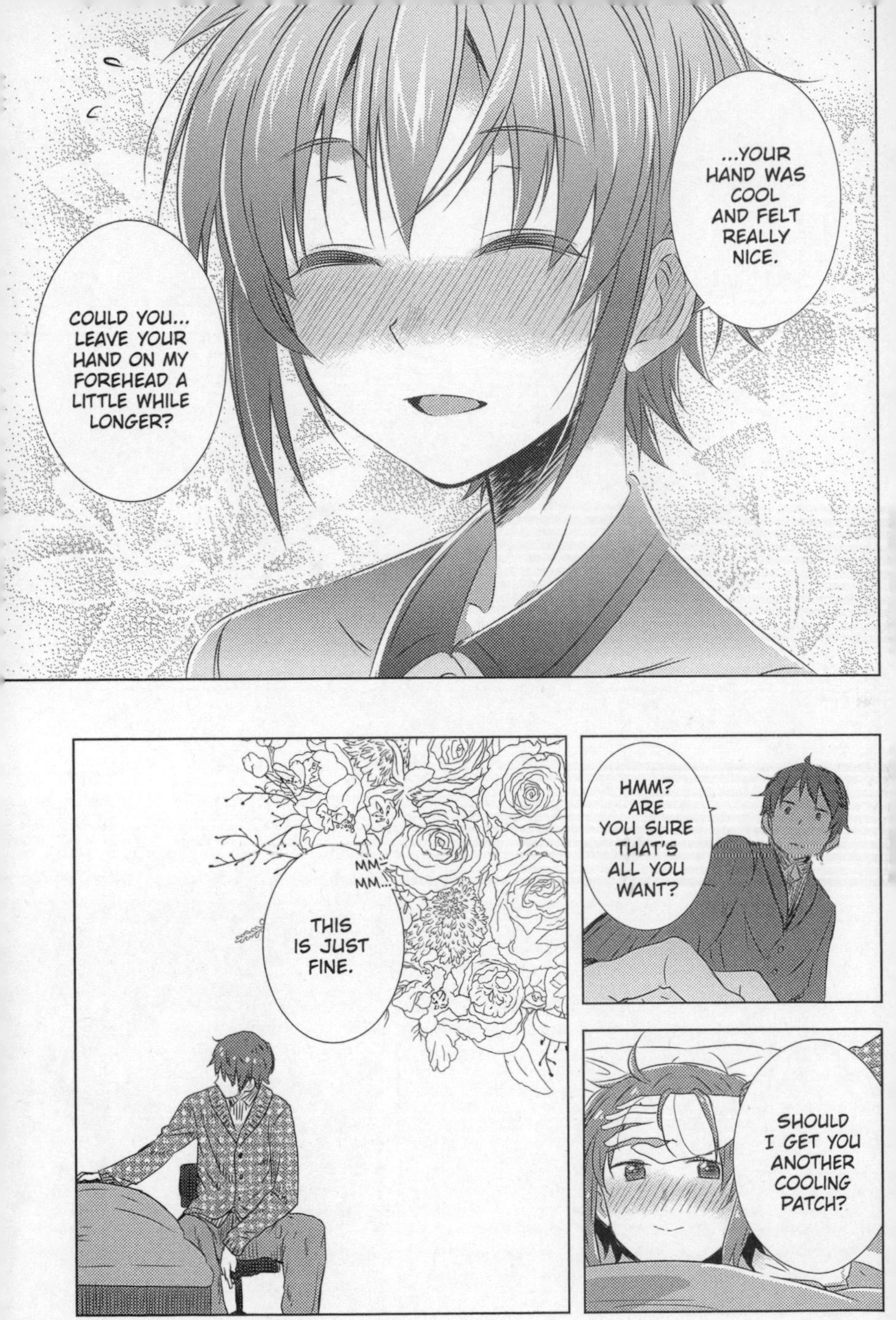
...YOUR HAND WAS COOL AND FELT REALLY NICE.
COULD YOU... LEAVE YOUR HAND ON MY FOREHEAD A LITTLE WHILE LONGER?
HMM? ARE YOU SURE THAT'S ALL YOU WANT?
SHOULD I GET YOU ANOTHER COOLING PATCH?
MM-MM...
THIS IS JUST FINE.

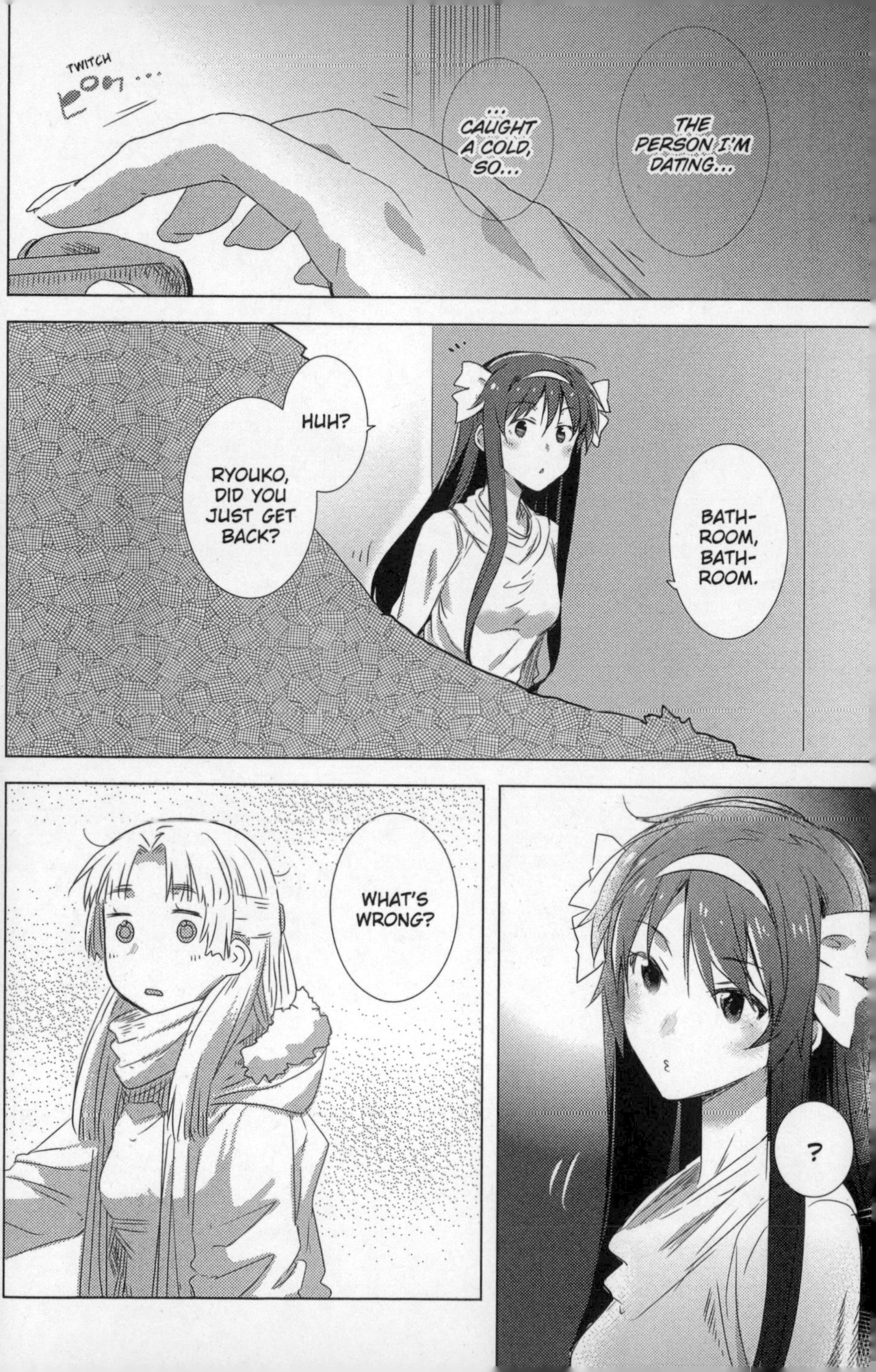
THE PERSON I'M DATING...
...CAUGHT A COLD, SO...
TWITCH
BATH-ROOM, BATH-ROOM.
HUH?
RYOUKO, DID YOU JUST GET BACK?
?
WHAT'S WRONG?

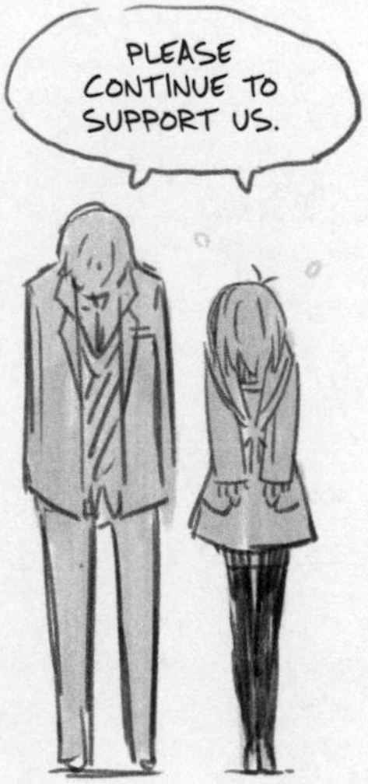
PLEASE CONTINUE TO SUPPORT US.

EXTRAAA.

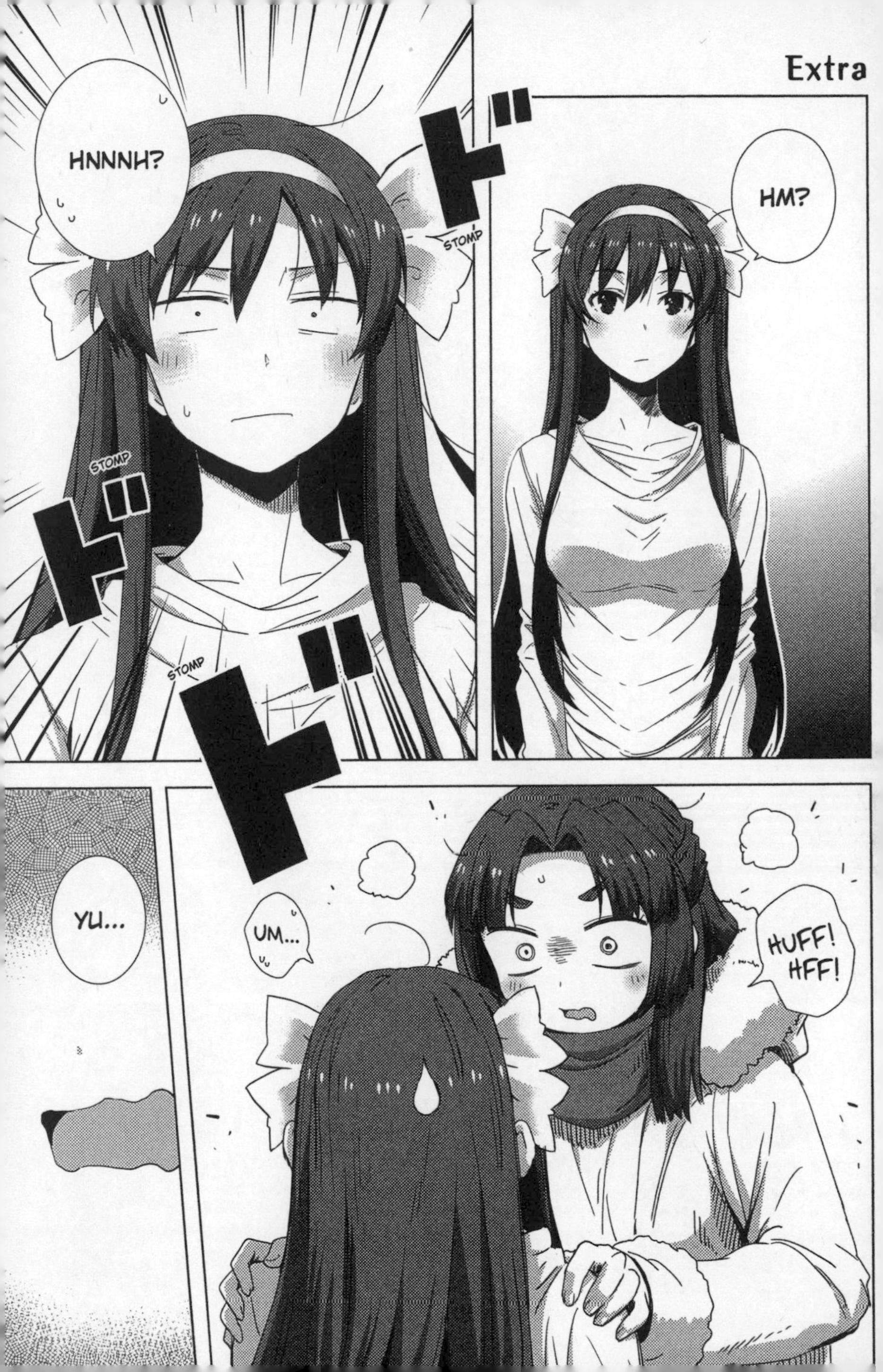
HM?
STOMP
HNNNH?
STOMP
STOMP
HUFF! HFF!
UM...
YU...

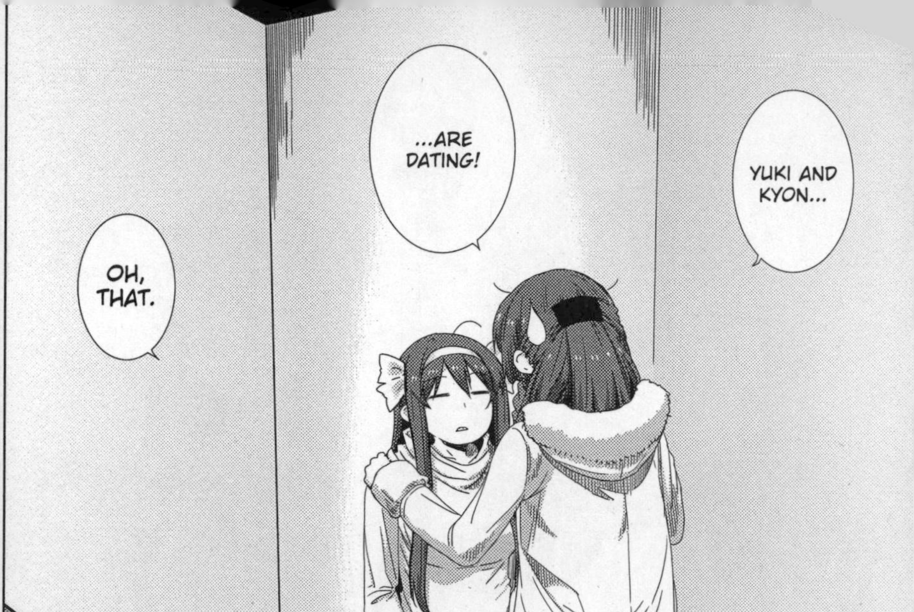
YUKI AND KYON...
...ARE DATING!
OH, THAT.

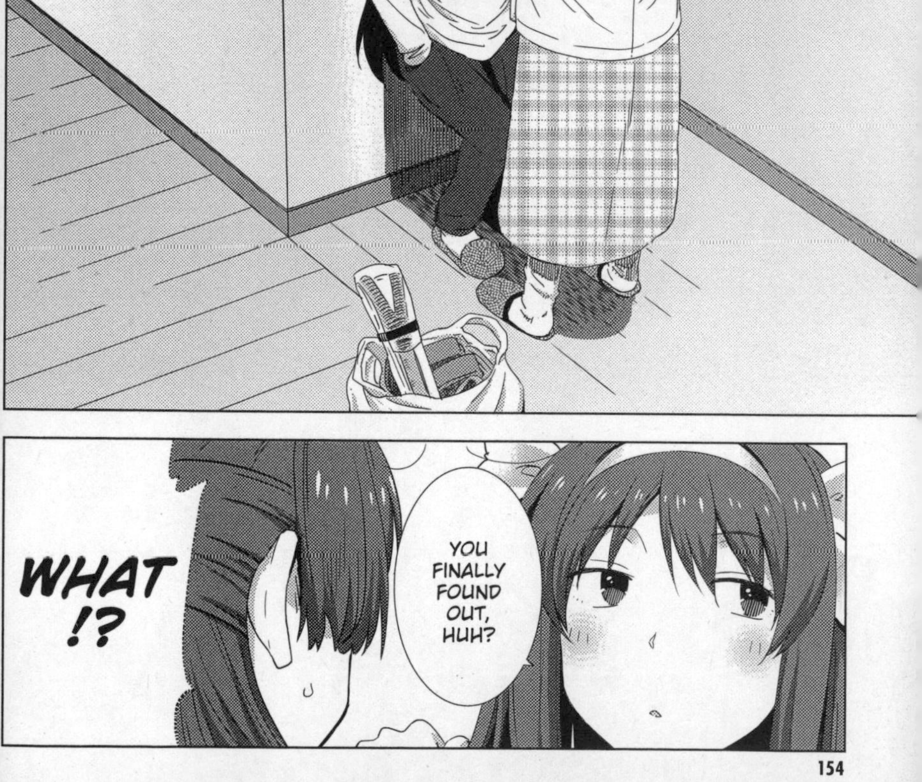
YOU FINALLY FOUND OUT, HUH?
WHAT!?

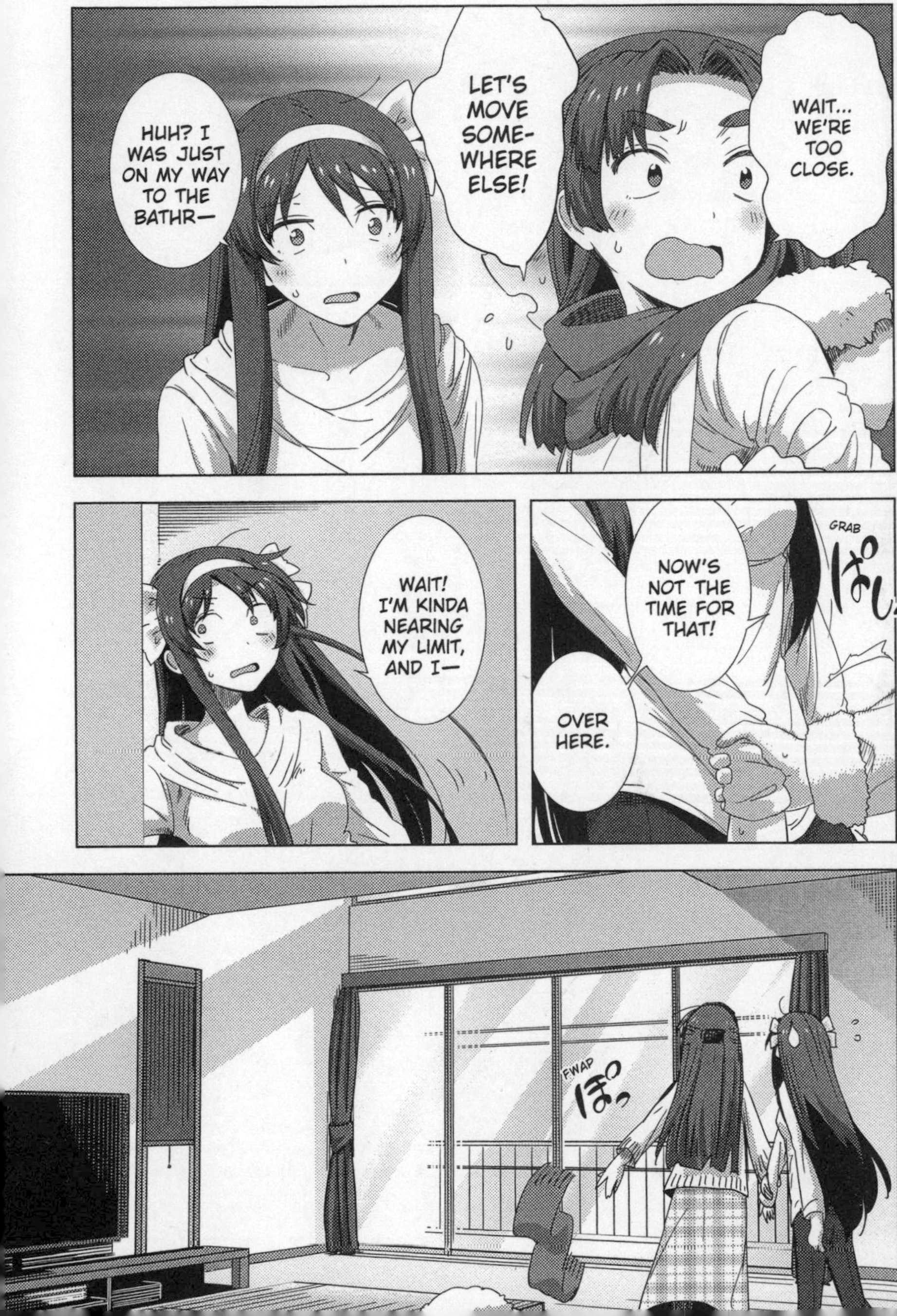
WAIT... WE'RE TOO CLOSE.
LET'S MOVE SOME-WHERE ELSE!
HUH? I WAS JUST ON MY WAY TO THE BATHR—
GRAB
ぱし
NOW'S NOT THE TIME FOR THAT!
OVER HERE.
WAIT! I'M KINDA NEARING MY LIMIT, AND I—
FWAP
ぽっ

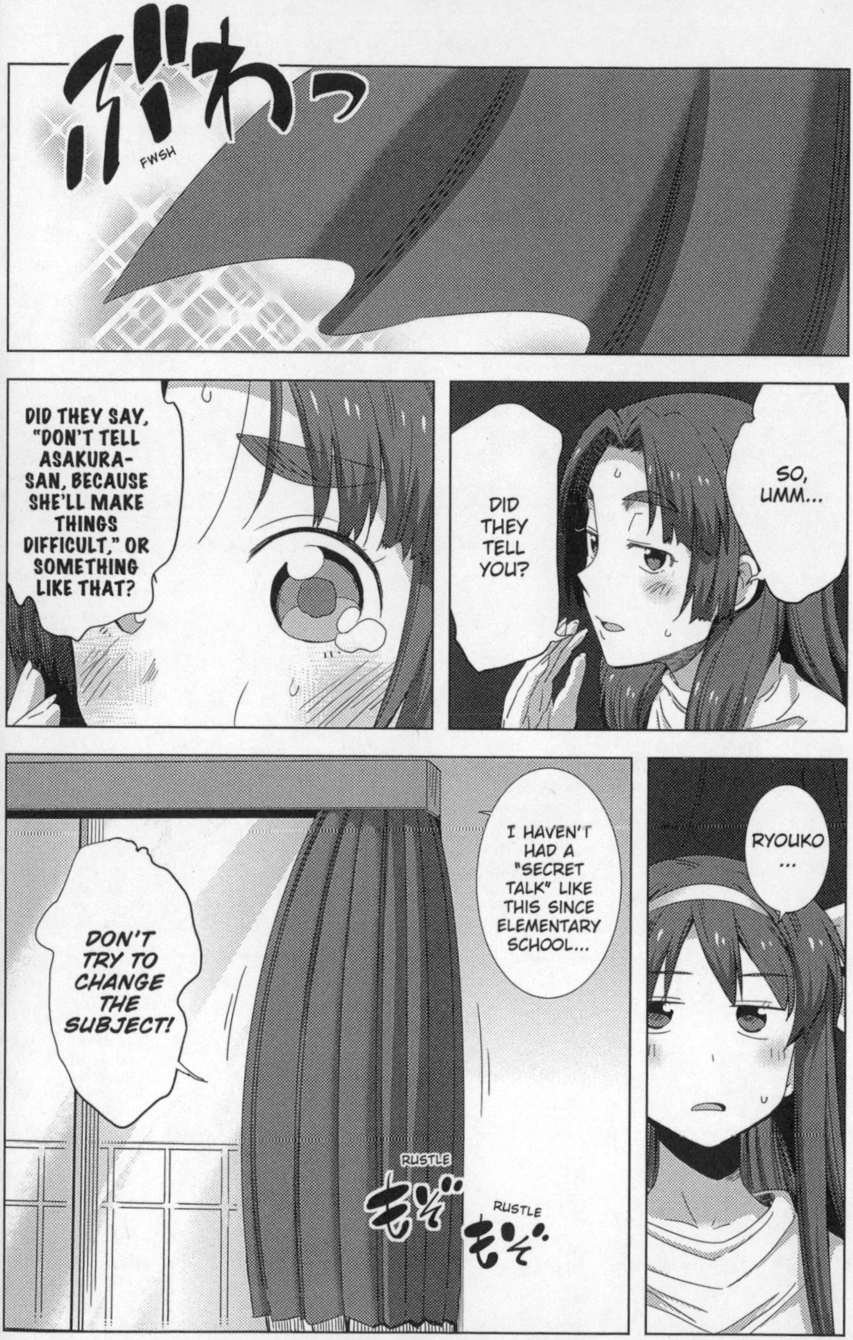

ぶわっ
FWSH
SO, UMM...
DID THEY TELL YOU?
DID THEY SAY, "DON'T TELL ASAKURA-SAN, BECAUSE SHE'LL MAKE THINGS DIFFICULT," OR SOMETHING LIKE THAT?
RYOUKO ...
I HAVEN'T HAD A "SECRET TALK" LIKE THIS SINCE ELEMENTARY SCHOOL...
DON'T TRY TO CHANGE THE SUBJECT!
RUSTLE
もぞ
RUSTLE
もぞ

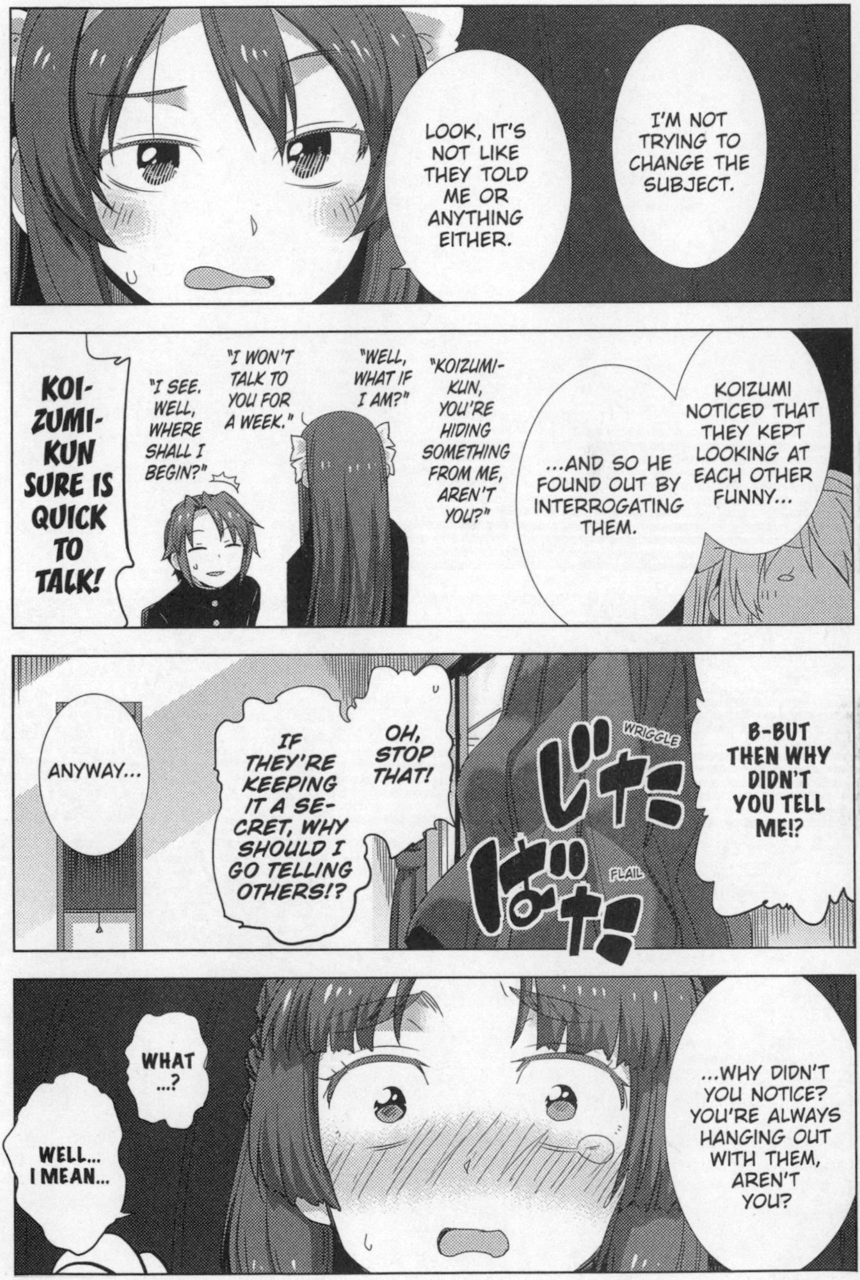

I'M NOT TRYING TO CHANGE THE SUBJECT.
LOOK, IT'S NOT LIKE THEY TOLD ME OR ANYTHING EITHER.
KOIZUMI NOTICED THAT THEY KEPT LOOKING AT EACH OTHER FUNNY...
...AND SO HE FOUND OUT BY INTERROGATING THEM.
"KOIZUMI-KUN, YOU'RE HIDING SOMETHING FROM ME, AREN'T YOU?"
"WELL, WHAT IF I AM?"
"I WON'T TALK TO YOU FOR A WEEK."
"I SEE. WELL, WHERE SHALL I BEGIN?"
KOI-ZUMI-KUN SURE IS QUICK TO TALK!
B-BUT THEN WHY DIDN'T YOU TELL ME!?
じた
WRIGGLE
ばた
FLAIL
OH, STOP THAT!
IF THEY'RE KEEPING IT A SE-CRET, WHY SHOULD I GO TELLING OTHERS!?
ANYWAY...
...WHY DIDN'T YOU NOTICE? YOU'RE ALWAYS HANGING OUT WITH THEM, AREN'T YOU?
WHAT ...?
WELL... I MEAN...

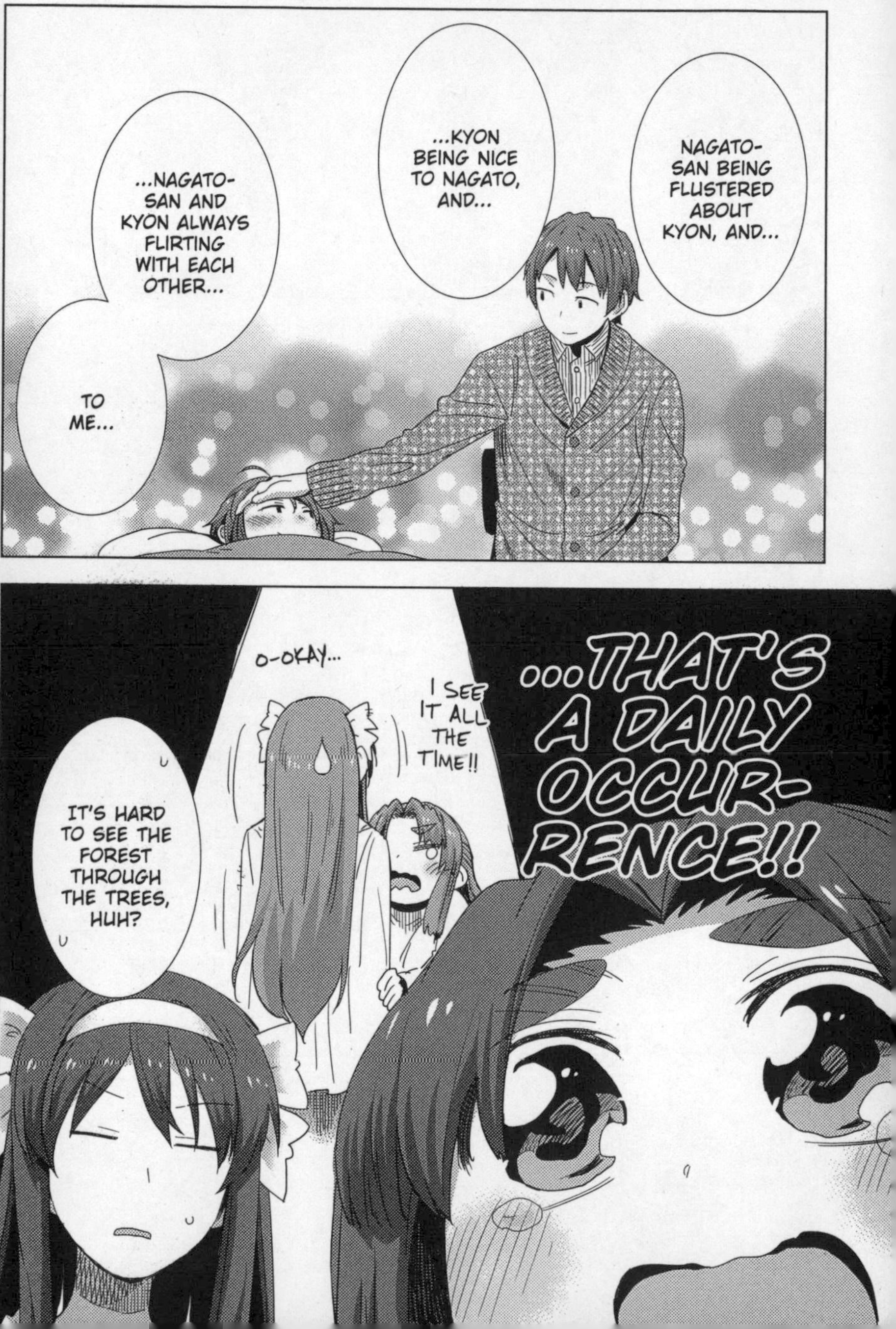
NAGATO-SAN BEING FLUSTERED ABOUT KYON, AND...
...KYON BEING NICE TO NAGATO, AND...
...NAGATO-SAN AND KYON ALWAYS FLIRTING WITH EACH OTHER...
TO ME...
...THAT'S A DAILY OCCURRENCE!!
I SEE IT ALL THE TIME!!
O-OKAY...
IT'S HARD TO SEE THE FOREST THROUGH THE TREES, HUH?

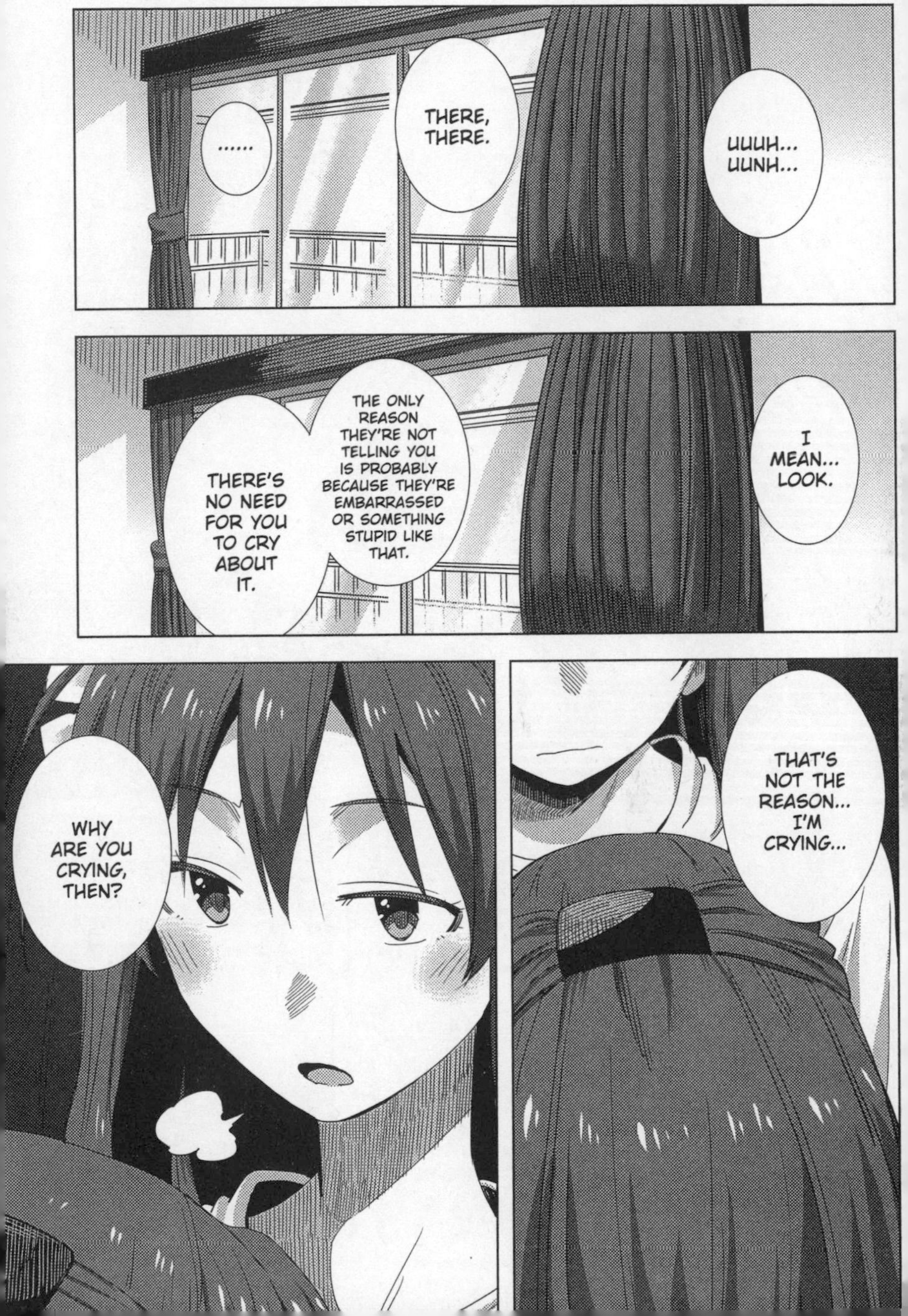
UUUH... UUNH...
THERE, THERE.
......
I MEAN... LOOK.
THE ONLY REASON THEY'RE NOT TELLING YOU IS PROBABLY BECAUSE THEY'RE EMBARRASSED OR SOMETHING STUPID LIKE THAT.
THERE'S NO NEED FOR YOU TO CRY ABOUT IT.
THAT'S NOT THE REASON... I'M CRYING...
WHY ARE YOU CRYING, THEN?

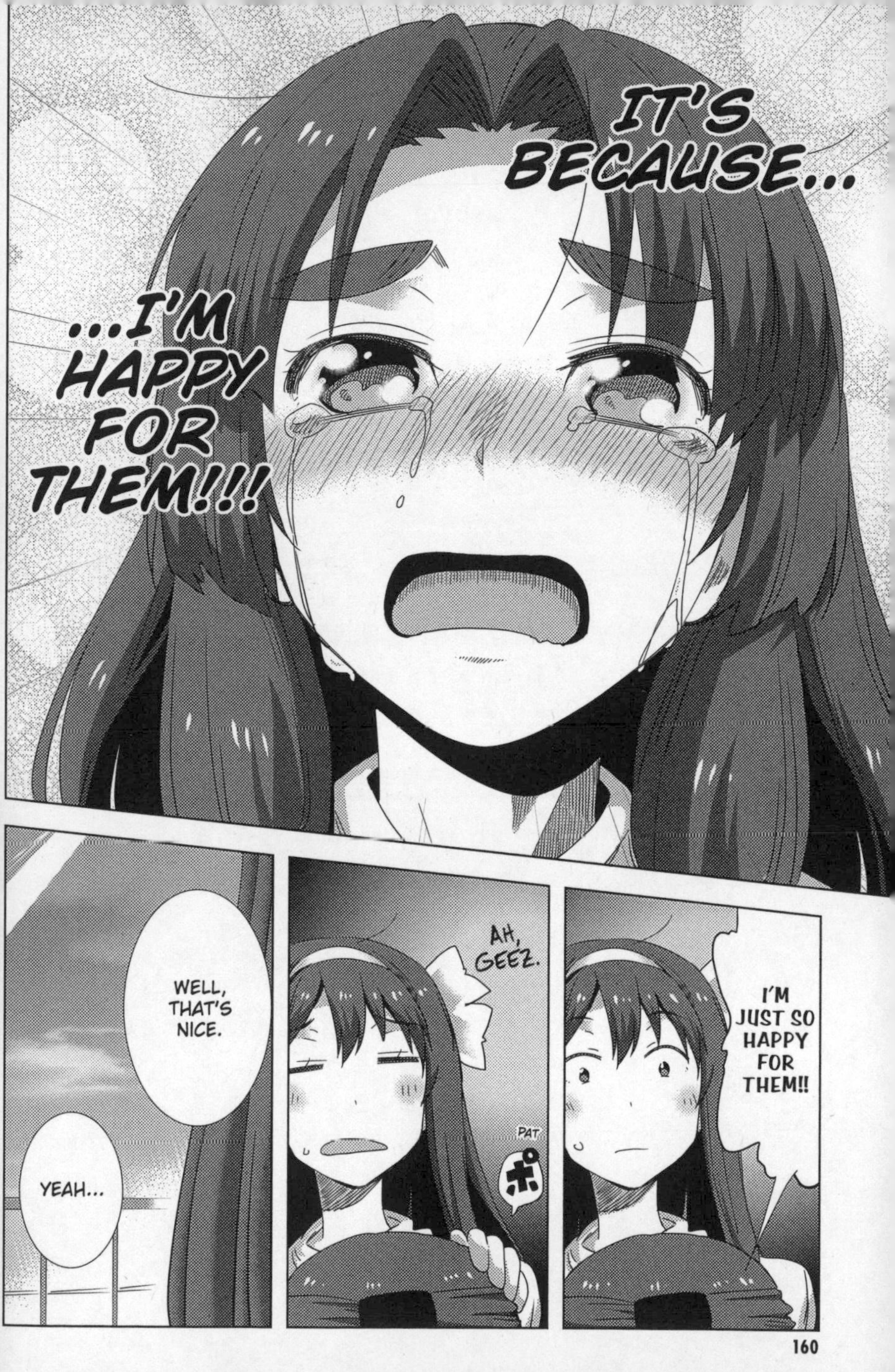
IT'S BECAUSE...
...I'M HAPPY FOR THEM!!!
I'M JUST SO HAPPY FOR THEM!!
AH, GEEZ.
PAT
WELL, THAT'S NICE.
YEAH...

SO THAT'S WHAT HAP- PENED...

TO BE CONTINUED.

THE DISAPPEARANCE OF NAGATO
YUKI-CHAN
8

Original Story: Nagaru Tanigawa
Manga: PUYO
Character Design: Noizi Ito

Translation: ZephyrRz
Lettering: Abigail Blackman

NAGATO YUKI CHAN NO SHOSHITSU Volume 8 © Nagaru TANIGAWA · Noizi ITO 2015 © PUYO 2015. Edited by KADOKAWA SHOTEN. First published in Japan in 2015 by KADOKAWA CORPORATION, Tokyo. English translation rights arranged with KADOKAWA CORPORATION, Tokyo, through TUTTLE-MORI AGENCY, INC., Tokyo.

English translation © 2015 by Hachette Book Group, Inc.

Yen Press
Hachette Book Group
1290 Avenue of the Americas, New York, NY 10104

www.HachetteBookGroup.com
www.YenPress.com

Yen Press is an imprint of Hachette Book Group, Inc.
The Yen Press name and logo are trademarks of Hachette Book Group, Inc.

The publisher is not responsible for websites (or their content) that are not owned by the publisher.

First Yen Press Edition: November 2015

ISBN: 978-0-316-35192-8

10 9 8 7 6 5 4 3 2

BVG

Printed in the United States of America